COMMUNITY LIBRARY
P9-CJW-262

THE
BOAT
RUNNER

THE BOAT RUNNER

A Novel

DEVIN MURPHY

HARPER ● PERENNIAL

NEW YORK ● LONDON ● TORONTO ● SYDNEY ● NEW DELHI ● AUCKLAND

THE BOAT RUNNER. Copyright © 2017 by Devin Murphy. All rights reserved. Printed
in the United States of America. No part of this book may be used or reproduced
in any manner whatsoever without written permission except in the case of brief
quotations embodied in critical articles and reviews. For information, address
HarperCollins Publishers, 195 Broadway, New York, NY 10007.

HarperCollins books may be purchased for educational, business, or sales
promotional use. For information, please email the Special Markets Department at
SPsales@harpercollins.com.

P.S.™ is a trademark of HarperCollins Publishers.

FIRST EDITION

Designed by Leydiana Rodriguez

Library of Congress Cataloging-in-Publication Data has been applied for.

ISBN 978-0-06-265801-2 (pbk.)

17 18 19 20 21   LSC   10 9 8 7 6 5 4 3 2 1

For Becca, my light maker.

THE
BOAT
RUNNER

"Our existence is but a brief crack of light between two eternities of darkness."

—VLADIMIR NABOKOV

A BRIEF CRACK OF LIGHT

1

I was fourteen when my father thought he finally developed the perfect inner coil for the lightbulb. He'd gone to Hamburg where he tried, again, to solicit a new account from Volkswagen. My mother was playing Chopin's Étude in Thirds on her piano downstairs when he came home. My brother, Edwin, older by a year, slumped next to me on the floor of our bedroom drawing with pastels on a large sheet of butcher paper. Fergus, our big leg-chewing mutt, slept upside down beneath the window with his feet against the wall. In his dreams he twitched and kicked himself across the floor, digging his claws into the plaster until a rut formed one foot off the ground ringed the room. My parents' voices were muffled until they walked into the den, where sound carried up through the heating register.

"I still think it's a bad idea." I knew she wanted him to stop crossing the border.

"This will set us up for the future."

"There is no future with them."

"They'll give me a chance to supply *all* their headlights. What else could we want, Drika? We need secure accounts." I could tell by the groan of a loose spring that my father sat on the Biedermeier sofa next to the metal clock, his feet probably resting on the wooden steamer trunk.

"It's a bad idea. Sell more here and in France."

"To whom?"

There was a cold beat of tension between them. This was an old fight and hearing them start up again felt like a nervous folding of wings deep in my chest.

"I got you something," my father said to her after a moment.

He always brought books home to us as presents. For my mother, he brought her books on music that she'd devour. She would come into the room, thrusting the opened pages into our laps for us to read, like she needed us to hold them to be real. I knew from reading all those books that the oldest song was the *Shaduf Chant,* sung by workers on the Nile River in Egypt. And that there was a concert in Breslau on August 2, 1937, that ended with sixty thousand people singing together.

"The world's largest choir. Can you imagine?" my mother asked.

I knew that in 540 BC Pythagoras introduced the concept of the musical octave. In 250 BC the first organ was invented in Greece.

"That long ago," she whispered. *"Astonishing."*

When my father brought back music sheets, my mother would race to the piano to begin practicing. Monteverdi's *Vespers*; Puccini's *Madama Butterfly*; and Stravinsky's *The Rite of Spring* all took shape in our home. With no warm-up she could play all of Handel's *Messiah*. She didn't tire, or the music gave her new energy. She never said. She rarely talked about her playing or responded when I praised her.

"The music plays itself," she said. *"The musician is there to make the transitions between loud and soft. Fast and slow. Slide along those scales and you can make it work."*

I knew she made it sound easy to tempt me to try, but I had no talent or patience for stringing one butchered note after another.

Books were sacred to my parents, who both longed to use them to break from what they perceived as their vulgar lineages. So my father gave books freely and we gathered as many as we could. Years before, when my father was struggling to launch the factory, he'd given me a set of illustrated Bibles. I remembered a picture from one of the books of a cypress-tree-filled valley between Nazareth and Cana. An ancient path my father said Roman generals marched over. I remembered nothing else from those books, because soon after I received the gift, when his manic efforts and drive were tipped by self-doubt and fatigue into some fatalistic downswing, he got roaring drunk, gathered up those volumes, and crammed them into the fireplace, where they curled into orange ash. As the fire bucked and flared, it cemented the written word for me as a higher power that could lift a person from basic human rage and lunacy, or drive them right back down into it.

"This is a nice book," my mother now replied to my father. But there was a flatness to her voice. Disappointment. A small beat of quiet that held the larger story of their lives I had yet to piece together. Back then, I didn't yet know how neglected she felt by my father, who gave her wealth and gifts instead of his time.

"Well, I don't know who you should sell to," my mother started in again, "but if things get bad we should shut down and leave."

"Now? When I'm so close? If I get this right it will change everything. This is it."

"This is it, this is it. You've been close for ten years. Things get better, but you're never happy. Never done."

"If I get this coil right they'll be our largest account. We'll supply almost all the vehicles in Germany. We can leverage that to sell all around the world!"

The teakettle clanked against the kitchen sink.

Fergus stood up, scratched at the carpet, walked a tight circle, and fell into a ball, knees and elbows clunking the ground.

"I also came up with a solution for keeping the boys busy. It will help with the Volkswagen account too," my father said loud enough so she could hear him from the other room. I leapt from bed and kneeled over the heating vent. Then my father walked into the kitchen, where it was harder for me to hear. Several minutes later the teakettle whistled, and I heard my mother yelling.

"Are you kidding?"

"Edwin, come listen," I said to my brother.

"Not now."

"Edwin. Listen."

"Not now."

I knew not to engage him when he was like that.

"It's a good idea. It will make them good citizens," my father said.

"Good German citizens," she screamed.

I looked at Edwin. "Did you hear that?"

"Hear what?" he said.

I went back to bed and patted the mattress. Fergus shot up and jumped up with me. He stood panting in my face until I scratched behind his ear enough that he sat down and eased his head onto my legs. He stayed like that as I went to sleep wondering what my mother meant.

In the morning I bounded down the stairs, where I found my father already awake and working in his lab. My mother's busy movements made it clear that they had avoided another fight and gone right to icy silence. For breakfast she served wild blueberry crêpes from a cast-iron skillet and covered them in syrup and churned butter. She wore her hair-strand gold necklace that held a pendant my father brought back from Norway and silver earrings from Poland. Edwin and I ate with our arms shielding our plates from each other. There were oil and vinegar bottles and a brandy decanter in the center of the table that we'd often douse the other's food with if he let down his guard.

I was desperate to ask my parents what they had been talking about, but asking questions would let on that we could hear them through the ductwork, so I ate and listened for my father.

My father founded the Koopman Light Company, which manufactured lightbulbs in the village of Delfzijl, in Holland. The village sat on the west bank of the Ems Estuary, across from the mouth of the Ems River in Germany and south of the open waters of the North Sea. The company was our town's largest employer, and he ran the business side of it from the factory's office in the center of town.

When my father wasn't at the factory, he spent his time in the dark laboratory attached to our home, where he worked on modifying his production lines and improving the factory's output. He was always working. My mother said he never wanted to be saddled with his father's farm so he worked in a frenzy, intent to get away from that life, and did what he could to surround us with art and industry to become as refined as heirs to the royal family. We would gauge his moods by how he came out of the lab. If he walked quickly, with eager purpose, it was because he was happy with the work he'd done and was ready to be with his family. If he came out slow, hesitant, he would usually be distracted for the rest of the day, his mind fogged by whatever needed to be done, done again, or done better. He'd spend a few half-present hours in our company, fidgeting constantly, looking out the window, hounding us about the daily vocabulary our private French, German, and English tutors assigned, saying, "Study your words, boys. You have to be able to name the world." Or, "The Dutch are the lords of languages." Then he'd stand up and head back to his lab.

If we were ever allowed into his lab it was because he missed us after traveling to secure sales contracts. He'd go as far east as Moscow, as far west as Morocco, and over to Britain, but he still did most of his business with Germany and already had their Auto Union account, supplying headlights to most Audi, Wanderer, and DKM models. Still, we all knew the thing that kept my father manically rattling through our house on edge, we all knew Volkswagen was the big prize.

That morning, as we finished our crêpes, he emerged from his lab and looked at us sitting at the table.

"Can we talk for a moment?" my mother asked.

"Of course," he said.

"In private."

"In a bit then, love."

Our mother mouthed some coded message to him as she violently stacked our plates and walked to the sink. I looked at my father, who, at a lean six feet six inches, towered over almost everyone.

"Boys. Come on in," he said and waved us into his lab.

Mysterious surgeon-like tools, curved like fishhooks, sprawled over his workbenches. Long blowing irons leaned in the corner.

Around them on the floor were unsuccessful gobs, each plum-sized, burnt, warped, reflective as uncut diamonds. On the shelf were books about Thomas Edison, Nikola Tesla, and studies in electrical currents. My father went right to work with a pair of long, needle-nose pliers and set a coil and filament into place. Then he placed the bulbous glass casing over the assembly and used a vacuum pump to suck out all the air.

Edwin and I always wanted to be his assistants in the lab and knew to immediately grab our safety goggles off the hook when allowed in. I put mine on and watched our father work. I was in awe of him then. He wore soft wool pants and a spun horsehair jacket fitted by a tailor in Amsterdam. The brown jacket was one of five he rotated through each week. His graying blond hair was brushed back by his tortoiseshell comb and held into an off-center part by an antiseptic-smelling pomade. As a nervous habit, he slid out a Swiss watch with a gold-plated case, gilt hands, and an enamel dial that was pinned to his vest by a chain, which he rubbed with his thumb, then tucked away neatly without checking the time, and kept tinkering at his workbench. We would study his every move. In a lot of ways I was afraid of my father. His size. His drunken meltdowns. The barriers he put up between his vocation and family. But I also loved him so much that it felt like my life and identity were built on the tangled interplay of those two emotions, resulting in a deep pull to be near him when he was working.

"Edwin, get me the small canister of black gas."

"You told us not to touch that one," Edwin said.

"Today you will."

Edwin went to the steel-mesh-covered gas locker, undid the latch, and returned with the cylindrical canister held away from his chest like it was some hot, holy thing.

My father fumbled with a glass bulb that fell to the floor and shattered. This happened often. Without a word, he picked up another, crunched over the glass, and walked to us. I studied the broken glass and imagined picking up several shards, laying them side by side by side to see different reflections of how we all fit together. A mosaic of our family. "Watch what I'm doing, Jacob," he said. He hooked up a release valve to the canister, filled the bulb with shimmying vapors of gas, sealed the bulb at the copper base setting, and screwed that fixture into one of the dangling sockets he hung for testing his lights. His open palms cradled the bulb.

"Now, Jacob, turn all the lights off."

When I flipped the switch the room went black.

"Now hit your switch, Edwin."

When Edwin hit the power, a searing white worm burned around the thin coil in the bulb before the filament ignited in an electric whorl, and it flashed into a pulsing glow that our father held out as if offering us some luminous bird. We stared into his palms like he held the crystal future—a future that would turn out so different from what any of us could have imagined in the lab that morning, huddled together.

It's only now, a lifetime later, I can find these first words about my family, which I always knew would bring the whole of it howling out like a fever dream.

"Boys," my father said in the lab, "a man I met in Hamburg gave me a good idea of something you can do this summer."

"Do we have to go work in your friend's factory?" Edwin teased.

My father took a mock swat at his head. "No."

"Do we get to go on the next trip with you?" I asked.

"I'd like to take you along every time I leave," he said. Then he reached his long arms out so a hand cupped the back of each of our necks. "But I'll tell you what. I have an idea that might be fun. Your own little trip. It's a summer camp. It might be good for you. You'll practice your German."

That night, after eating dried apricots and apples roasted over the fireplace, I tried to get my brother to talk about what the camp might be like. Neither of us had ever been away from our family long. I wanted to talk it over with Edwin, to express my concerns, but he began to draw and soon his attention faded from me. He covered another large sheet of butcher paper with etchings, working in circles so his finished project looked like a constellation wheel.

His side of the room was covered in stacks of smooth and textured papers, sketchbooks, knives and peels of pencil shavings, brushes, tubes of paint, a jar of turpentine, and an easel that looked like a giant praying mantis when I caught it out of the corner of my eye in dim light.

Edwin had a book called *The Greatest Drawings of All Time* that he slipped his own sketches between the pages of.

"Just to keep them pressed," he said.

"Our sports almanac is just as big."

"I'll use that one next," he said, but page after page of his own work found their way between the covers in what must have been a small allowance to his own sense of talent.

I understood why he did it. I daydreamed about being a prodigy like my brother. I imagined greatness in sports, art, music, and industrial invention, and if those dreams came with tangible scraps, I would have squirreled them away in lofty bindings too.

Edwin spent hours that night working on his hands and knees. I woke much later to the scent of beeswax candles and saw his shadow hunkered over some new dream image he couldn't wait to bring out of the paper. The lump of his body dark and still, his extended arm swaying and twitching, conducted some unfolding vision to life. Behind him the old steel radiator jutted out of the wall, a bleached-white square rib cage that hissed and ticked and warmed his midnight painting sessions. He filled an old cistern with water, wet his fingers, and rubbed dabs over the ink lines so they blurred. The shapes loosened at the corners, and the color bled across the watermarks like he created some new set of rules for form.

Our father bought him the easel, but he still preferred to do all his drawing leaning over the floor. He kneeled on the paper, somehow never tearing it, as if when drawing or painting he became weightless and floated over the work.

"Edwin. What do you think that camp will be like?" I tried to break through. "Why doesn't Mom want us to go?"

Edwin gave me a look like I'd said something really stupid, and kept drawing.

I got out of bed, snuck down the stairs, and shuffled into my father's lab. I lay down on the floor in the dark. The smell of burnt chemicals hung in the air, and slivers of glass speckled the floor. It became a sort of dare to myself to lie down without getting cut, and I never succeeded. Some jagged shard would always drive beneath my skin. Those little wounds made me feel closer to my father, like we both understood something about his work that went beyond words.

No light came through when the door was shut. I turned a flashlight on and swept it across the floor and the glass shone back like a crystal rug. The beam of light lingered on the tops of chemical canisters and gas welding tanks. I pictured my father bending into the shower of molten orange as sparks bounced off the dark faceplate of his helmet—the blue-tongued coalescence of metals drawing him closer to something that only he could see among the raw materials. I studied the beaded melding points of the castings and bases he made, and how each joint somehow balanced the metals in intricate and subtle curves.

I picked up the welding rod and imagined the blue flame liquefying steel and binding it together in more fascinating ways. An art form. I thought we were all supposed to have some kind of art form. My father had his lights, my mother her music, and Edwin, who beamed with talent and potential, took wide slabs of butcher paper and mimicked every shape in the world, as if practicing for some larger swath of canvas, maybe even a cathedral ceiling, that would surely come later. In the dark I imagined turning the blue tongue of fire on my own chest to crack it open, to pull out my own hidden talent, my own art form, whatever it was.

Late the next evening, I was reading at the top of the stairs, petting Fergus, when my mother's younger brother, Uncle Martin, came to our house. In socked feet, he stood almost as tall as my father, near two meters, but he had muscular arms and a V-shaped back from years of hauling in fishing nets. Under his raincoat he wore a gray French seaman's sweater for which my mother had sewn thick black elbow patches that cracked white at the bend. Under his sweater was a host of faded gypsy tattoos covering his chest and arms. A compass sat on his right shoulder, a large portrait of Neptune stretched across his stomach, and a bare-chested woman with wings and blue-tipped nipples soared across his rib cage. A paragraph in Latin scrolled along his upper forearm, and between his shoulder blades sailed a schooner at full mast with the words *Flying Dutchman*, etched in bold blue India ink, arched over the topmast. The top of the *h* crawled up the side of his neck like an arterial vein.

"Don't get any ideas," our mother said when she first saw us idolizing his tattoos.

He'd taken his shirt off while wrestling with Edwin, me, and our best friends, Ludo and Hilda. He let Hilda knock him down and took it easy on Ludo, whose left arm had dried up and coiled from a bout of polio he'd survived as an infant.

When we asked about his inking, our mother said, "He didn't have a proper upbringing, so he couldn't help himself. But you boys dream of it, and I'll scrub the ink off of you with a fistful of sand and gravel."

Like my mother and father, almost everything I knew about Uncle Martin's life came from stories other people told of him. He rarely, if ever, spoke about himself, which gave him a sense of mystery, as if mystery were the language he moved in, his mother tongue.

Not asking my parents or Uncle Martin about their early lives was one of those things I knew. Whispered to me at birth. Traced on my skin by my mother's fingers. It was just in me. But of course, that led to the creation of a great antenna to gather any fragments of news about them I could find into my own private mythologies.

I knew Uncle Martin left home in 1912, when he was fourteen, to get away from his fisherman father he never got along with. This part was shrouded in silence as my grandfather's name only rose to my uncle and mother's lips with vitriol. I knew Uncle Martin joined the crew of a schooner ferry that ran cargo between Rotterdam and England.

After that, he did his time in the Dutch Marines, which according to him was the happiest he'd ever been. He went back to sea after the marines because that was all he really knew. For years he jumped ships that followed old whale roads to the Dutch colonies and around the world. Then, when I was six, he bought a fishing trawler and started running it out of Delfzijl to be close to us, the only family he had.

He often took us fishing. Once the lightbulb factory started turning large profits, and our father could spend more time doing what he wanted, he began coming out with us on Uncle Martin's boat. We'd cruise together into the Ems, past the Frisian Islands, and into the North Sea. Our father became so enamored with the water he bought a leisure boat for himself, which was the first of its kind in our town's harbor.

"I have a gift for you guys," Uncle Martin said as he walked into our home that night. He held out a dusty-looking bottle of liquor. "This is Prohibition-era American liquor. So good it was forbidden."

"Where'd you get that?" my father asked. He held the bottle up to the light to study the label. Gray with black letters. *Old Hermitage Sour Mash Rye. 62. Broad Street. Boston.* They went into the living room and sat on the couches. I lay on my stomach and leaned down the stairs to see them. My father still held the bottle. "It's contraband."

"No, nothing to worry about," Uncle Martin said. "Let's give it a taste."

My mother caught Uncle Martin's eyes and nodded her head toward my father.

"You know. I came over because I thought maybe the boys could come out on the boat for the summer?"

My father turned the bottle so he could read the back. "I've made plans for them already."

"Oh yeah?"

My father looked from the bottle to my mother. His jaw was set, and even from where I watched I could see the pounding of blood at his temple. "Yes. They'll be working at the factory as well."

"He's worried about his Volkswagen account. Everything's about Volkswagen."

"Drika."

"Well, it's true."

"That's because it will set us up for the future."

"That's what you said about Auto Union."

My father swung toward her. "Auto Union paid for this house. Built the factory. Go ahead and say something bad about that."

"You have most of the country's cars already, Hans."

"Stop it, Drika. Just stop this. Like I don't see you setting Martin on me like this."

My mother turned and saw me at the top of the stairs. "Go to your room, Jacob."

"Okay. I'm sorry," I said.

My father looked up and anger melted from him at the sight of me, the way it always did. He hated being angry, coarse, or drunk in front of us and skulked around like a shamed dog after behaving so.

"Go study your words, Jacob," he said and smiled.

From the heating vent, I heard them talking about the camp. Mostly my mother protesting sending us away and pestering Uncle Martin to help change my father's mind.

"You could go out on the boat with them, Hans," my mother said. "Spend some time with your boys."

If my father heard her, he said nothing.

Edwin pencil-sketched a dark silhouette cutting through a stand of trees. The trees had enough depth to draw the eye into the suggested shadow. That was something he practiced. Shadows. I caught him after he put one of our mother's dresses on Fergus and chased the dog around the house to study the way folds in the fabric played with light.

"You fancy dogs now?" I teased him.

He didn't respond and acted like he didn't hear me. I wondered if he registered any of the tension below the floorboards the way I did. That antenna of mine caught every shifting speck of frustration and pulled it into the endlessly burbling core of my body.

In the end, after my uncle left and my mother and father had a screaming match that felt like it would split the foundation of our home, but crested and fell into the long, apologetic chords of exhaustion, it was agreed that we would go out for a weeklong fishing trip with Uncle Martin, return home to pick up our father who would accompany us to the camp, then come home from camp and work in the factory until school started.

It was a compromise of sorts. A neat and orderly parceling of our time.

2

I n early July, my father brought us to the docks to meet Uncle
Martin's boat, the *Lighthouse Lady*. On our way through town,
we saw Father Heard, the parish priest, who was also one of my
father's best, if not only, friends. The two of them founded and kept
afloat what seemed to be the only Catholic Church in the north. Father Heard led a man named Samuel to the church by his left arm.
Samuel had no control over his right arm. It shot out over his head
and frantically scribbled, as if writing some great, unknown sentence
in the air. Everyone called him the air-writer. Samuel mostly wandered the town all day and lived in an apartment his father had set
him up with before he died. His father had left money in his will to
have Father Heard keep watch over his son. My father hired Samuel
to clean the factory and the town's church so he had something to
do. My mother said Samuel had been touched in the head, but Ludo
called him retarded when no one else was around.

Ludo lived with his mother and father in a row of brownstones
three kilometers beyond the church. Ludo's father was a carpenter. His
mother worked at Koopman Light on the factory floor.

The morning shift was starting soon, and the town seemed alive with people flowing to the factory. Most of them I'd known long enough to pick out their gait at first light. There was Edward Fass, who was thick-chested, rough-hewn, and as scarred up as a cutting block. He worked the assembly line and was known for his loud mouth. Gerard Van Den Bosch and his wife, Annie, both worked as accountants for my father. They walked from the early morning café with an old widow, Maud Stein, whose husband was one of my father's first employees. Most of the town had some connection to my father's factory, which meant he was often treated with a sort of deference that came with an emotional remove from other families.

When we got to the dock we boarded the boat. Uncle Martin was going to bring us back in six days' time to pick up our father and Ludo, who had persuaded his parents to let him come to camp with us. Then we would cross the Ems and board a train to the summer camp in Germany.

During our first morning on the *Lighthouse Lady*, Edwin and I set out long nets and spent the afternoon picking cod, herring, friar fish, hake, flounder, mackerel, and an occasional squid from the gill nets and tossing them down a chute to Uncle Martin who sliced them up and pitched the entrails over the side for the seagulls.

We started close enough to shore to see long-legged shorebirds run back and forth at the edge of the surf. Oystercatchers kept following the waves so they could dig with their beaks into the newly packed sand before they raised their wings and ran away squawking from the next incoming wash. All day they danced like that.

The estuary was eighty kilometers across at its widest point. Uncle Martin knew every ledge, sandbar, and current around the clock and tried to teach us about navigating a vessel. "You have to be able to picture the wind on the map too. How it works on water," he said as I looked at all the charts.

He let me steer the boat straight across the channel where there was a shelf underwater that dipped to the deepest point of the Ems; we couldn't see land on either side. To me, the Ems itself seemed alive and I wanted to keep going as far out to sea as possible.

On our second night we passed over the drop-off after the West Frisian Islands. The water was deep, gunmetal blue and calm enough that we could see it sloping off the horizon before sunset. We'd been hitting on a ten-kilometer shoal of herring when Uncle Martin came out on the decks and said, "We'll set the nets out one more time," and he tongued the gap where his canine tooth and bicuspid used to be before he lost it in what he called "a collision with a lead pipe." Spit in his mouth made a popping sound from the suction between the pock in his gums and his tongue.

Ahead of us herring broke the water, jumping and falling back. When we wrapped up the net with one of our holds full, we went farther out than I'd ever been before, as far as Den Helder.

I walked into the wheelhouse, where Edwin tried to keep up with Uncle Martin's exercise routine. Uncle Martin was shirtless. His tattoos pinched and strained as he did deep lunges, push-ups, sit-ups, and then bent-knee pull-ups from a bar he'd mounted on the overhead.

"Did those hurt?" I asked. "The needles, I mean."

Martin ran his palm along his forearm. "Needles. Is that how you think I got these?"

"Yes."

"No." He lifted his fists to his face and rubbed a knuckle into each eye socket. "Do you know how the sun can turn your skin pink, then red before it peels and flakes off?"

"Yes."

"Well. I spent too much time on decks without a shirt on, is all. Lost so many layers of skin I started seeing these faint images emerging." He traced inked lines on his flesh with his fingertip. "They got clearer with time, as more skin burned away."

I studied the fluted and hooked tattoos.

"So we have pictures etched into our bodies?" I asked.

"Deep down. At the truest version of ourselves." Uncle Martin winked at me.

I didn't know what to say, but liked the idea that drawing as he did, maybe my brother was able to see the pictures beneath other people's skin?

Through the window, we saw the large shadow of a German navy ship cut across the swells like an enormous gray dorsal fin.

"We'll be seeing a lot more of those, I suspect," Uncle Martin said.

Even from a great distance the ship dwarfed Uncle Martin's boat, though his was one of the largest trawlers in the Ems's fishing grounds. He had had it custom-built, a thirty-two-meter, steel-beam trawler, with a high-whaleback bow and slow-turning high-torque engines to power it through rough waters.

Uncle Martin kept exercising as the ship slipped into the horizon.

The knife he always wore on his belt was on the console. I picked it up. An American sailor had taught him how to make the scrimshaw handle. Whalebone. Sanded smooth and polished. He pencil-drew a rudimentary drawing of a man hugging tight to the upper mast beams of a rigged ship. To me, the picture symbolized some ultimate freedom I'd yet to really understand. Though of course I was young. I would have drawn the sailor with his hands out to the wind. What did I know about holding on for dear life? When the drawing was as good as he could make it, he carved along the pencil lines with an old dentist tool, then poured and wiped away ink until it dyed the grooves.

"Should have had you draw that one for me," he said to Edwin and pointed to the knife I held.

"Was I born yet?" Edwin asked.

"No. I guess you weren't. Though even as a baby you could have done better than that. That one took me a heap of hours to make."

I held the heft of the handle and swung the blade in front of me, back and forth, back and forth, always keeping the steel moving the way Uncle Martin had shown us.

"Have you been to the South Pacific?" Edwin asked.

"Yes," Uncle Martin said.

"Is it like the paintings?"

"Which paintings?

"The Gauguin paintings."

"I don't know those."

Edwin put his hand on the gunwale, looked out at the water, and was silent for a moment. "Is it so bright and lush that the colors seem distorted?"

"I'm not sure that's what I was looking for onshore." Uncle Martin grinned at me.

"I'd like to travel like you did," Edwin said. "Bring an endless sheet of canvas and hundreds of brushes to capture everything I see."

"Well. You can go anywhere if you've got enough fuel or wind. That's the secret of boats. The world opens up to you. Though to be honest, it can be as much a curse as a gift."

"How so?" Edwin asked.

"You see the whole world, but you do it alone."

That was the first time I really thought of how in the middle of the sea there is no break, no leaving. Prior to this, boats always meant the roar of props pushing water. All the science and industry behind each rivet that composed a vessel felt like a poem to people in motion, to wild souls pushing offshore.

Uncle Martin spread his legs shoulder-distance apart and began another set of deep-knee bends. Edwin jumped in and tried to keep up but lost his balance on the pitching deck. I sat down and watched the water. For as much as I loved this boat, my uncle, and the sea, I knew I'd be more comfortable working in my father's lab when I grew up, where I was a door away from my family.

"What was your favorite place?" Edwin asked.

"I liked South America. Argentina, Brazil, and Dutch Guiana. There are Dutch that settled there. Some of the women have Dutch and native blood and are so exotic it's impossible not to fall right in love with them. Those were hard places to leave. But I'm a North Sea man. This place calls to me. Besides, I need cold water to keep my heart primed."

I walked into the holds. On the table sat a pile of small tools, a microphone, and a disassembled green radio housing I hadn't seen before. I picked the radio up but dropped the microphone.

"Don't touch that." Uncle Martin's voice boomed down the stairwell.

I put the microphone back and lay down in my bunk as we traveled farther north. When the engines slowed, I went back to the wheelhouse. Off the port stern a small vessel headed our way. Uncle Martin lifted his binoculars and studied it.

"Coming fast," he said.

Edwin and I went to the window as Uncle Martin slowed the *Lighthouse Lady* down even more. When he looked again, he put the binoculars down and started down the stairwell. "A patrol boat."

"How can you tell?" I asked.

"The spine of the bow is riding high out of the water."

I heard him belowdecks shuffling around with the disassembled radio. Something fell on the floor, and he swore. A hatch opened and slammed shut. He climbed back up the stairs.

"Edwin. Pull back on the throttle. Bring us to idle til they catch up."

Edwin sprung to the helm and eased back the throttle. The engine noise settled to a slow thrumming below deck.

"They're coming for us."

"Why?"

"We'll see. Edwin, you stay at the wheel. Jacob, go tend the lines at the stern, and I'll get the spring line."

Before I walked out on deck, I noticed the green radio on the table was gone. A tiny screwdriver lay on the ground. Out on deck I coiled up a docking line to ready it for the PT boat's approach.

The PT boat idled its engines when it came alongside.

"Ahoy," Uncle Martin yelled and lifted a throw line over his head to show the sailors on deck.

When the boat pulled parallel to us, Uncle Martin tossed the spring line over to them, and a sailor grabbed it and tied it off to a cleat.

"Where you headed?" a sailor asked in German.

"Northwest for herring grounds," Uncle Martin said in Dutch.

"There's no more going north of here," the sailor replied in Dutch.

"It's prime fishing up there," Uncle Martin yelled.

"No more."

Several soldiers leaned over the railing and studied our decks.

I think I picked up on Uncle Martin's wordless anger and was channeling it as I wanted to tell them to piss off, but I kept from making eye contact with any of them. Not making eye contact was something my father had noticed as a timid habit.

"*Stand straight. Look straight,*" he'd said, and even his having to mention it, a fault I felt, made my eyes snap to the floor and I'd apologize like a meek little I'm-sorry machine. I'm sorry, I'm sorry, I'm sorry, I'd chant to tamp down any sparks I perceived between us. I'd do this to try to keep the peace between everyone, though I hated every time the words crossed my lips.

"Is there some sort of trouble that way?" Uncle Martin asked the sailors.

"Sealed off."

Uncle Martin smiled. He turned toward me, and I could tell his smile was fake, *lubricious,* one of the vocabulary words my father had given me. My uncle's neck flushed crimson like he was choking back anger. He must have been furious at the notion that someone would try to stop him from moving freely.

"Well. Not sure what I'm supposed to do to make a living if I can't go fishing there."

"Fish south," the sailor said.

"You guys can't let us slip by for half a day? I'm sure no one out here would crawl up your asses about it."

"I cannot let you go farther."

"Well then. I'm sure you got your reasons." Uncle Martin's knuckles whitened as he gripped the gunwale. "Maybe later in the season?"

"Maybe," the soldier said. "Maybe you'll be allowed a permit."

"Okay then," Uncle Martin said. "You guys be safe out here."

"You as well," the sailor said and tossed the spring line back onto our deck. The line was as thick as my wrist and pieces of barnacle shells ground into the fibers from rubbing against pylons sliced my skin.

Uncle Martin climbed up the back ladder into the wheelhouse and started to turn the *Lighthouse Lady* around.

"A permit! Who are these bed-pissers? Bunch of bastards with misshapen peckers, probably."

"Why'd they stop us?" Edwin asked.

"Who knows. That big ship must have radioed to shore about us. Sent those guys out to check on us." He pushed the throttle forward and muttered to himself. "Permits. You're kidding me with your permits."

We turned the *Lighthouse Lady* back south and fished those waters until it was time to go get my father and Ludo. Once they boarded we headed east to the port town of Leer, where the three of us boys would meet the train.

That night, onboard, we played card games: spades, whist, and gin rummy.

"Hilda will be mad she's missing out on these games," I said. We all grew up with Hilda, who I was desperately and secretly in love with.

"But she'd hate cutting up the fish," Ludo said.

"For sure," I said, like I knew anything about her.

My first sex dream was of holding Hilda's ankles in my hands and letting the sole of my foot press and rub between her legs—an area that in my mind was as smooth and featureless as a mannequin. I had not yet seen a naked girl and didn't know what to do. The confusion only worsened, then shifted to a shame because I woke with painful erections pushing on my shorts, or worse, a gooey mess crusting in my underwear, which I would strip off, ball up, and cram deep in our hamper to hide.

While Ludo and Edwin played, I went out on deck, where sequins of fish scales glinted on the drying nets. I walked into the wheelhouse where my father and uncle were arguing.

"I can't believe you'd let them do this, Hans."

"They'll have fun."

"But there?"

"Come on, Martin. Don't you give this to me too. The boys will have a good time."

"They just stopped my boat. They want to control everything." Uncle Martin waved his arms in front of him as if shaking off some ugly thought.

I went and stood between them, to be a good son, a peacemaker.

"I can't believe you'll let Jacob do this," Uncle Martin said. My father looked at me standing there, and held back anything else he had to say.

That night I slept on a wheelhouse bench as Uncle Martin steered, studied the charts, and referenced his liquid compass and echo recorder. The sound of the diesel engines pumping the props through the wind and rolling white caps shook the whole ship.

In my half-sleep I thought I heard one of my father's stories. He would always tell us stories about a character he invented named Thump-Drag, a clubfooted hunchback. When he swung his dead foot, it clobbered the ground, *thump*, and then he dragged it behind him as if it were an anvil. We grew up hearing about Thump-Drag's knotted hump, which was really a giant extra muscle, and about how dragging that foot around made him incredibly strong. The steady rhythm of his walking, *thump-drag, thump-drag*, was the one constant to all his stories.

Thump-Drag was born a millennium ago as a Celt, my father told us, and the stories of his adventures, strength, and humility grew nightly as our father put us to bed. One night he gave moral lessons akin to Father Heard's at church. The next, Thump-Drag became an outcast for his deformations. As we grew, Thump-Drag's travels took him all over the world and through time. One day Thump-Drag was a Stone Age troglodyte and the next he fought in the Great War. In this way, he became the Wandering Jew, a Spartan, different Greek mythological figures, and a Byronic hero.

My father walked into the wheelhouse waking me fully up. "There you are," he said. "Don't you want to sleep in your bunk?"

"Can I stay here?"

He sat by my feet and rested a hand over my ankle.

"Can you tell me a story?" I asked.

He looked at Uncle Martin, who nodded.

"A short one," my father said. He began speaking of Thump-Drag in the sailor Ulysses' story.

"Thump-Drag was cast from the sea and told by Poseidon to put an oar over his shoulder and walk inland until someone asked what he was holding. Then he was to plant his oar in the ground and build a church to the god of the ocean."

My father went on, but of all the stories, hearing the start of this one now pained me the most because now I saw no matter where he went or who Thump-Drag came upon, he was perpetually moving away from his home. As my father spoke I understood Thump-Drag would see the whole world, but do so alone. I turned to the hulking shadow of my uncle steering our boat through the night. In the dark, my father's voice went on and then braided his own truth into this story. I wish my father told a different story altogether, one that would not come to resemble his own.

3

Uncle Martin was still at the wheel our last morning aboard. Out the windows, the sun was like a great rolling cat's eye. Waves crested and crashed into each other until they reached the thin strip of shoreline. I opened the door and felt the briny air all around the *Lighthouse Lady*. Ahead of us, channel markers led the river up to the town of Leer. Next to the harbormaster's house in Leer was a large scaffold pyramid.

"That radio tower is probably where the navy cruiser called our location in. They used the tower to order the PT boat to come turn us back."

"That really got under your skin, didn't it?" my father asked.

Uncle Martin nodded and gave my father that put-on smile he had given the German sailors.

Our father and Uncle Martin walked us through town. The three of us boys ran ahead and then doubled back in our excitement. We each had our backpacks stuffed with camp uniforms, a tin of biscuits, and a sleeping bag crammed into a small canvas sack my mother had sewn that we could fill with spare clothes and use as a pillow. We detached our sleeping bag pouches and heaved them up in the air where they drifted upward before freezing for a moment at their peak and dropping back into our arms. We ran ahead, laughing and tossing our bags up like it was our voices lifting the sleep sacks upward. The drab lemon morning light slid up the brick buildings in town and made the dark, earth-colored walls shine like honey.

At the station Uncle Martin gave us a silly sailor's salute with a wobbly left hand. "Don't buy too much into what these people are going to tell you."

"Stop that, Martin," my father said.

"All right. All right. Just a little advice."

The two of them ushered us onto the train steps. "Drop this in the post when you arrive," our father said and handed Edwin a letter.

"*Eisenbahn,*" our father said.

"What?" Edwin asked.

"It means happy travels on the iron road," our father said. "And, please, practice your German." He cupped the back of our necks one at a time. Ludo's too. "Do well," he shouted as we entered the second-class passenger compartments. When I looked back, the two giants of my youth waved good-bye to us.

Once we were moving, the train leaned into curves. Groaning metal rose into our cabin as we picked up speed.

Ludo kept saying, "Look at that. Look at that," as we clattered across bridges, through tunnels, and over several canals that were emerald green with scum. Had we been close enough, we could have reached out and written our names on the surface until the sour algae pulled our letters under like secrets. We ran parallel to the blue outline of a river in the distance that cut through lush, green patchworks of barley, alfalfa, and potatoes. Dim silhouettes of medieval towns flashed by through the clearings of trees.

Edwin drew in a notepad, sketching the tapestried landscape; elm trees, low hills, church steeples, gray-blue wisps of smoke from the Tudor farmhouses with high rectangular windows. I was nervous about what lay ahead, but Edwin's steadiness and focus on his drawing put me at ease. I peeled back the flap of the letter my father gave to Edwin so as not to tear it and be able to seal it back together. It was nothing interesting. A note to a Mr. Gunnelburg, an executive at Volkswagen: *In hopes to continue to grow our business together and to more years of good relations.* He thanked the man for telling him about the camp. Said we *were very excited about attending.* I folded the letter back to look unhampered and watched the countryside roll along.

The train rode through dense forested areas of old-growth elm and pine trees before slowing at the edge of a tan, umber, and rose-colored town. When we got off the train, we entered the train station, a large stone building, its roof black with age. Birds nested high up the wall in veiny cracks through the mortar. Inside we used a rest room next to a bakery. The toilet smelled like urine and dense, black artisan breads. The square in front of the station filled with boys our age. Across the square, bicycles leaned against tenement buildings that were covered in ivy which wrapped around the grillwork of their balconies. The sky was drained and pure and I was so excited to be in this new place that I remember it all very clearly.

"What do we do now?" Ludo asked.

A group of older boys were in front of the station. They wore gray socks up to their knees, gray shorts, and white shirts with brown suspenders and soft brown cloth hats. They were mostly lean and blond with wide, tan faces and glistening mouths. It would be easy to think they came from the same family of two dozen blond brothers. Compared to my own brown eyes and pale form, I couldn't pass for a distant cousin. One of them yelled out, "Camp boys. Form a line here."

The three of us merged with the other boys and were led out the front of the station to a row of buses. We were counted off by tens and told to board the third bus, where one of the older boys was to mark us off on a clipboard. A sprig of hair fell down and bent like a stork's leg over his forehead. His mouth was full of yellowed teeth.

"Edwin Koopman."

"Koopman, Koopman. Ah, you are Dutch."

"Yes," Edwin said.

"Well, good to have you here."

"Jacob Koopman," I said, stepping up to the older boy.

"Jacob Koopman," the older boy said. "A pair of Dutchmen, very good."

We got on the bus, and I heard Ludo behind us.

"Ludo Shoemackher."

"Look at this," the older boy said. "The Dutch are coming to their senses and joining us." The boy with the clipboard patted Ludo's weak left arm. "What's this?"

"Nothing," Ludo said.

"It doesn't look like nothing."

Ludo tried to walk onto the bus but the boy extended his clipboard and blocked the stairs.

"What's wrong with your arm?"

"Nothing."

"An injury?"

"Nothing."

"It's nothing," I called back from the bus's steps.

"Tell me," the boy said.

"Polio. From a long time ago."

The boy stepped back. "Can that make me sick?"

"It's no different than an injury," Ludo said, stepping by the boy and onto the bus.

Over two hundred boys boarded the row of buses. Some of them already wore their camp uniforms, and others looked like they came from a day playing in the woods, sweaty, dusted in dirt with mud tracing the seams of their shoes. When the three of us sat down, a boy in front of Ludo whose neck looked scoured by sandpaper turned toward him. He had the flattened nose and thick neck of a young boxer. His features seemed set with a chisel and hammer. Deep-set black eyes. Long furrows across his forehead. He kept licking his lips like a parched lizard.

"You know, you won't be able to compete with any of us," the boy said, eyeing Ludo's arm.

Ludo turned to the window. His right hand cupped his left like the lid of a sugar cup.

The buses took us to the camp offices, about fifty kilometers away from the train station, where we had to be checked in.

We were each given a clipboard and told to sign the loyalty oaths. To the camp. To the National Socialist Party. Without reading it, we did.

In the main congregating ground around the flagpoles, we split into groups. Each group was assigned an older boy as a group leader. Edwin, Ludo, and I were, thankfully, placed together. We were led to a cabin that slept ten boys. Our cabin had a row of five cots with chests at their base on either side and a large window at each end.

Our group leader for the next five weeks was Günter Zimmer, a seventeen-year-old boy with blue eyes, nubby ears, and black hair, oiled and parted down the middle. His breath smelled like smoke and mint. His uniform of gouged wood.

"Unpack, change into uniforms, and meet outside in ten minutes," Günter said.

When Günter went outside, the rash-necked boy from the bus assessed his bunkmates. "Great, our group has been invaded by defective Dutchmen." The few boys next to him leered at us as we continued to unpack.

"Don't worry about him," a boy in the cot next to Ludo said. The boy looked at Ludo and put down a colorful three-tone quilt he unfolded from his bag. "I'm Pauwel," he said. He had glossy, volcanic pimples around his nose and chewed at the peels of raw skin around his thumbnail.

"Ludo Shoemackher, and these are Edwin and Jacob Koopman."

"Nice to meet you," Pauwel said. He had a pear-shaped face with doughy cheeks that made him look like a chubby little Viking. "You'll settle in fine."

Outside, we were lined up for uniform inspections by Günter, who had us stand straight, tuck our shirts beneath our belt lines, and fold back the tops of our wool socks. He stood in front of me and ran his hands over my shoulders to smooth the creases.

"Look up and ahead. Not down."

I looked up and let my eyes lose focus and cursed myself for being scared of people talking directly to me, like anyone, at any moment, might spark into a rage if I said a word.

After inspection we were ready for our first tour of the grounds

and marched single file by the rows of bunkhouses, and a giant building that was the camp officers' housing and offices.

"This is the parade ground with the flagpoles," Günter said. A red
flag with a black, hooked swastika flapped in the breeze, snapping as it
fully extended before folding back on itself.

Beyond the main grounds were sports fields that pushed all the
way back to a dense stand of woods. In the woods were obstacle
courses, firing ranges, and an area where previous campers had built
bunker forts and concrete pillboxes to border the camp's property.

We marched around the campgrounds, then we teamed up for a
football match where I ran myself ragged from the pure joy of having
so many other kids to play with. After the game, we ate as a giant group
at long wooden tables set end to end in rows outside so all five hundred camp boys could eat together at once. I had never seen so many
boys, and wondered what had brought them here. For the most part it
was the sixteen- to eighteen-year-olds who were in charge of the camp,
although there were several camp officers. *Alten Händen*, they called
them, Old Hands, who we were told had survived hard times on the
front lines. They marched through the grounds, scanning, supervis-
ing, instructing on *Kampfgeist*, fighting spirit, or *Labenscraum*, living
space, and then disappeared into cabins near the main office.

Most of the German words were thick and heavy in my mouth.
Ludo and Edwin took to nuances of the language we hadn't learned in
lessons, but I was quite clunky at it.

That first night we had campfires and played games. Tests of courage, really. Boys jumped over bonfires. Older counselors carried out giant circular canvases with handles woven along the edge. When rolled
out, the canvas was large enough for two grown men to lie end to end

in any direction. Thirty campers from my troop gathered around the tarp as one boy crawled into the center. Then everyone lifted his edge of the canvas so the boy in the middle launched off the ground. Günter counted so we knew when to dip and lift the canvas. To his cadence, we launched the boy in the middle up into the air, a free-float ascension until he peaked and sailed back into the taut and ready trampoline. This was how we learned one another's names. The flying boy shouted his name, and the rest of us repeated it as we heaved.

Ed-win.

Lu-do.

Tim-o-thy, the rash-necked boy.

Garth, another bunkmate.

Pauw-el.

The names felt endless. Our voices lifted the boy upward. When it was my turn, I flew over the whole troop and saw the quick glow of other fires and other boys being launched around the campground before falling back into the soft, giving tarp, my body sinking into it, and then springing back off of it, back into the air. They pitched me into the summer night to the sound of one deep cadence and the voice of thirty other laughing boys.

"Ja-cob. Ja-cob. Ja-cob," they shouted.

Before going to our bunkhouses for bed, the older boys told us stories about great German soldiers and fairy tales, which were entertaining, sure, but no match for my father's. His always made me feel like I moved underwater, like the world my body was in was not the world of sight at all, and that it was the world of his stories that mattered most. His stories were so vivid and real, so dangerous and profound, he could have easily scared the piss out of any of these boys.

My father had a habit of gathering all the kids in our church around him for storytelling after Mass ended. Every kid in the village and Samuel, the air-writer, knew to make a crescent moon around him after our mother finished playing from Dieterich Buxtehude's Fugues, always the final organ song. At first, the kids kept their distance from him the way their parents did, but his stories lulled them close.

My father would tuck his arms against his ribs and whisper as we leaned toward him, and as he raised his voice and lifted his arms, we'd lurch back as if in concert with him. To me, my father telling these stories in church was its own kind of worship. For a half hour every week, he was the babysitter while the children's parents would talk among themselves. Samuel's arm waved over the sitting children's head like a spastic blessing. Edwin and I hung in limbo, somewhere between the adults and our father, trying our best to grow out of the stories we'd heard our whole lives, one ear cocked to what the adults talked about—recipes, fishing grounds, and something about fascism, which I barely understood—and the other searching out new twists to old stories, or captivated by the occasional new tale he'd offer up, letting the children knead them into their own fantasies. The last church story I heard had Thump-Drag stumbling into a darkened church where the Devil was doing a wild dance, his disguises changing with each twirl. The Devil shape-shifted from a giant shaggy dog to a snake with legs, and finally, to a beautiful woman who reached out and pulled Thump-Drag into her dance.

Storytelling was how my father communicated with us, and I remembered every detail of his tales. I felt them enter my bloodstream and become a part of me. Thinking back, if there was any art that truly became part of my life, my father's stories were it. Their fictions were the magic of my childhood. When I shut my eyes, I'd pick up their tracks, like the paw prints of a fox out in the early morning snow.

My first night in the cabin I lay awake for hours getting used to the shadows and sounds of other boys breathing. Günter got up from bed and walked outside to relieve himself. His hard-on made a tent of his underwear. I hated seeing that as it made me feel by contrast a puny, hairless boy. The screen slapped shut behind him as he spit a gob of phlegm into the grass.

The morning revelry call woke me up, but Edwin was already drawing in his notepad, sketching the boys running to the fields, the cabins adorned with the sharp red, black, and white flags. He had sketches of Ludo at play, his arm shriveled on the paper too. He drew me as well. I was a close and easy model, so perhaps it was all that repetition, but my brother had me down exactly. I'd look down at a sketch and recognize myself immediately. Page after page. Jacob. Jacob. Jacob. There I was.

We met at the camp's main flagpole during revelry. Pauwel was part of the drum line, and he marched down among the campers, pounding on his drum as if he were a thunderclap. He was by far the best player, and the rest of the drum line softened their playing until they almost faded entirely while his beat picked up for a solo. He carried four drumsticks, two in reserve tucked into the loop of his snare drum's carrying strap. The band came back on the same note, and the whole parade ground of several hundred boys practiced their marching.

"Eyes left," and we snapped our heads to the left, so that we moved together, shoes clopping in time to Pauwel and his drums.

After that, the large gathering broke into cabin groups. We studied how to plot our positions with maps and compasses, and how to shoot targets attached to fifty-gallon steel drums. Rifle training required us to become accustomed to the weight of weapons. We learned marksmanship with air rifles and trained in bolt-action .22s. Those boys who had been to camp in previous years were excellent marksmen. The boys shot the hell out of the targets too, exploding cans, boxes, and barrels, and each little explosion scattered dirt on the slope of the backdrop. The *plink-plink-plink* of bullets on targets echoed across the field all day, which carried the scent of spent gunpowder.

The most accomplished marksmen received *Dienstdolch*, daggers, as rewards, which were the envy of everyone who had yet to earn one. The older boys and camp counselors all had service daggers attached to their belts—a major status symbol. All the boys wanted their own daggers and worked for them every day. The daggers said, *Blut und Ehre*, Blood and Honor. Each came with a steel scabbard attached to a thin leather strap. The blade was six inches long and one in width. The handles were steel with black grip plates screwed in. At the center of each grip plate was the red-and-white diamond insignia around a swastika. The older boys compared their RZM numbers, which had been put on by the natural-material-control office. "Mine is M7/25/37," one of the boys said as he read the etchings off the blade.

I leaned in closer, eyeing the numbers. I desperately wanted one for myself. I felt that it would rival my Uncle Martin's scrimshaw blade and imagined the whir of one in front of me. Keep it moving. Keep the steel moving.

We donned gas masks, cinched them tight, and then played tug-of-war with the masks on. If two people from one side got their masks on and ran to the rope and only one from the other team made it, then that one person had to anchor down and hold the line until the others on his team got there to help. I got to the rope at the same time as Edwin during our first tug-of-war match, but Günter tapped Edwin on the shoulder and pulled him out of the line. He dug a finger into the side of Edwin's mask where it wasn't sealed properly.

"You're out, Koopman. Dead men can't help their teammates pull." He looked at me then. "Jacob. Fine work." I swelled with pride over doing well among so many boys that would play and compete and not start raving if they were kept from their drawing.

We dug parallel trenches out in the field and threw wooden potato-masher grenades at one another. Until they showed me how to let it glide out of my hands, I whipped mine with such forced, jerking motions that my shoulder muscles hurt for days. The last one standing won. That was the goal with most of the games we played—be the last one standing.

At night, we had a large group gathering by the main building and listened to speeches and music from the gramophone. My mother would have loved the music. Every Sunday evening at home she made us dress up. Me, my father, Edwin, and sometimes Ludo and Uncle Martin would clear the center of our living room of furniture and her sewing machine, and all take our seats on the couches as she started her gramophone. The room was modeled after a British Victorian sitting parlor. Built-in bookshelves lined the walls. One by one, we each danced with her. She was thin-boned, loose-jointed, at ease as she glided across the hardwood, leading everyone but Uncle Martin, who was the best dancer among us.

"This makes your mother happy," my father told us when Edwin protested having to dance. So, we each took our turns. When it was my turn she swept me off the couch, spun me around, twisted me along with her graceful body, and delivered me seamlessly back to my seat.

"Thank you, kind sir," she would say.

When it was Ludo's turn, she shifted her hands so his weak arm could stay relaxed at his side as they slid around the room together, as easily as the rest of us did. Fergus's uncontrollable excitement led him to swing around the dancing couple, his nails scratching the hardwood floor. At camp, there were enough boys my mother could have danced from one boy to the next, across the field grounds for the rest of her life, her flower dress spinning on and on. This image has stayed with me my whole life—my beautiful mother in perpetual motion.

During the third week of camp, the buses took us to meet up with boys from other camps on the shores of the North Sea. In total there were over two thousand boys, and for an hour we marched on the sands showing our formations and marching skills to one another. Then we had to face up to the dunes where a procession of military officers gathered around General Spitz of the Luftwaffe, who had come to give a speech to all of us. His chest from collarbone to navel was covered in so many medals it looked like a toddler had gone wild decorating him.

"You are a fine group of young men," he said into a microphone. "You are making your families proud. Keep having fun. Learn as much as you can, and you will make this nation a phoenix, rising with the scalding light of redemption to bring prosperity back to our people. When you are called, your hearts will know to rise."

The boys around me shot their arms up so their palms faced the top of the dunes so I did the same.

"*Sieg Heil,*" the thousands of boys said in unison, and their chorus could have beat back the surf with its force.

When the general finished his speech, the camp counselors said we could strip down to our shorts and leave the rest of our clothes folded at our feet.

As we stood there I looked to see which boys had the first trails of hair plunging from their belly buttons to their pant lines. Who had ribs and veins protruding or developed muscles or was flabby and pale. I was comparing everyone with my own body and the general's words were already far from my mind.

"Now, raise your hand if you cannot swim or if you are a poor swimmer," Günter said.

The few boys who raised their hands were asked to come stand behind him. "Now, when the general's whistle blows, you boys who are good swimmers can go swimming. Those behind me, we will go down to the beach and you will *learn* how to swim."

When the whistle sounded, I hardly heard it, but waves of boys peeled out of their ranks and ran across the sand toward the surf. Bodies crashed into the water by the dozens when Edwin, Ludo, and I at last realized we were free to run; the others had expected the whistle from years before.

The three of us turned and ran across the flat sand to the water in a wild stampede of yipping and yelling to one another. The hard crash of my body into the ice cold water knocked the wind out of me, but I dove farther in, closer to the crowd of hundreds of milky-pale boys playing in the North Sea. We began to wrestle one another.

One boy dunked himself under, and came up with globs of wet sand that he threw up into the air, yelling "Incoming!" as the boys around him dove under the surface to avoid the gritty spray that fell in after them.

Other boys yelled "Incoming!" and "Fire!" and "Save yourself!"

Their voices carried down the strand. *Einfall! Angriff! Alle mann van bard!*

Then, Timothy, our bunkmate with the rashed neck, jumped on my back and pushed me under.

"Take that," he said.

His meaty hands pinched at the muscles of my neck and I thought, You fucker, and tried to swim free and kick up, but he kept me pinned down until I swallowed mouthfuls of water. Then he placed his foot on my back and kicked me into the sandy bottom where I felt his other foot press between my shoulder blades. Then I thought, Jesus, I'm going to drown.

But Edwin came to my rescue. He pushed Timothy away. When I jumped out of the water and gasped for air, I heard the last of my brother yelling at Timothy.

"What's wrong with you?"

I worked my way to shore and for a moment wished the sand under my feet were the soil of Delfzijl—of home.

Later in the day, after I recovered on the beach, Pauwel, Ludo, Edwin, and I wrestled in the water. We teamed up to get on each other's shoulders and tried to push one another off. I grappled with Ludo, who kept pushing me into the cold water despite his dead arm, which was thinner at the bicep than the knot of bone at his elbow. We did this until our bodies were blue from the cold and red from the sun. I imagined pictures rising from our bones to our skin. Then we were instructed to come out of the water, dry off, dress on the sand, and board the buses, which we rode home with our skin tight from the salt and sunburn.

Timothy turned toward the three of us on the bus. "I'm surprised the Dutch boys didn't drown."

At night we watched a movie that had been set up in a giant tent.

The film was about a teenaged Nazi martyr named Hitlerjunge Quex, who grew up in poverty in Berlin. It showed him in 1932, during the pit of the German Depression, when his out-of-work father, a supporter of the Communist party, sent him on a weekend camping trip with a Communist youth group. While there, Quex found the Communists were undisciplined and rowdy. They smoked and drank, danced late into the night, and served their meals by tossing hunks of bread at a hungry crowd that fought for what they could catch. One of the games the Communist camp counselors set up quickly turned into a game of holding each other down and slapping the other's private parts.

When this scene appeared, the boys who had been to camp before yelled, "Filthy animals," in unison and then they leaned into each other and laughed.

Quex sneaks off to another part of the park and finds a group of Hitler Youth camping by the lake and he spies on them. When the German boys appeared onscreen, the boys around us started cheering.

"Watch and learn, Quex. Watch and learn," the boys yelled at the screen.

Quex saw the Hitler Youth working together to make a fire and cook a hot dinner. They listened to speeches, sang patriotic songs, and shouted in unison their support for an "awakened Germany."

On cue, the boys in the movie tent yelled, "Awakened Germany!"

When Quex returns home, singing one of the Hitler Youth songs, his father comes on the screen, and at this point all the boys in the tent began to hiss.

Hissssss.

Quex's father beats him and signs him up to become a member of the Communist party. However, Quex informs the Hitler Youth that the Young Communists are planning to ambush them during a march using guns and dynamite. Quex's warning is found out, and he becomes a pariah to the Communists and a hero to the Hitler Youth. His distraught mother tries to kill her son and herself by extinguishing the pilot light and leaving the gas on in their one-room apartment at night. She is killed. Quex survives. His father, crushed by what happens, begins to wonder aloud whether his son isn't right—maybe National Socialism is better for Germany than communism.

The boys in the movie tent all yell, "Of course it is! Of course!"

Edwin, Ludo, and I had seen plenty of movies together. We all nearly pissed our pants when we saw *Nosferatu*. During *The Hunchback of Notre Dame*, I yelped when Quasimodo abducted Esmeralda, and Edwin and Ludo giggled out loud when he was crowned as the king of the fools. Still, neither of those was interactive like this.

By the end of the movie, Edwin, Ludo, and I were all trying to anticipate what the group would yell at the screen next, hoping we would guess right, and could join in.

"You're a hero, Quex," the boys yelled when the film ended.

After watching that movie, something shifted in me. That night, in my cot, I imagined I was Quex saving the Hitler Youth boys. Brave despite knowing I was on a *Himmelfahrts Kommando*, a trip-to-heaven mission. I wanted to be a hero too.

"I loved that movie," I whispered over to Edwin who propped his flashlight on his pillow so he could see his notepad as he sketched.

"Well. Remember what Uncle Martin said. Don't buy too much into what these people are telling you."

"Why not? We don't have this many friends at home."

"Which are our friends here?"

I pointed around the room and my finger fell on Pauwel's bunk.

"Who else? Who else, Mr. Soldier Boy?"

"You're just mad I'm doing so well and can figure out how to put on a gas mask."

Edwin swung his legs out of bed, reached a hand to my shoulder, and dug his fingers into the flesh above my collarbone until it felt like he held me by a handle.

"Am not," he said.

"Okay. Okay," I murmured, squirming to get away from him.

"To sleep!" Günter yelled from the far end of the cabin.

Asleep, my dream self cared only for the heroic. I had been called to perform. Before camp, I went to sleep most nights dreaming of my mother's organ music, the spark and glow of fresh new lights my father had brought into the world, Thump-Drag, or Hilda, my grip on her ankles. Now, I'd been called.

The next morning at breakfast, where we were fed scoops from a vat of brown goulash and boiled and pressed sugar beets, Timothy and three of his friends sat across the table from Edwin, Ludo, Pauwel, and me. The boy straight across from me, Garth, was pudgy with pinched, close-set eyes. His hands dimpled at the knuckles. There were different-colored stains down the front of his shirt.

"You strike me as someone who would slap another boy's privates if you got the chance," Timothy said. "And you," he pointed at Ludo's bad arm, "you weaken the race."

Edwin sat perfectly still. Then he spit his juice out of his mouth in a whalelike blow across the table. Spray settled and rivulets of juice converged and dripped from Timothy's chin.

"I thought I tasted a spider," Edwin said, and turned back to his juice, washing down his breakfast as if nothing had happened.

I was shocked at my brother's nerve. He sat there calm and easy. Though for the first time I noticed the gray skin under his eyes from staying up every night drawing.

"You just made a mistake, you Dutch *du Hurenschn*." Timothy pulled a dagger out from the side of his belt and slammed it down into the wood table. The blade ate an inch into the wood, and the black handle—with the red-framed black swastika in the middle—shook for a moment between the two boys. Etched on the blade were the familiar words *Blut und Ehre*, and no sooner had I finished reading them, Timothy yelled, "Now!"

He and his three friends jumped up onto their benches, stepped onto the table as if they'd choreographed their movements earlier and dove at us. One of the boys kicked Pauwel right in the mouth. One jumped on Ludo, and Timothy sent an errant kick toward Edwin who sidestepped it and swept his other leg off the solid wooden table. I didn't see Timothy smash onto the breakfast tray, as at that moment Garth jumped off the table, landed on top of me, and slammed me to the ground. In moments, red-faced Garth was snarling hysterically and pounding his fists on my arms where I covered my face and tried to fight back.

The counselors pulled a boy off Pauwel and peeled Ludo and Edwin off one boy with a bloody nose they had wrestled down. Ludo was in a rage and spit flew from his mouth. "I hope you piss green worms," he yelled.

"Halt this immediately!" Günter yelled.

Günter and his fellow counselors lined us guilty boys up so Edwin and Timothy's allies were mixed up and standing shoulder to shoulder. We breathed heavy. Missing hats. Our shirts untucked, dirty, and blood-splotched. I had split knuckles. Red crescents from hitting teeth leaked into the webbing of my fingers.

"So you all want to be fighters? That's good. But we will have to teach you when to fight and who to fight. Now all of you face forward. Turn left. Now march—march—march."

Günter led the eight of us boys to the flagpole at the revelry area. "Remember what Quex learned, boys? You work together. You are brothers. But wrongs must be punished. Now who started this fight?"

Timothy and Edwin both stepped forward. They both looked right into Günter's eyes.

Again Edwin's nerve astonished me.

Günter motioned to the two other camp counselors who had marched with us to the flagpole to join him in front of the boys. When one of them was each positioned in front of Edwin and Timothy, they hauled back their arms and slugged each of the boys in the stomach, toppling them to the ground.

"Now that you're down there, make fists and lean on your knuckles. The rest of you get down and do the same," Günter yelled.

On our knuckles we were forced to do push-ups in the grass while chanting after Günter, who spouted off about a reawakened Germany beneath the waving flag.

Well after lights out that night, I woke to Pauwel screaming, and shot up with a sudden spell of nervousness. It was late and the cabin rumbled from thunder several kilometers off. Two other boys bolted up. The one closest to me, Lutz, was stock-still, his eyes locked on the plywood roof, his chest heaved from sudden fear. His silhouette, a high forehead, stumpy nose, and jutting jaw. A flash of lightning came through the windows and sank away in his eyes. Pauwel paced back and forth mumbling to himself. I didn't get out of bed but lifted my body up on my elbows to see the shadow of my new friend moving at the foot of his bunk, holding the three-tone quilt with blue, red, and black squares that his mother had made for him.

Günter woke up and whisper-yelled to Pauwel, "What the hell are you doing?"

"There's too many pieces," Pauwel said. "Too many."

"What?"

"Too many."

Günter got out of bed and walked to Pauwel.

In his wild dreaming, Pauwel's eyes were dark, emotive, and arresting as they held a hint of some exotic blood—Hungarian or perhaps Italian. His face had a strange elasticity to it. One moment it was expressionless, and then it would open up into an oversized grin that twisted his features and showed his large, square teeth and swollen upper lip.

"It fell apart."

"What did?" Günter asked.

"It will take forever to put them all back. I won't have enough time to do it."

"Do what?"

"All these squares. They fell apart. There are too many pieces." Pauwel was holding up the blanket and looked near tears.

"Your blanket?"

"Too many pieces."

Günter put his hand on Pauwel's forehead, and said, "It's okay. Let's get you back to bed," and he led Pauwel back to his bunk by the bulb of his elbow, pulled the quilt over his body, and told him to go back to sleep. Günter, who had been so harsh earlier, was kind and gentle now, and the soothing sound of his voice surprised me.

"The blanket's fine. It's together," Günter said.

"It will take my whole life to fix."

"No. It's okay," I heard Günter's reassuring words for quite a while that night.

I sat in the dark as the rain searched for a way inside and heightened the smell of the pine trees and musty wood floorboards. I was the last of the boys to fall back to sleep. I looked over the others. I presumed their dreams were like mine, both innocent and bloodthirsty.

After the bugle wake-up call, Garth teased Pauwel. "My blanky broke. My blanky broke." He rocked back and forth with his hands on his stomach like he had terrible gas. He gave a fake laugh, "I'm sorry we were all there to see you go nuts last night."

"You shouldn't tease me," Pauwel said. "I'll tell everyone how I walked in on you pulling on your crank."

"I don't remember that," Garth said.

"You were busy," Pauwel said.

The rest of the boys laughed. I was happy to see my new friend hold his ground.

After breakfast we played tug-of-war with gas masks on. The glass eye lens of my mask steamed over from straining for breath. I let the fog sit but Edwin wiped his away by sticking a finger inside the lining seal.

"You're dead, Edwin," Günter yelled. "Step out of the line. Dead men still can't help their teammates pull. When are you going to learn that one?"

I kept pulling with the other boys. Part of me was happy to be better at something than Edwin. Ludo, however, had mastered tug-of-war. He looped his strong arm over the rope, grabbed it from the bottom, and leaned backward so his bicep curled into a coiled snake.

After a lunch of fish stew that tasted like the salt sheen of a tidal flat, our troop cabin went to the firing range and began practice for what we were told would be the camp's final games. For which we would practice every afternoon for the next two weeks.

In the evening, we lounged around our cabin reading magazines that had been placed in the bunkhouse. They were a thrill to read. The Hitler Youth were regularly issued *Wille und Macht*, Will and Power Monthly magazine. The other publications included *Die Kameradshaft*, Comradeship, which had a version for the Bund Deutscher Mädel, the League of German Girls, called *Mädelschaft*, and a yearbook called *Jungen eure Welt*, Youth, Your World. We took turns reading to one another. Sometimes we read from the girls' magazine.

Timothy lay shirtless on his bunk. His head rested on one hand and with the other hand he rolled the few soft brown armpit hairs he had between his thumb and forefinger.

"I'm going to get myself a job at a girls' camp. I'll perform virginity tests. Get to feel how warm they are. Hold up a breast. Feel its weight. Do the other breast. Stuff like that. I'll be busy for years."

The thought of him touching anyone was revolting, but even hearing the word *breast* made my prick stiff.

Of course I thought of Hilda then. Hilda's red hair. Green eyes. Lean, porcelain limbs. She lived in the first farmhouse down the road from us. Her kneecaps had soft golden hairs that I wanted to place my palms over. Let them sit there. Feel the bone. The warmth. When we walked home together, surreptitiously I ogled the slight, nearly imperceptible movement of her breasts beneath the fabric of her sweater.

That night Günter and the other older camp counselors met outside and huddled behind the cabin smoking cigarettes. They stood, posing as soldiers.

While they were out, Timothy woke up a group of his friends and for some reason tapped me on the feet to come with them. Edwin, Ludo, and Pauwel were still sleeping. I was scared of Timothy and his friends, but wanting to gain their approval, I got up and blindly followed them outside.

I could hear the counselors talking from behind the cabin.

"The Russians have smelly old pussies where their hearts should be," one said and the rest laughed. One choked midexhale and then coughed out a laugh.

The phrase "smelly old pussies" set into my mind on repeat. I imagined it set to music. Organ music. "Smelly old pussies. Smelly old pussies." The phrase blasted over parishioners and then circled back as an echo. Over and over the perverse music played out in my head until we were past the cabins, and I realized Timothy and the boys all held flashlights in one hand and rocks in the other. When I saw that I froze.

"Come on," Timothy said.

"I think I'll head back," I said.

"No. Come on."

"I'm going to go back."

"No. Come with us."

Timothy must have sensed my fear as he handed me an extra light and a stone of my own. "Here. Come on."

We snuck to the edge of the burn pit where camp trash was tossed and stood in a line shoulder to shoulder.

"On three," Timothy said.

I wanted to run away before they tossed me in.

"One. Two. Three. Now."

The boys all flashed their lights on and as they spotlighted rats they heaved their stones.

"Got one," Garth said.

"Me too," Lutz said.

"Turn your lights off," Timothy called.

In the dark, we only had to wait a minute to count again. When we flashed the lights back on the rats were already back scurrying over the trash and ash.

"Now," Timothy yelled again.

Everyone threw their stones. I was so relieved this wasn't some hazing punishment focused on me that I tossed the stones with the easy arc I'd learned to hurl potato mashers.

"Oh. Oh. The one I got looked just like the Jews in the poster. Did you see it?" Garth asked.

I hadn't known many Jews, but those I did I had no problem with. My homeroom teacher, Mrs. Von Schuler, was Jewish. She'd float into the room every morning. "*Yeladim. Yeladim.* Time to sit, my *Yeladim.*" It was the Hebrew word for children and she said it like it were a song. The word a breathy hug. The word—my favorite word—that to me sounded like it should mean lights. Bright, radiant lights.

"Did you see it?" Garth asked again.

"I think I hit it too," I said. It was one of those nothing, braggart things I said as a boy and forgot about for years, until it rose up in memory and my face grew hot with shame.

Our troop was up early the next morning and was brought to the camp's main entrance. I remember being exhausted until we were led to a line of BMW motorcycles with sidecars. Drivers wearing trench coats and dark goggles snapped tight above the rims of their helmets stood in front of each motorcycle.

"You want to have a ride with us?" one of them called.

I got the last one in the line and sat in the low bucket of the sidecar. The rider pulled his dark goggles down and started the engine. We gained speed quickly. Several of the first boys raised their hands over their heads to catch the wind in their palms, but I had to pin my knees and elbows against the side to keep from bouncing out. Dust kicked up by the other riders swept over my face, but it was fun to move so fast. Fun to be a boy around so many other boys with games, movies, swimming, and great machines like this one to capture our attention. The driver shouted something but I couldn't hear him over the smooth thrumming of the engine.

We drove around the entire camp to the western edge, which I hadn't seen before. It was an annexed farm and my driver stopped on the road to let me look over at the horse barn. I'd overheard a small group of older boys talking at the lunch tables about mucking horseshit and piss-soaked hay from stalls. I saw they'd also built an obstacle course in the western paddock.

The same group were down there now in a single-file line in front of the barn. One by one they approached a grown man in riding boots who held his arms out in a circle the boys dove through. He caught the back of the boys' heads with one hand and the bottom of their stomachs with the other, and spun them like they were sturgeon at a fish market. The boys tucked in midair, hit the ground, and rolled from their shoulders back to their feet before running to the back of the line again.

"They're practicing falling off of a horse," my driver said.

"Why?"

"They'll be horse soldiers. A garrison of about twenty, I'd guess."

He looked down at me and perhaps saw my surprise. "We train for everything. There are glider pilot units. Naval auxiliaries. You'll find something good."

He started the engine and we buzzed along the back side of the camp. It would be much later that I'd think, dear Christ, whoever put the camps together had thought through every minute of what would hook and bend a boy's imagination into becoming a soldier, including feelings for girls, who were to be meticulously organized and regulated. Though at the time, my pubescent mind probably latched onto the idea of Timothy training to perform virginity tests.

For the final games, Günter pulled our troop into the cabin and had us sit on the edge of our cots.

"Now, if we are going to survive the final games, we have to work together. There have been problems between some of you, but I need our best six athletes for the main event, which means we have to team up."

Günter had Timothy and Edwin stand side by side in the front of the cabin and put Pauwel between them. Then he had Ludo and Garth, who had jumped on me during our fight, stand behind those two. Then Günter called my name.

The main event of the games was a competition called Roman chariot. It took six boys to form one chariot. Three boys would link arms at the elbows, with the two outer boys having a leather loop hanging off their shoulders. Two more boys linked arms, bent their heads forward, and leaned into the linked three so the five of them faced one direction and fit together like a rugby scrum. The sixth boy, the charioteer—me, because I was the smallest—climbed up on the bent shoulders of the two boys in back, reached for the leather loops from the boys in front and leaned backward, letting the rope strung around the boys' shoulders hold me from falling. My feet pushed forward, easing the two boys below me into the three boys ahead of them, so we were all tensed and held together as the five boys started to run. My hands pulled on the lines to guide Timothy and Edwin in the front and Ludo and Garth in the back as we practiced running all over the grounds.

My body was ropey and strong, but the first times we tried to move together I fell backward as if bucked from a horse. Then I overcompensated and sailed face-first over Timothy's scoured neck. My brother and the rest of the team crashed on top of me. Then we switched Ludo so his weak arm faced out and didn't affect his stance. Once I got the feel for shifting my weight, and warned the boys holding the straps in the front before leaning back, the whole group straightened out. Günter had us run the full circle around the camp. The team ran under my feet. Their ten legs pounded the dirt.

When we were back in our cabin, Edwin painted an animal on each of my teammates' forearms, a wolf, a bear, a hawk. On mine he drew Thump-Drag, a hunchbacked silhouette.

"What is that?" Timothy asked.

"That's Thump-Drag," Edwin told him.

"Who's that?"

Timothy's question threw me off. I forgot not everyone knew about Thump-Drag.

On the first day of the camp games, foot racing, target shooting, and singing tournaments began. Older boys played a violent group game where cabins put on red or blue armbands and had to hunt one another down and steal all the other team's colors to win. But the camp-wide highlight was the Roman chariot races.

By then we were practiced enough that we swept past the whirl of cheering boys around the oval track. My whole body shifted to keep balance as the balls of my heels dug into the backs of the boys below me. My rear-end drooped low, and my arms reached straight ahead, yanking in with my right hand and slacking the left to turn, and like one fluid creature, the six of us circled the course. We won our first three meets because other teams kept crashing. One boy broke his arm after a fall, and that put us in the final race with four other teams. The race was held the last night of camp, once it got dark. The campers who were not in the final race lined the track and held flashlights and torches made with wadded, oil-soaked cloth, so winding lines of fire and iridescent light bordered the whole course.

I remember thinking that some of these bulbs must have come from my father's factory.

Before the race started, Edwin and Timothy talked about how to take the corners. They had begun working together after Timothy made a joke about how the two of them were the only ones who knew that the counselors punched like girls. When they were bound together, they let me climb onto their bent shoulders.

I looked ahead of me at the curve in the track, and the layered flames on both sides of it. The idea of launching off the backs of the boys into the flames suddenly scared me.

"Ready," I said.

At the starting line other charioteers boxed me in on both sides.

The boy to my immediate left smiled, and the boy to my right was already squatting back, legs shaking, and ready to begin.

Günter was at the starting line cheering us on. The camp director, donned in the full military uniform of an SS officer, walked to the front of the racers and held up a Luger. When the gun fired, the boys below me jerked forward and I eased back so the lines in my hands snapped taut. The voices of the boys lining the course pushed against me as we ran past. Wisps of smoke from the burning oil filled my lungs. At the start of the race we were in third place. We made it halfway around the track when one of the teams ahead of us crumpled on a tight turn. On the last stretch, with my screaming matched by all five of the boys below me, we passed the remaining chariot in front of us by the length of my brother's head and stayed locked for fifty meters before we pulled ahead and won.

Günter met us at the finish line and hugged Pauwel and Timothy.

"We did it! We did it!" he yelled. Then, as if remembering himself, he stood back and raised his hand high in front of our team to salute us.

The noise of all the boys who watched was deafening as they cheered and closed in around us in a dizzy whorl of lights and flames. The camp director ordered everyone to the main revelry grounds, where there was a giant pile of wood. All the boys walked forward and touched their torches onto the pile. Once the bonfire was stoked, the camp director ordered the winning chariot team forward.

"You young men have shown great strength and honor today. Your family and country are proud of you," the officer said.

Then Günter handed each of us a dagger. I unsheathed mine and held it in front of me so the firelight shone off the blade.

"As is our tradition, the winning team gets to do the final march of heroes."

Günter and another counselor came forward with a giant shield that had a broken thunderbolt on it.

"We get to carry the fallen soldier," Timothy told Garth.

"It's an honor for us," Günter added.

We lined up at the flagpole, where they had me lie down on the shield. Edwin, the other four boys, and Günter lifted the shield over their heads and started marching. The camp director led everyone in the songs we had learned over the course of the last five weeks. With my dagger pinned to my chest, my head rolled from side to side to see the tips of the torches lit around me. The voices of hundreds of boys, singing in unison about the valor of fallen soldiers, lifted into the sky. I lay on the shield as if I were Quex, and let the singing and firelight soak into me, basking in what would be the first but not the last time Hitler's nationalists would celebrate me.

4

The buses arrived the next morning to take us back to the train station. I had spent all night imagining myself as a war hero, leading my troop from the Hitler Youth camps east through Russia. We marched, now hardened men, until we hit Stalingrad. I army-crawled on the cool forest floor, and the scope of my gun lined up faceless individual soldiers who didn't see me hidden behind trees, sniping away at them from a distance, chanting, Smelly old pussies, smelly old pussies, as each figure dropped to the ground.

After the long train ride, we found Uncle Martin and our father waiting for us at the station by the loading docks. There was too much to tell them all at once, but all three of us started shouting to them about it anyway.

"We won the camp games!" Ludo announced.

"We learned how to take target practice," Edwin said.

"Look what I won," I said to my father and held up my dagger for him to admire. "Look at this." The blade glinted like a blue fang in the sunlight. The pad of my finger traced the RZM numbers.

"Jesus," my father said.

"We did orienteering and grenade fights," Ludo said.

"Jesus, you did that?"

"We loved it," I said.

Uncle Martin and my father looked at each other, and I could tell a coded family message passed between them.

Next to the harbormaster's office, the scaffold radio tower we'd seen before had collapsed into a pile of charred lumber and steel.

"Look at that," Ludo said.

I looked at my uncle, who didn't turn but walked ahead of us to the boat.

"Wires must have gotten too hot," my father said.

I was disappointed my father wasn't more excited for us. The more animated we became, the quieter he and Uncle Martin got. Later that day, when we cruised the Ems on the *Lighthouse Lady*, I overheard my father and my uncle talking.

"This is more craziness," Uncle Martin said.

"What would you have me do?" my father asked.

"You can take them somewhere else for a while. You have the money."

"But then what? I'd have to shut down the factory. I have to stay and keep that up."

"There'll be more trouble. More fighting."

"They can't fight anymore. They've done that already and ten million people died."

"You're naïve," Uncle Martin said.

They stood for a long time in silence. I stopped listening and turned to Ludo and my brother, who basked in the glow of how well camp had ended for us. They carried their daggers on their belts just like me.

Hilda met us at the dock and walked home with us. She'd been riding her horse and was dressed in riding breeches, laced boots, and a black, felt-covered helmet.

On our walk, Edwin slapped at his shoulder.

"Got the sucker," he said, and cupped a fly in his fist. "I can feel the wings banging against my fingers.

"Can I have a strand of your hair, Hilda?" he asked.

"What?"

"A strand of hair. Can I?"

Hilda took off her helmet, let down the little bun she kept her hair folded up in and started to preen through the hair flowing between her shoulder blades. She singled one out, yanked it, and held it out to Edwin.

"Make a sliding knot in that," Edwin told me.

"It's too delicate," I said.

"The way you taught me," he said. "Loop it and cinch it until the loop is half the size of a guilder."

I'd never taught my brother anything in my life and when I looked at him he winked at me, a put-on mannerism I now see he took from Uncle Martin. I twisted Hilda's hair, and imagined my hands running through the rest of it, what the full heft of it would feel like. When the loop was knotted, Edwin took the strand. Still holding the fly, he let his pinky and ring finger pinch the fly to his palm and held one end of her hair strand with his thumb and pointer finger and the other with his other hand. He slid the knot of hair under his pinched fingers to where the fly was, and started wiggling the strand back and forth, working the fine hair and little bug. When he opened his hand the fly jumped out and flew, then stopped in midair, and started moving like an inverse pendulum in perfect circles around the tips of his thumb and pointer finger where he pinched the little hair tether.

"Here you go, Hilda," Edwin said, "flies make good pets."

"Gross," she said, but held her hand out to pinch at her own hair.

The fly circled around in front of her as we walked. It lifted and flitted, the constant buzz of it moving with us.

"Jacob, you showed him this?" Hilda asked. Some voltage of light cut loose in her cool green eyes. I was paralyzed by her red mouth, a momentary softening of her features, this glimpse of youthful beauty.

"He sure did," my brother said, patting me on the back. "This one's full of great tricks."

I blushed under her stare, and looked at her and the fly on a string that mystified me as much as Hilda did. Hilda was distracted by the fly in front of her, and I studied the part in her hair, the deep green flecks in her eyes, and wished the road would go on forever.

After camp, half the summer was left, so Edwin and I started working full-time at our father's factory. Our first day, he gave us a tour of everything we'd seen hundreds of times. His office had a picture-frame window that looked down onto the factory floor. The glass furnace, rollers, and cooling tanks were against the far wall. The ribbon machines and assembly lines stood parallel to each other. Production flowed from end to end, then serpentined back in the other direction on the next line until the finished bulbs were ready to be packaged and stacked by the case for shipments. The window filtered out the noise of wheezing

machinery and workers calling loudly to one another over the mold-
ing press tamping out copper bases for the lights. Once he formally
showed us the entire factory, he started describing how Gerard and
Annie Van Den Bosch ran the books, the ledgers; what each person
in the office did. Then we moved to the factory with Ludo's mother,
Edward Fass, and dozens of others.

"Boys, if you're going to understand this business, you're going to
learn it from the bottom up, not the other way around," he told us.

I tried to picture myself making this my life, standing behind the
glass up in the office and watching the output of our own industry.
We started by loading the cases of bulbs onto outgoing trucks. "This
is when you protect all of the hard work that went into making them,"
he said, showing us how to stack the boxes close and tight and to cover
each pallet with padded cargo blankets.

"These are the first for our trial run for Volkswagen," he pointed to a
growing stack of light pallets. "A long way to go, but it's a start."

Then Edwin and I unloaded supply trucks, and filled and organized the warehouse supplies. When that was done, he had us follow Samuel around. Samuel stopped every ten paces and let his right
arm flail up over his head and scribble some frantic thought in the
air. He'd force out some inarticulate grunts that were drowned by
the factory noises. On breaks that week, I followed Samuel up the
cobblestone road from the harbor to a bench where he sat and fed
the birds. Pigeons gathered around his feet, jumped into his lap, and
settled on the back part of the bench as he crumbled old crusts in his
palms. He looked calmer when he was with the birds. His spastic arm
didn't shoot up as often, but when it did the pigeons leapt away from
him, and lingered for a moment in a wild flap of wings before falling
back toward him. He had them tamed. Big shorebirds often swooped

in and made off with large chunks of bread but he kicked his foot at those, preferring the oil sheen–ringed crowns of the pigeons.

After I followed Samuel around, Edwin and I were put on the assembly line to shadow the workers there. Most of the men on the line had hands too thick to do such delicate work. Edward Fass, who manned the first station, had a deep fishhook-shaped scar on his forearm that formed a meaty ridge. I stared at the scar as we screwed in copper bases.

"You're going to learn it all," my father told us, and he meant it. He had us getting more involved at his home laboratory too. He kept trying to create new lightbulbs, new chemicals, and new methods; his ambition seemed boundless.

Taking time away from drawing and painting drove Edwin wild, and he spent all his free time with his artwork. He had a book called *Fish of the World*, and he would pencil-sketch different fish, detailing each fish down to the scales, copying the models from the pages. Sometimes he'd add an extra fin, a change that was not noticeable, but just as often he'd add a set of arms or legs so the fish could easily crawl off the page and run across our room.

"Did you know fish never shut their eyes?" Edwin said while flipping through his book. "I'd like that. Not missing anything. To always be able to take everything in."

At night, during a storm, Edwin was on his hands and knees leaning over the paper and drawing a giant picture of a fish swimming in a huge lightbulb. "That could be our family crest," I said, admiring the details of his drawing as Fergus came in trailing the scent of damp fur, and began running around the room, howling in fear of the thunder.

"Oh god, Fergus. You stink," Edwin said and pushed our dog away from him.

Fergus treated the woods as his buffet: dead birds, squirrels, and the occasional skunk carcass. Each in turn his body processed late at night, coming out one end or the other. Most of the time his wet heaving woke someone in time to shuffle him out back. If he ever found something too foul to eat, he rolled in it and came back stinking of animal feces, rancid meat, and swamp scum. Edwin and I had to take turns holding him and brushing away the filth and knotted burrs, but neither of us had bathed him in a long time.

Fergus howled again, and ran across the butcher paper, his claws tearing the paper before he retreated to some other corner of the house.

"Oh no," I said, worried about his creation.

"That's okay. I'll make a better one next time," Edwin said.

Our father constantly read the papers for news about Germany. While we were at camp, Volkswagen had given him a massive order to test his lights and ability to supply them. If everything went well, they would give him the majority of their business. He worried about getting the order ready. His clothes were wrinkled. His hair stood up as if licked against the grain. He looked nervous, though he kept his concerns from us. When Uncle Martin came over to visit or eat dinner, the two of them went into a separate room and whispered about what they should do if "the worst" happened.

Then, on September 1, our father spread a late edition newspaper onto the kitchen table while we ate dinner.

At 4:45 that morning, 1.5 million German troops invaded Poland along its three-thousand-kilometer border with German-controlled territory. Simultaneously, the Luftwaffe bombed Polish airfields, and German warships and U-boats attacked Polish naval forces in the Baltic Sea. The paper had a transcript of Hitler's address to the Reichstag claiming the massive invasion was a defensive action.

"What does this mean?" Edwin asked.

My father paced the kitchen muttering. "We should have known better. That man was not to be trusted. Of course he wasn't going to stand by the treaties."

Edwin and I didn't know what to make of the news. It would have been boys like Günter who crossed the border into Poland.

Over the next few days the papers said that France and England didn't believe Hitler's rationale for the invasion, and on September 3, 1939, they declared war on Germany.

"We are in the middle of this madness now," my mother said. "We'll have to leave, there's no other choice."

"Drika, I have sixty employees. That's sixty families to tend to. I have to stay."

"I don't care. You have to ask what you care about. What's important here?"

My father didn't look at her, but at us.

My mother walked from the room and I followed to comfort her. She sat in the den on a bench next to her candle-making kit and looked out at her flowers. She made candles by dipping wicks into large cans of molten wax and letting them dry after each dip. They came out slender, tapered, and the color of tulip bouquets when she hung them from small nails on the wall.

"Can I do something for you, Mom?"

She looked at me and shook her head no. Her eyes were welling up, and I knew she had an expanding bubble in her chest that kept her from talking. I wanted to swallow her bubble of mute hurt and keep it buried in my gut so she could breathe easy.

She ran her finger under the drying candles, which touched one to the next like a faint wind chime.

"They add atmosphere to a home," she'd said. Birthday cakes, summer meals, almost every room, and especially her and my father's bedroom were covered in her candles, like she wanted to always see and be seen in light that swayed.

"Do you remember what you used to tell me about your flowers?" I asked and tapped on the glass to point at her garden.

She snorted and tried to smile.

To make sure Edwin and I wouldn't pick her flowers she'd told us that forest pixies didn't have cradles for their infants so at night lay them in the tulips to have the breeze rock them to sleep in the chalice of the bloom.

My father walked into the room. "Maybe I can have Martin take the three of you across the Channel if things get any worse."

"Of course they'll get worse. We're between two countries at war, between all this madness," my mother said.

My father was silent but held his arms out and she stood, walked to him, and let herself be folded into him.

Ludo, Edwin, Hilda, and I each took a box of extra lightbulb casings from our father's lab, carried them out back to the fort we'd made from mildewed wooden factory pallets, and used them to play a war game where we treated the small glass casings as grenades. Fergus followed as we chased one another in circles through the forest. We pretended the bulbs held light inside of them as we arced them behind our backs and hurled them. When Edwin hit me square in the spine, the glass exploded, dropping me to my knees. Hilda ran up to me and kneeled by my side. She put her hands on my chest and her hair hung down and grazed my cheeks. Her rich smell—sweet grass, lilac, sweat—fell over me, *pinioned* me. *Pinioned*, another of my father's assigned vocabulary words. I tried to memorize her in this moment, how the sunshine gleamed along the palms of leaves overhead, down the sharp needles of the pine boughs. The world glowed as the image of her face made room for itself in my memory where it would move like a fish, fluid and glinting, down the river of my life.

Fergus howled and yelped every few feet among the trees. He stopped after a yowl, sat down, twisted behind himself, and jammed his back foot into his mouth as if trying to swallow it whole.

When we ran out of bulbs, we hid the empty boxes in the fort, said good night, and went home for dinner. Our mother was in the kitchen making the homemade noodles she used for casserole. Puffs of flour dusted the counter. She leaned into the wooden roller and flattened out sheets of dough. She cut the sheets lengthwise into small strips that she then draped over all the open cupboard doors. Raw dough noodles hung limp over everything, as if the shelves were bursting with food. The cupboard was stocked with molasses, rye, dry yeast in little tins with sealable glass lids, cloves, vinegar, dried fish, and chocolate bars my brother and I would nip when we thought they'd go unmissed.

"No, no, out, get out, take that stinky dog with you too," she said, chasing us out with the roller raised over her head for show. When she was in the kitchen's doorway she stopped and looked at the ground behind us. "What happened?"

Fergus had followed us through the front door, across the main entrance carpet, and into the kitchen where he walked in dainty little circles behind Edwin, who hadn't noticed the small blotches of blood each paw print left behind.

5

After Germany invaded Poland, my father read the newspapers with greater fervor. He'd drop the tightly coiled paper on the table, and Edwin and I would scoop it up to read what little details there were about Russia and Germany dividing up Poland. We secretly wanted to be part of the army, but were confused why the Germans would do such a thing with the Bolshevik Russians everyone at camp had talked so poorly about. We read about England going to rations and evacuating cities, about Germany bombing Scapa Flow naval base in Scotland, and the British air attacks on the German navy. My father and Uncle Martin had charted and been practicing our escape plan for months.

"What will happen to them if war begins?" our mother kept asking. The question radiated from her. "We should send the boys somewhere."

"Drika, where?" my father asked. "We don't have any family to send them to."

We had no extended family. My father's parents were dead and he had no siblings. My mother's parents were gone as well, her only two distant cousins killed during the Great War, and talk of any of that lot had been veiled and avoided. As for friends, owning the factory in town came with wealth and privilege, but everyone saw us as employers, acquaintances at best, and we had no one we could send our own to for protection, for keepsake. That was the unspoken trade for our fortune.

If the Germans decided to cross the Rhine into Holland, my mother, Edwin, and I would board the *Lighthouse Lady* and work our way along the coast, sneaking through the North Sea to northern England, away from any cities. My father would stay behind to shut down the factory and come later with his banking and business books on his own boat. We drilled on what to take and where to meet. My uncle and father stocked the hulls of their boats with food and spare clothing. They told us we were not to discuss our plans with anyone else, not even Ludo or Hilda. It was imperative to our safety that we remain quiet. But every time we went through the plan, I secretly played out my own amendment of sprinting to get Hilda, and the two of us going to gather up Ludo. If I was going, they were coming with me.

Holland was promised neutrality by the German government. However, all along, the Dutch people seemed to intuit that Hitler would eventually invade our country. It was a case of proximity. Either out of fear or denial, our government didn't properly prepare for any war, and when the sense of an impending German invasion mounted, they started to scramble, drafting as many men as possible into the army.

"The boys are too young to get drafted," I heard my father say through the heating ducts.

My mother's reply was unclear.

"I know, but everything we worked for is at stake here," he said. "The factory, the house, all of it."

On April 9, 1940, when the Nazis invaded Denmark and Norway, they set up a sea blockade around Denmark that stretched to the Frisian Islands north of Delfzijl. Uncle Martin had been working his way back from a North Sea fishing trip when a German navy ship stopped him, checked his papers, and searched his ship. They set up a naval blockade, and from what he could gather, it covered the escape route we had mapped out to England.

I remember sitting with my parents after we found this out. They were side by side, holding hands, which I always found comforting.

"What are we going to do?" I asked.

I think I only ever wanted us to be together, for the war to pass us by and everything to be a smooth sheet of ice for us to glide over.

"I don't know," my father said.

My mother took her finger and traced small circles on the inside of his wrist.

"You know," my father said, softly, as if to himself, "on April twentieth, the Führer's birthday, merchants decorate their store windows with oil paintings of Hitler looking sternly into the distance. They use these large red wax candles to illuminate the paintings like he were a new god to worship."

A second plan was then made. My father's factory was finishing the giant Volkswagen order; he would have it shipped to Rotterdam via train and then to Germany in early May by steamer. He would finish the order and see it to Rotterdam in person, where he would look for a boat that could take us to England.

Three weeks later, on May 9, the lights were finally done and ready to be loaded onto the train. Our father took me and Edwin with him, and if he could find a boat, he would wire for our mother to join us. We would leave and wait out whatever would happen in England.

"I'm not going without Hilda and Ludo," I said.

"They can't come with us."

"Sure they can. Buy them tickets."

"They have their families. Look. We'll be back soon. Think of it as a vacation."

"Then can I come later with Mother?" Edwin asked. He had started a canvas painting and didn't want to leave it. The paint was expensive and he used it only when he had a sketch he loved and felt worthy of the materials.

"No. I want you to come with me. You'll want to see the shipment off. It will give you an idea of the whole process."

"I already have a good idea, and I have something here I want to work on."

"What? A drawing? Come on. You'll miss your whole life if you keep your nose in a sketchpad."

Edwin pulled at the sleeve of his shirt, a habit used when he was hurt or angry. He looked straight at my father and almost snapped, "I'm capturing life."

"You don't want to go to camp. You don't want to go to the city with me. You probably just want to paint all over your skin and go to the sea. Draw the waves all day."

"That would be no different than tinkering with lights all the time."

"Edwin," my mother said.

"That tinkering with lights created a secure life for us. A place for this family in the world. Your painting can wait. Your friends can wait.

That's the end of it," my father said. "You'll come with me and see how the lights travel. And besides. Mr. Gunnelburg may be in Rotterdam, and if he is I'd like you boys to tell him how much you enjoyed the camp. It was his idea. It would be helpful to me."

"Is that why you're really taking them, Hans?" my mother said.

"No. They wanted to travel with me last time. This will be good for them. And might be our way out."

We rode in the passenger train while my mother stayed behind and saw to the loading of the shipment on the cargo train several hours afterward.

The train stopped in Amsterdam, where we had a three-hour stopover.

"Edwin. I want to make up for forcing you to come," my father said. "Follow me."

We walked out of the train station, passed the canals full of riverboats tied stem to stern, storefronts with diamond traders from Antwerp, and narrow brownstone homes with iron balconies built wall-to-wall with one another. I saw a smutty flyer for a dancing girls show on the ground and when my father and brother weren't looking I bent down to snatch it up and folded it into my pants pocket. As we walked that day I kept pulling it out to sneak a peek of the pencil drawing of the woman with leggings up to her thighs, a flowing camisole with a hooked line of cleavage, long black hair, and plum-colored lips.

I kept my fingers pinched on the flyer in my pocket. The pad of my thumb traced the flat line of the woman's image, desperately imagining the contours.

"Here we are," my father said as we approached the giant Rijksmuseum. "We'll have to hurry, but you'll love this."

We walked through the Renaissance palace, under horseshoe-arch doorways and down the giant marble corridors in barrel-vaulted rooms where Edwin stopped in front of at least one piece of artwork in each display. He squared his shoulders to a Vermeer painting, a maid with a white bonnet pouring a pitcher of milk, and let his eyes fall over the lines.

"Why don't you just lick it?" I said, but he didn't break his gaze, his admiration.

I was quiet after that and watched as he leaned in closer, studying the direction of the brushstrokes, the flow of brush hairs. He tilted his head to study how those strokes changed tint with the angle of the light. It would not have surprised me if he reached his fingers out to touch where the color floated from the cracked paint on the canvas, or if he fell to his knees before the frame. Vermeer. Van Gogh. Dutchmen. Masters. Keepers of my brother's heart.

After the museum, we made our way to the train and finally got to Rotterdam as the sun went down. The nut-brown faces of foreigners strolled along Stieltjesstraat. Outdoor cafés angled toward the harbor with its giant ships and schooners. The men smoked cigarettes and the women in black gloves spun umbrella necks resting against their shoulders so that discs of cloth twirled over their heads.

"Has Uncle Martin been on boats like those?" Edwin asked.

"He's been on almost every kind of ship you could imagine," my father said.

The sun dropped to the water and disappeared below it. It made all the sailing boats look like lean, long-necked birds paddling on the horizon. Along the main roads potted trees with russet branches with small, green buds punching out lined the canal, where deeply weathered canal boats were moored side by side.

Edwin kept eyeing the harbor and the ships. "I'd love to be out on one of those," he said, slapping at my shoulder and pointing from one vessel to the next.

We ate at a pancake restaurant along the water. At the tables around us were women in dark blue dresses and men in gray and brown suits, similar to our father. A counter on the way to the kitchen had four large wheels of Gouda cheese; the waiters cut thin wedges from them to deliver to each table. My father cut our wedge into slices, and we passed them around until our orders came.

A girl my age sat at the table behind my father. She had loose yellow hair and a tight little face. Her bones seemed so close below the skin. She took a chocolate from the table, unwrapped it, and put it in her mouth. Her fingers straightened the paper on the tablecloth, pushing out the folds. She didn't chew. I imagined the chocolate on her tongue. A communion of sorts. Her head was down but I suddenly wanted to see her teeth, the curve of her white throat, the specks of her eyes. I wanted her to glance at me.

We each ate thick pancakes with apple, bacon, and syrup. Then we shared a fillet of pan-fried herring covered in olive oil and crushed almonds. My father drank a glass of red wine served from a straw-covered bottle. We shared an artichoke that had been boiled and soaked in melted butter, and we each ate two oranges, leaving a pile of husked artichoke leaves and quartered orange rinds in the middle of the table. Strange accents hung in the air. A girl on a bicycle ticked past. Rims rattled over cobbles. Her basket was full of flowers. Horse carts clopped along the cobblestone between the cars.

At dinner, we decided that our father would leave first thing in the morning to go back to the rail yard to see the shipment of lights from the train to the harbor, where the boat was scheduled for a midmorning departure. We would meet him at the same pancake restaurant for lunch before going to meet his contact at Volkswagen, Mr. Gunnelburg.

Finished eating, we worked our way to the hotel, which was a five-story brick structure that shared walls with the office buildings on both sides. It had a wall of windows in the lobby, a key rack and letter rack with pigeonholes behind the reception counter, and a frosted globe chandelier by the fireside. On the hearth's mantel was a large wooden carving of two eagles that we ran our hands over as our father checked us in. Each set of the eagles' wings spread out wide, and their heads faced each other in a fierce wooden stare, one on top of the other with their talons interwoven. They were both rising and falling, competing and fighting—locked in some thrall that engaged each, locked in a moment that would mark them forever. When my father had the keys, we followed him up the marble stairs instead of riding the groaning cage elevator. He walked ahead of us with the keys dangling like an ornament from his hooked finger. My father went to sleep in his room, and Edwin and I went to our shared room.

We stayed up well past normal looking into the street and the surrounding buildings. Edwin sketched how the angle of the buildings descended down the road. I pulled the flyer from my pocket and studied the picture of the woman, imagining the place where this figure, or smoky women like her, might walk slowly toward me, gather up their long hair, and drape it over my body. How I'd get lost in the scent of her cascading locks before they pressed into me.

We had planned on sleeping until we had to wake and go meet our father. But that didn't happen.

Very early the next morning, we were awakened by the loud hum of approaching airplane engines, followed by heavy artillery gunfire. I lay in bed, trying to remember where I was. Voices came in from the hallway. Doors swung open. People yelled to one another. Others ran down the corridor, their footfalls manic and heavy.

The strange noises washed over my bed.

"Jacob. Get dressed," Edwin yelled, and then something in me snapped to attention. I pushed the covers off and pulled clothes on. We stepped into the hallway. My father had already left to oversee the light shipment. People ducked down the stairwell and we followed. The stairwell sounded like Pauwel's drum line at camp. There must have been thirty people hurrying down to the lobby, where the hotel workers pointed everyone into the basement.

"Down the steps, down the steps," a bellhop yelled. Behind him, through the hotel's main glass doors, came the steady and terrible howl of an air raid siren.

The hotel's basement was an unfinished room full of guests in their nightclothes. Most were silent except for a woman our mother's age in the back who kept praying in quavering utterances.

With each crack of gunfire, dust shook loose from the corners of the walls. Several of the people huddled up and started wrapping their arms around one another. Some of them must have been strangers, but they hugged like old friends. Their faces sour with fear, arms around shoulders, heads tucked into each other's chests. The room became one giant tangle of a frightened body. The noise of planes overhead echoed down through the skeleton of the building.

"What is this?"

"They're coming."

We stayed in the basement for several minutes. I thought about the general talking to us camp boys on the beach about how one scalding push of violence would put the world back to its proper order. I had not imagined that heat touching my own country.

"We have to go get Father," I said to Edwin.

"He'll come back for us," Edwin said.

"We told him we'd meet him, we have to go the restaurant to meet him," I pleaded. Chaos pounded from outside, but if it was the Germans who were coming, we would be fine. We were dagger-carrying members of the youth camps, after all.

This. This is what I honestly thought. Now, I can track any memory back to this moment. This moment when I proved to be such a fool.

"This changes the plan, Jacob. He'll know to come back here." My brother hunkered against the basement wall, bobbing on his bent knees, coiled to spring up. His hair was messy on the left side from resting on the pillow. His eyes were recessed pools of dark liquid as he scanned the room.

"No. We have to go get him, we have to," I insisted. "We have to go," I continued until Edwin agreed to at least go up to the lobby.

"Boys, stay here," a woman said.

"Go, go." I pushed Edwin.

At street level a young bellhop leaned against the corner of the door and looked down the road. We ran up and crouched next to him. The sun rose and cut the street with slanting light. Streams ran over the cobblestones.

"What's the water from?" Edwin asked the bellhop.

"Either the artillery hit and broke a canal wall or we opened it as a defense, because some of the dykes are opened and the streets are flooding." He had pouch cheeks, aquamarine eyes with long lashes, and thick, dark eyebrows, each the size of a mustache.

"We won't be able to get to him," Edwin said.

I gripped his arm. I felt the rush and lift of panic—a feeling of total powerlessness of not finding my father worming around my chest. "We have to."

Edwin looked up and down the street, then at me for a long time. I don't know what he thought of me in that moment—if I wanted to be brave and save my father or if I truly needed him near to save me. In truth, it was the latter—but whatever Edwin saw in me made him act.

"Do you have your identification papers?" he asked me.

I nodded.

The water in the street in front of the hotel didn't look very deep. Edwin peered at me closely again. The start of a light silk mustache shadowed his upper lip. He looked up and down the street again and then back at me.

"All right," he said. "Come on."

Outside, the rattle of heavy machine-gun fire echoed from every direction. When the first major wave of planes stopped flying overhead, Edwin started down the street toward the port. Nothing was said between us. We walked with our shoulders touching the wall of buildings along the road. Over the rooftops, a paratrooper floated under his inverted bowl-shaped parachute. The white, silk chute bloomed out of the sky. A limp body descended the last hundred meters onto the street, landing between us and the road to the port. The man crashed hard and his parachute covered him as if he had never been there. I froze. My legs locked, my shoulders squared toward the man. The canvas of the chute ruffled with the breeze as we passed. It was the first dead body I'd ever seen.

"Don't look at him, Jacob," Edwin said. He grabbed my hand and pulled me away, but his eyes never left the dead paratrooper. His eyes were wide open. I imagined soon I'd be seeing such men drifting down slabs of butcher paper, through charcoal clouds.

At last I came unstuck and walked on, passing a dozen other similar lumps on our way up Plantagestraat to the market. People huddled in the wedges of door frames. Faces gazed out of shop windows as we walked along the edge of the canal. Sewers brimmed over. The water in the canal surged. Some levies had been shifted to control the flow. It rose up along the brick walls toward street level.

Our father had taken us to the docks the day before while he signed the incoming shipment over to the customs workers. He would have been by the docks waiting to see off the freight.

Small artillery cracked from the foxholes the Dutch Marines had dug around the city's bridges. The few people on the street moved toward the waterfront. The whole city, which had feared the Germans coming, hunkered down or crept toward the dock, seeking safe passage elsewhere. Several blocks from the hotel along the Plantagestraat, the street level dipped below the canal. The canal wall tunneled in that portion of the road and held the water back. But the water had flowed down the canal too fast and surged over the lip down into the cup of the road. Water roared over the wall and flushed the street out for about fifty meters. Beyond the washout, the brick road angled up and rose out of the brown water, and there was the pier building and restaurant we had arranged to meet our father, but the three intersections between us were washed out.

Water poured over the flooded road, ran up the tree trunks, spilt over the wooden entrances of first-floor shops and the lower lips of windowsills that had shattered from the pressure. Torn strips of leather and random wooden shoes floated out of a broken storefront window at a cobbler's. Water crept up our shinbones as we moved to another doorway. Ahead of us, a man moved through the water in the street. On his shoulders was a little girl cradling a dulled gray pillowcase. As soon as the man with his child cleared the sunken street, other people started running after them. It got deep at the middle of the intersection, but it was doable, and looked only about knee-deep nearer the dock.

"What a stupid defense plan," Edwin said.

Water covered a bicycle rack. A row of handlebars stuck above the surface and each cut a little V in the current. Dirt and trash floated to the high-water mark, which kept rising. A Packard 180 shimmied toward the lowest point of the road. We watched the hood shift, dip backward, and submerge, which lifted the automobile's grill and headlights for a brief moment before the whole thing disappeared.

I felt a swampy heat in my armpits. I was too scared to go into the flooded street and decided to tell Edwin. We were wrong to have come looking for our father. I was wrong. I'd tell him before the tree branch floated by. Before the wooden sign. Before . . . But I didn't say anything. My mouth formed the words, but I had no tongue, windpipe, or lungs to push them out.

"Swim where it gets deep so you don't get caught on anything underwater," Edwin said. He moved forward and marched into the flooded street. I followed. The water was knee-deep right away. The heavy flow rushed against my wet pant legs. The brownstone buildings on both sides of the street became canyon walls rising out of a river.

Edwin was ten meters ahead of me. "Watch out," he yelled without looking behind him as a small birch tree came floating down the street. It got snagged on something underwater, spun around, and floated off again.

Others walked through the flood behind us like we were a pilgrimage of instant refugees. Some crossed the way we were and others tried to move in the other direction.

"Keep up, Jacob," Edwin yelled.

He looked back. Beside him was the black steel hood of another big car. It was in the middle of the road as if it had been abandoned while moving. The hood of the car reflected the first of the morning's sunlight, a silver glow laying down on this water that seemed to run through the heart of the city, possibly the whole country. Dead men continued to fall from the sky. The crack and echo of gunfire bounced off the buildings before settling into the mortar and marrow of Rotterdam. Edwin kept looking back and must have seen me among all that—struggling against the current, slipping so my chest and face kept dipping into the water. Every other step now my brother turned back to make sure I kept up.

When Edwin was next to the car we made eye contact. Then he turned, took about four steps forward so he was even with the car's front bumper, and he started walking the road's incline out of the water. The water level sunk from his waist, below his pants pocket, and off the back of his knees as he stepped forward. He looked back again like he knew that seeing him was keeping me calm. The water was at the centerline of his shins when he turned back to the port.

Then, in midstride, Edwin plunged straight down—dropping below the waterline.

A white rim of bubbles from where he'd sunk swept to the surface and flowed toward me.

"Edwin!" I ran hard to get out of the deeper water, dove forward, and swam until my knees scraped the road. Some larval shifting of fear roiled through my stomach. Next to the submerged car, I plunged forward again. My head was out of the water and my hands searched the contours of the road. The brick cut the heel of my palm and scraped at my skin. Then my hands found the circular lip of an open manhole and reached down into it. A stronger, quicker moving current beneath the street sucked at my arm, buckled my body in half, and folded me over the steel lip of the hole, and I had to fight from getting swallowed into that hidden river.

My hands ran around the lip. The quick flowing water over the street must have jarred the cover loose and pushed it away. I pinned my armpits against the lip and dove my head into the hole. Everything underwater was black. The current pushed hard against my neck, and it took all my strength to hold myself in that position, underwater in both the flooded road and this unmapped world. My hands circled the water, reaching for anything, each finger striving loose of the knuckles. I thought of Samuel's manic arm. No sunlight sunk beneath the street. I willed my body to let go, to let the current pull me to Edwin. My abdominal muscles locked in a folded U against the lip. My mind kept telling my feet to kick my body the rest of the way in—just kick.

Air bubbles rose up the side of my head as I exhaled in a gasping scream. Above the surface I took wild fish breaths for air, howled for help, and dove again, but couldn't bring my body to let itself go with the current. *Let go. Let go. Let go.* But I stayed like that, diving into and breaching the flooded street, reaching, but not finding anything in that dark underground flow.

"Help! Please help! I need rope."

The water sunk in through my ears and nose and skin and saturated everything.

I ran to where the road level was above the canal to see if there were any sewer outlets. If there were, they were underwater.

Tributaries slunk off in quick streams and rivulets. In the water a dead rat floated past me. Up ahead where it was dry, there were more gunned-downed paratroopers on the street.

Another man crossing the water had a small child on his shoulders. Beside them was a younger boy.

"Young fellow," the man said to me. "Keep moving, get out of the street."

"Please, help me," I begged, weeping from hot, incoherent rage. That helpless anger stayed with me, it rose and receded in my throat and coated me like a second skin.

"Come on. Keep moving," he said again.

"What happened?" the boy walking behind the man asked me. The boy's face was slack and dumb-looking, like he had no context for the city all around him, exploding into flood and noise and death.

"I think we flooded the streets," I said, standing and following the man and his children toward the piers, walking like a ghost, floating free of who I had been. As I wandered, I was not myself—could never be myself again. I was now the person who had persuaded Edwin to take to the street with me.

My father was leaning over a wounded man and wrapping gauze around his shoulder when I got to the restaurant where we had planned to meet.

I walked inside the barrier of the sidewalk seating.

"Papi," I said, using the name for him I hadn't used since I was a child.

When he saw me, he ran over and hugged me. "Damn it, I knew you boys wouldn't stay where you were, I knew it. Why are you all wet? Where's Edwin?"

"Papi," was all I could say.

"Jacob, where's your brother? Jacob. Jacob, where's Edwin?" My father looked right into my eyes—all the way to the deepest reaches of my life. "Where's Edwin?" he yelled and shook me by the shoulders. "Where's Edwin?"

He saw that I was incapable of forming words. That a swelling of garbled cries clotted in my stomach. He shook me even harder.

"Where?"

"He fell."

"What?"

"Under the road. He fell under the road."

The wounded man lay on the patio floor next to a table. Blood already soaked through the bandage wrapped around him. The sunlight reflected off the window, and the golden glow filled the wrinkled edges of my father's desperate face.

"Jacob. Tell me what happened."

"The road flooded and he fell under it, through a manhole and got swept away."

"Where?"

I pointed behind me, down Plantagestraat, to the section of the street where I lost my brother.

"Show me."

He pulled me along and we worked our way back to the spot where Edwin fell. I led him to the hole under the water. A slow current flowed into the lowest point of the road. Another parallel current ran faster just beneath it, to some unseen place beyond our reach. When we found the hole, my father dropped to his knees and felt out the opening. He plunged his hands in and the currents pulled them away. He sat back up immediately.

"Jesus," he said. "Jacob, hold on to my belt."

My fingers clasped hold of his belt as he leaned into the hole, the leather strap popped tight against my palms as the water pressure pulled on him. His legs kicked forward, trying to plunge himself into the hole, and I heaved him back to keep him from being carried away too. My father resurfaced, gasping for air.

"How'd this happen?"

There was no answer I could have given him then. No confession I could have mustered. Instead I plunged my hands back into the hole and started waving beneath the road from the force of the underground river. I sensed that my arms would now always be searching and wished they would come loose from my body and float away from me.

After my father examined the hole, he ran in a full panic to the shops that lined the street and asked everyone where the sewer system let out. When no one could tell him, he led me to a corner store that had flooded ankle-deep and rooted around for a map that showed the canals fanning out from the harbor. He was on some other plane of existence then, silent, navigating by instinct, pulling me along by some magnetic force.

"Jacob," he said, "start yelling your brother's name, and don't stop until we find him. Don't stop."

For three hours I yelled "Edwin" at the top of my lungs along the canals, until it felt like my heart would never stop echoing that call, that name. That whole time my father had not said another word, just run his finger over the map in his hand, then started taking those incredibly long strides of his around the ruined city, along every waterway, scanning the banks.

Through the roads running along the canal, we passed more dead paratroopers in their ready-made burial tarps. They were dressed as Dutch Royal Guardsmen, but were German soldiers. I looked closely at every heap on the street. I imagined myself hiding away from my father under one of those white, billowing chutes, until I was no longer trembling, wet, and cold. On one corner a parachute snagged on a broken tree trunk. The trunk cut through the tarp and held it in place. The parachute lines pulled taut downstream where they fell into the canal. At the end of the lines, a body bobbed face-down on the surface like a giant fishing lure.

We circled the flooded area a dozen times, before widening our search and walking the rest of the city. People fled in droves, heading to the bridges. In one of the small shops the radio that someone had pushed against the sill of a broken window was broadcasting. We stopped to listen for a moment. My throat hurt from yelling. My chest hurt. I was trying to rest when the broadcaster said, "German forces to bomb city of Rotterdam if the Dutch do not surrender."

My father sank to his knees and let his body crumple onto his haunches. "Jacob," he said from the ground. "I can't find your brother. I can't find him, and we're going to have to get out of the city."

My father looked at the map like it baffled him, like the answer to where to find his missing son had to be hidden on that surface. Eventually he stood up, and we walked toward the eastern bridge out of the city.

Rotterdam was now a giant anthill stirred up by a boot. Thousands of refugees fleeing the bomb threats filled the roads in cars, buses, lorries, wagons, mules, and horses. A drunk old man yelled from horseback for everyone to go back and wait it out as an old lady leading the horse by the reins walked with the flow of people. A boy about my age drove a cow from his bicycle by gently swatting at the animal's flanks with a stick to keep it moving. People carried everything they could in pathetic bundles piled on carts drawn by tractors. A canary sang from its cage slung from the side of a Packard. Crates of fowl laced together by hastily tied knots swung off roof racks. Little children carried huge loads and panting Alsatian dogs harnessed to wheelbarrows dragged heaps deemed essential in such a panic. They all crossed the bridge as if it were a gangplank dropping them out of their own lives into something bottomless and unknown.

Dutch Marines had dug foxholes around the next bridge and let only a single-file line of residents pass over. A marine with a machine gun stood at the start of the bridge where everyone lined up.

"Have your hands visible as you cross," the marine yelled. "If you do anything threatening to the bridge, you will be shot."

"Stay in front of me," my father said. The people around us wore business clothes, or smocks from working in restaurants. Two men covered in ash looked like they'd run out from working in an aluminum smelter.

Once we crossed the bridge, my father looked along the bank and his focus locked on something triggering him to run downhill away from me. His long, awkward stride caught me off guard as he headed to the water. He lost his balance, stumbled, slid down on his back, and got up again in stride.

"Halt," one of the marines yelled.

My father kept moving toward the water. A few steps ahead of him a dark bulge floated against the bank. His back obscured my view as the marine yelled again.

"Halt," the soldier boomed down off the concrete lip of the bridge.

"Wait. No," I yelled.

Then the man aimed the muzzle of his gun at my father running to the base of the bridge and let off several rounds. Dirt ahead of my father jumped up in little clouds and disappeared like dark dandelion puffs. My father kept running and almost dove to the edge of the water. His hand reached out and pulled something up on the shore. By the time he had a good grip of it and was pulling it up I was running down the hill after him. The marine who fired his weapon didn't yell anything at me as he must have seen what my father was after. At the bottom of the bank my father's back curved over his lap as if he were sinking into the shore. He held a soggy wet burlap sack in his lap. Easy to mistake for a body—just a bag that was filled by the current and hung up on the rocks.

For a long time we sat by the banks of that water with the wet burlap resting over his lap.

Eventually, he took the burlap sack and placed it back in the water so it filled up and drifted off downstream, hanging under the surface until we could no longer see it. Then I helped him walk up the hillside, almost pushing his hunched, sapless body.

Everything was different then. Everything would always be different after that.

We spent the rest of that day asking everyone among the refugees if they knew where the canals or sewers let out in the city. My father paid to have a message telegraphed to my mother.

Stay put until you hear from me. Hans.

Later on, after the guns had been silent for hours and we had not heard any more airplanes, we persuaded a soldier to let us cross a bridge back into Rotterdam and we went to City Hall to look for help, and then the police station, but there was nobody there. Not in either place. Everyone was hiding. All that day we searched, and at night we didn't sleep. Anyone we passed we asked if they knew where the water let out. If they had a guess, we followed it. We walked along the harbor where all the boats had quickly made way after the morning attack.

"The ship I paid to take us across has left," my father said as he stared at the empty slips in the harbor. He turned back to me. "We're going to be trapped here."

Past the harbor we found a huge drainage pipe opening up along the shore. The giant pipe led into a dark hole tunneled under the street. A stream trickled out. In his wet and ruined three-piece suit and sopping shoes my father walked right into the blackness and disappeared. I ran after him and yelled out my brother's name, which echoed away from us in the darkness. I followed after the splash of my father's sunken feet as we walked under the city. The passageway ran into smaller grated-off pipes that I put my head against, calling for my brother.

All that night and into the next day we searched. We wandered the city in a stupor for several days after that, following and backtracking along the city's canals and eventually ending up at the morgue, where people already began cataloging the new dead. My father made me wait outside while he walked the corridors and looked into the blued faces of strangers.

I sat on the bench, pulled the rumpled flyer of the woman from my pocket, and felt a bloom of shame and disgust in my gut for wanting something so physical. Vomit rose to the back of my mouth. I crumpled the paper into a wet ball and tossed it into the street.

At night in the city before the raid, nothing was shrouded in darkness. Streetlights and lights up in the buildings had cast shadows on the city where something was always happening. "Those lights up there feel like glowing money," my father had said. But since the raid, all was dark. Night came much earlier. The buildings' shadows slipped away. That darkness seeped into me as we passed those few nights, stopping only to let me sleep in a doorway or on a park bench for an hour here and there when exhaustion set in firmly enough to overpower the wild feeling of wanting to keep following my father, to constantly call out my brother's name, my phantom hands ever grasping fistfuls of water.

It was still dark when I woke on a bench outside the morgue. My father sat on the ground against the seat where my feet were. He rubbed the sleeve of his jacket across his face. When he turned to me, his eyes were red and inflamed. If he'd been crying it would have been the first time I'd ever seen it. A distant expression pinched his brows close together. Resignation, perhaps. When he saw my eyes open, he shook his head.

"I found nothing inside. Your mother is going to be worried to death. We have to at least get you home safe. At least you," he said again.

We crossed the bridge out of the city and looked for someone who would drive us all the way back to Delfzijl.

We found another shop to wire a message. My father looked at me as we stood at the counter. "I have no idea what to say to her."

I thought of my mother then. My poor mother waiting for heartbreak.

Late on the evening of the fourteenth, we found someone to drive us home. It was getting dark outside, and despite all the houses the driver passed in his old Fiat, almost none of them had their lights on.

The world had gone dark and I sensed then that the world and I moved in different directions—separated by complicated crosscurrents, soon to be strangers.

"I don't want you thinking this was your fault. This is bigger than you," my father said while we drove. He tried to be kind but his words confirmed my own conclusion, that this was *completely* my fault. I had made Edwin leave the hotel. "Much bigger than you," my father said, his familiar hand reaching out to cup the back of my neck.

The Germans were going through with their invasion.

By the time we reached the outer limits of Rotterdam, it was pitch-black, and we heard what sounded like a large machine engine digging into the road ahead of us. The driver pulled the car over at the easternmost side of an expansive field. We all got out of the car and listened to the sound getting louder.

"Let's find cover," the driver said.

We followed him to the tree line as wave upon wave of airplanes swooped over our heads, barreling toward Rotterdam. Then suddenly we heard the sounds of firebombs exploding in the distance. We hid away from the car in the trees and watched the fiery, orange glow in the west, rising out of the pale darkness where Rotterdam—where we—had been. From the edge of the field the subtle percussions in the distance, I felt like the world shifting to make some great change.

The sky emptied of plane noise. Then, leaving behind the angry, red gloaming of the firestorm, we started the car back up and headed east without our lights on to avoid whatever else might be coming. We headed east, back to our home, our lives, missing one.

6

When we arrived in the village of Delfzijl, my father and I had the driver drop us off in the harbor so we could see if Uncle Martin's boat was in. The *Lighthouse Lady* was moored to several other boats. All of the fishing fleet was now docked. A group of fishermen talked by the pier. My father went up to them.

"What's the news?" he asked.

"Didn't you hear," Dieter Clapson said. "We surrendered this morning."

They all kept talking over one another.

"Germany wants our country for our airfields."

"Soldiers crossed the River Meuse at Maastricht on the eleventh."

"Luxemburg went right away. The Belgians had help from French and Brit soldiers, but couldn't hold up. Louvain was destroyed."

"I have a cousin there."

"They rolled through Flanders."

"Are you okay, Hans?" Stevens Von Heller, a fisherman and one of our neighbors, asked. "We heard about some excitement up at your house last night."

My father pulled my wrist and turned me toward home. We walked quickly but with a mounting dread of facing my mother. I wanted to run ahead, to keep going past our house, even past Hilda's family farm, out of town, anywhere to avoid being there when she found out about Edwin. I didn't want the conversation to land on who persuaded him to leave our hotel.

In the driveway we crossed the stepping-stones from the side of the house to a square frame used for beating carpets clean. The front door of our house opened and my mother ran out to us. I stepped toward her and instinctively knew, but could not articulate then, that this was the first step on the trail that led right out of childhood. Right behind her was Fergus, who sprinted past her and headed straight for me. Then Uncle Martin appeared in the doorway.

"Hans, you had me terrified this whole time," she said as she ran across the lawn. Fergus jumped at my feet. She hugged my father and reached out to pull me into her. She grabbed both sides of my face and looked right into my eyes. Fergus's frenetic body crashed into my legs.

"Where's your brother?" she asked.

I lifted my hand and covered her eyes so not to see them the moment she heard. My throat constricted from the full burden of the last five days; from not sleeping, not eating enough, the crushing blow of guilt and loss that had been wracking me since Edwin slipped below the surface of the road.

"Drika," my father said. "Drika."

She turned to him. His eyes welled up and he shivered. Then he shook his head.

"What do you mean?" she said. "What does that mean?" She looked back at me. "Where's your brother, Jacob? Where's Edwin?"

Uncle Martin walked across the lawn. Fergus ran circles around me, sniffing at the ground, the reddish brown gloss of his coat in constant motion. Our house, so big and well placed in the center of all our land, looked peaceful. The monument of success my parents had intended it to be, with dark tar panels of roof layered on top of one another, as neatly pleated as feathers on a wing.

"Oh god, no!" my mother screamed.

The little yellow and blue cloth cap she wore wrapped tight over her hair had a strap that squeezed her skin forward into a second chin. Her eyes widened as she knelt down in front of me. The faint smell of cinnamon carried on her breath. Tears gathered at the corners of her hazel and gray eyes, each a bowl of seawater after a storm. She grabbed both my arms and squeezed to the bone. I watched her face redden and thought she might have a heart attack as she let go a piercing cry: a hand in open flame, a brutal wind on a rotten tooth, the last breath of a pained creature. Then she clutched her fingers at the hem of my shirt, buried her head into my stomach, and began heavy, uncontrolled sobs that shook both our bodies.

I went numb.

I became a stranger to her and she to me. Everything settled into my mind like a stack of photographs of each second, but something inside of me went cold—the deepest part where language and feelings form. If I looked at her, her pain would have sunk me and ended me in that driveway. I didn't want anything to be mine: no love, no longing, not hurt, nor disappointment, guilt or responsibility; just to live beside strangers or nobody at all.

I ignored her nose tucking into the soft middle of my stomach, ignored Uncle Martin and my father picking her up and leading her to the house. I stood in the driveway for a moment, a cold, unfeeling creature. Then, when they were all inside, Fergus doubled back and barked, which snapped me out of it and all those feelings of shame and endless hurt rushed back in.

Inside the house Uncle Martin sat my mother on the couch in the living room. As soon as she was down, she shot up and started screaming at my father.

"What happened? Tell me what happened!"

Fergus had followed me inside but now ran from the room. Uncle Martin kept his giant hands gripped on my mother's shoulders. "What did happen, Hans?" he asked. "She deserves to know."

My father leaned against the mantel and rubbed his palms over his cheeks, drawing the skin down. He seemed impossibly tall at that moment, though his spine had already started to curve.

"There was a flood the first day of the attacks," he started.

I leaned into the old ottoman as he told them about Edwin being lost underground. It was where I'd often sat and watched my mother dance with the men of our family. When everyone stopped talking, my mother curled up fetal on the couch. Uncle Martin's teeth clenched so tight the muscles in his jaw bulged. Blood flamed up from his neckline until his skin went scarlet.

"And did you get your account?" my mother whispered. "Did you get your precious Volkswagen account?"

"Drika."

She stood up and screamed into his face. "Volkswagen. Volkswagen. Volkswagen. Is our family all set up for the future, Hans?"

"Drika, please."

"Please nothing," she made a deep warbling sound like swallowing vomit from her throat. *Bilious* is the word, I thought.

My father took a step closer to her and she reached up and slapped him hard. Her handprint spread like sunburn across his jaw and cheek.

My heart was a rush of sparrows, as for a moment, I thought he was going to hit her back, though that was not my father. My giant father stood where he was without moving, as if inviting her to strike again. Neither said anything. My father stood dumbfounded in a dust-mote-filled shaft of light by the piano, and stood there like a statue long after she turned and left the room.

I turned away. Out the window I saw a giant crater of upturned earth in the backyard.

My uncle saw me staring out there. "That happened last night. Some plane must have dropped it by accident. A few landed in town. One knocked out all the church windows."

The pit appeared to be about a meter deep and twelve meters wide. There was a twin-trunked sessile oak tree in the backyard that Edwin and I climbed on. My father had tried to take a picture with us sitting in the two wedges, but neither of us could sit still long enough to get a good photo. There were a few blurry photos of us when we were younger looking squeamish while cradled in the oak. The bomb's blast had snapped one of the limbs off from the thick trunk and it lay across the yard. I pictured myself walking into the yard and lying down in the middle of the pit so my family could bury me there, suddenly longing for the pressure of earth to pack me away into some long, quiet darkness.

In the days that followed, Uncle Martin went to Rotterdam to hunt down any traces of Edwin. My father walked around handicapped by guilt over the loss of his son. Some part of him shriveled up like a salted slug and he no longer walked as tall. He went those first days home without sleeping, and then he collapsed across the bed and fell asleep, his clothes still on, one long arm dangling to the floor.

Father Heard came to our house every day. "I'm so sorry, my friend," he said and hugged my father, then my mother, then me. Despite all his efforts, he brought little comfort.

When my mother urged my father to talk about what happened, probing for more details, he gave the facts, stripped of any emotion as if he pulled some birdcage down over himself to lock that all away. Though parts of it bulged out between the iron gating. His voice cracked. His eyes glassed over.

"The road flooded. The water knocked a manhole cover loose. The boys were . . ." He paused and glanced at me for a moment. "They were trying to find me. I should have gone to them. To the hotel." As soon as he finished repeating the story, he left the room.

My mother screamed after him. "You were supposed to protect them. Keep them safe."

She and I remained sitting in the big, vacant stillness. The large wood-burning stove inhaled and cracked, breaking the silence; it seemed as if the house was already opening its doors to ghosts who moved in the distant corners of each room.

Over the next week, she threw a bowl against the wall, then pulled a blanket over her head. She walked up to my father, silent as a knife, and he braced himself to be hit, his body straightened for a moment and went hard, but she reached up and wrapped her arms around him.

"You poor man," she whispered.

Later she walked into his office and I could hear her curdling voice. "To hell with you and your lights!"

At night my dreams were of my brother's last breath before he slipped under the water, and how it was so giant, it sucked up all the air around him, and he was now adrift in some underground river, immersed in water, shifting somewhere under Rotterdam, or under the country, his fingertips rubbing against the underside of the continent. His eyes wide open. Edwin never sang, but in my dreams, he had gills, sang, and his words bubbled above him and soaked into the soil roof of the river. The rhythm of his song shifted the earth. His words rose and whispered softly up through the grasses. In my sleep my brother was very much still alive. So each time I woke clutching a pillow into my hollows, the deep fear and guilt of having lost him or having left before he resurfaced descended all over again.

When the red flare and glow of the German bombs on Rotterdam entered my mind, I pictured my brother tucked safe beneath the streets, or carried off to some floodplain or leach field clear of the city's firebombed limits, where he worked his way home.

When we got back from Rotterdam, the papers said that Germany had dropped one thousand paratroopers on Den Haag and several units on Rotterdam on the night of May 10, all dressed as Dutch Marines in an attempt to capture our royal family and government. Then, when that didn't work, they issued a warning that they'd bomb Rotterdam if we didn't surrender. It was only the day after they bombed us that we did surrender. Queen Wilhelmina and her family had been put on boats and escaped to England, but she swore on a public address over BBC Radio that her government would do its duty for us, for Holland.

Reliving that first night when we ran into the streets, I flashed over the memory of my pleading with Edwin to go find our father. Edwin had cursed our country for releasing the dykes, which, in my mind at the time, computed to it being our government's fault that that paltry section of road had flooded. I tried to make sense of it in my bed at night, but ended up listening to my mother getting out of bed and wandering the downstairs of the house. Soon after that, my father would descend the stairs, and they would both spend the dark hours of the night passing each other below my room. They did this nightly, until their footsteps and whispers became poisonous to me, setting off my stormy moods instead of letting me fall asleep.

"I had to protect Jacob." My father's voice carried through the house. "I couldn't stay there any longer without putting him in danger."

There was a long silence. In that silence I wanted to cry out my brother's name. In every silence I wanted that.

"I'll go in the morning," my father finally said.

And in the morning after refusing to let me come along, he did go back to Rotterdam. He wired Uncle Martin to meet him at the train station that night. Uncle Martin had no news so far. My father went to the factory to make sure the shifts kept running, and then he took the train that afternoon. It rained hard as I saw him off. When the train left, I went to Uncle Martin's boat in the harbor and imagined my brother on the deck, bossing me around or telling stories about our time last year at the youth camp.

On the way home I stopped at the church, where the organ played. After we had returned without Edwin, my mother started going to the church every afternoon to play sad songs on the organ. She played the first movement of Beethoven's "Moonlight Sonata," Mahler's "Kindertotenlieder," and Schubert's "Wiegenlied," which was about a mother singing over the grave of her infant. With all the stained-glass windows shattered from the bombings, there was nothing to keep the sound inside. Her music rose out of the building while she played, often improvising and making some new melody, a continuation of song. She was trying to call my brother home.

I tucked myself along the back wall so the roof's overhang would protect me from some of the rain. Her song reverberated through the walls and the notes ran link by link down the knuckles of my spine. I didn't know what to do for my mother. I felt losing Edwin was my fault and if I said one word about him to her I'd tip us both into an abyss. Along the road behind the church, Stanislaw Heigel walked with his wife toward the lightbulb factory. The second shift was about to start. With their heads down in the rain they didn't notice me.

"That woman's grief will cause her to lose her hearing," Mrs. Heigel said.

A senseless and sudden urge flared up in me to run after the older couple and push them face-down in the mud, standing on their backs until they flopped around like beached fish for making light of my mother's suffering. My anger was an arrow that hadn't yet landed.

I walked to Ludo's house, a three-level brownstone a few blocks west of my father's factory. I hadn't seen Hilda or Ludo since returning from Rotterdam, in hopes of avoiding having to tell someone else about Edwin. Besides, Ludo would have heard by now, and he hadn't come over. Everyone by then had heard. Ludo's mother opened their door. She was a sturdy brown-haired woman, short, with heavy thighs and extra weight around her bottom and hips. Her arms engulfed me and she made an exasperated cooing sound and patted her meaty hands against the middle of my back as she pulled me into her foyer.

"You sweet boy," Mrs. Shoemackher said. Behind her on the floor a scarlet and beige runner covered a polished oak table. I wanted to pick the fabric up and wrap it over my head so it would muffle her sympathies, swallow all noise.

Mr. Shoemackher, the carpenter, came to the door then. He was a quiet, short, gaunt man, tanned and windburned, dressed in brown trousers and a soiled gray shirt. He walked up to me and put his rough, wood-scented hand on my shoulder. His eyes were pale blue and sympathetic, and I couldn't look into them for long.

"Let me get Ludo." Mrs. Shoemackher turned and walked to the back of the house.

When Ludo came out, he held his youth camp dagger and a block of wilding wood he had carved into. When he saw me his eyes dropped to the floor. "I'm sorry I haven't been by yet."

"That's okay."

"I didn't know what to say."

"It's okay. I understand."

Ludo rocked back on his heels, shy and unassuming like he always was. Being an only child had made him eager for friends, and as I was suddenly an only child, I felt the same longing for his company that he must have felt for mine and Edwin's.

"I have something to show you, if you want to go for a walk," Ludo said.

The two of us walked in the rain across town, back to my house. I watched the cracks and gouges in the road fill with water, eyeing each little one and realizing the whole world had such little fissures. When we got to my house, Ludo led me into the woods.

"I came here earlier this week but didn't want to bother you or your parents." He walked me back to our fort. Twenty meters past, in a small clearing in the center of a cropping of Dutch elm trees, Ludo pointed to a large stone that had been rolled onto the grass. The stone had been polished smooth by the rain. On the wide face of the rock there were letters chiseled into it.

"Because they never found him, I figured we could mark a place for him like this," Ludo said.

The lettering on the stone read, *Edwin Koopman, Charioteer.*

This made my brother's absence finite, marked some conclusion to him as a being in the world, and I couldn't have that. I wasn't ready. He was still adrift in my dreams and that, at least, was something; that was somehow infinite. My hands leaned against the rock and pushed it over and then over again until it rolled out of the clearing.

"Why?" Ludo asked.

"He's not dead." My words took shape around me and faded. "He's not dead," I said again, this time trying to believe it. Uncle Martin and my father hadn't yet found a body. Uncle Martin sent daily wires updating us on finding nothing, so there couldn't be any gravestones yet.

Ludo looked hurt. I pictured him holding a chisel with his weak arm, which must have been difficult for him. "Thank you, Ludo," I said. "We'll put it back if we know."

On the morning of May 24, a troop of German soldiers spilled out of three carrier trucks in the center of Delfzijl. They formed two columns and marched over the main brick road. Their arms swung at their sides, their faces empty of any telling expressions as they passed without letting up on their march, without changing speed. Each wore a dark raincoat down to his knees and black jackboots. They were interchangeable in those outfits, with the iron cross on their hats like it was their sole eye, and their gloved hands showing no flesh.

"The only problem with Germany is that there are twenty million too many Germans," I remembered Edward Fass, the assembly line worker with the red, angry scar on his forearm, saying; seeing jackbooted infantrymen in my small town made that statement ring true.

People came out to watch the soldiers fan out across the village.

Several locals stood next to the road and raised their flat hands over their heads, the way we'd been taught at summer camp. That surprised me and I took note of everyone who raised their arms.

Ludo came with me as I followed the soldiers from a distance. We lurked behind buildings and hid behind trees. The soldiers were stationed across town by two men wearing charcoal gray coats. The men in charge were SS, and they had lists of buildings and roads they wanted the soldiers to guard. They took the schoolhouse as their new bunk barracks and commandeered the outdoor market street for what was said to be a new loading area for incoming German boats.

"What do you think they're going to do here?" I asked Ludo.

"I don't know."

"Well, should we do something? Should we go introduce ourselves?" I was desperate for anything to break the terrible routine of mourning my brother, to shift my focus from the submerged flow of sadness cutting through me.

"Why?"

"I don't know. Tell them we're the winners of last summer's games."

Ludo kept watching the soldiers. "I'm not sure what we're supposed to do."

When the soldiers spread out, I waved Ludo to follow me and we ran up to two soldiers broken off from the group.

"Hey, guys. Guys," I called to them in German.

When they stopped and faced us with the full seriousness of their charge, something in me deflated, and I looked from one to the next so quick I think I made them nervous.

"What is it?" one said.

I just stood there. Ludo said nothing.

"What do you want?"

"Nothing. Nothing. Never mind. I'm sorry," I said, letting those pathetic little words dribble free again.

"Well, go spread the word that total blackouts at night are now mandatory."

I still stood there. His jacket was held tight by a thick black belt worn high over the hips, a rectangular buckle pinching where his belly button was. What a big goddamned buckle, I thought.

"Got it?"

"Yes," I said.

"Get on then."

"Okay," I said and turned back into our town that made light but would now have to go dark.

We followed the soldiers from a distance for a few hours and then I ran home to tell my mother what happened. Tucked under the front door was a letter from Mr. Gunnelburg from Volkswagen. I walked into the house and placed it on top of the piano. My mother needed to wire my father in Rotterdam and let him know about the letter and the soldiers so he could figure out what it all meant for the factory.

When I turned around, I found her sleeping naked on the couch by the sliding glass windows. Her head rested on her folded arms, leaving her heavy breasts exposed. The last of the full light of the sun shone through the windows on her, on all her scars, highlighting how she'd aged without my ever having realized it. Then the true enormity and emptiness of our house settled on me, and I wanted to go curl on the floor at her feet, to participate in my family's downfall.

I crossed the room and pulled her blue robe over her.

"Let me take you to bed."

Her cheeks had begun to sag, and her features blunted. She pulled the bottom hem of her robe over her knees where she used tweezers to pluck at the fine hairs sprouting over her shins and calves where a road map of dark, forking, varicose veins leaned out against the skin.

When she sat up on the couch I helped her up, holding her elbows, and then led her up the steps.

"Thank you, Edwin," she mumbled in her half-sleep. We stopped and both stood there dazed until she realized what she'd said. Her head dropped into her hands as she walked into her bedroom and slumped at her dressing table.

Her robe hung open as she reached for her case full of jewelry bought over the course of years on my father's trips. She opened the sleek, felt case and picked up a necklace thin as a strand of hair. She sat back in the chair facing her bedroom dresser mirror and began to put all of her necklaces on. Then she took everything else out of the box. One by one, she put on every piece of jewelry. An ivory rose. Pearl brooch. Gemstone clasps. The necklaces touched one another on the back of her neck but hung at different lengths, the silver rubbing the gold, the gold rubbing the strings. She hung her loop earrings from her ear holes and then hooked every other glass earring she could into the loops until the clusters pulled her earlobes down toward her jawline.

"Mom," I said. "Mom."

But she kept at it and then she took out her rings, which were now loose on her, and one after the other she slipped them on until they locked her fingers straight. Her hands were suspended in front of her as she gazed into her mantle mirror. The strange gathering of chains and pearls about her neck was a layered coil of subtle light. Something ungovernable in her heart had saturated her mind. She looked at me then but her eyes were unfocused and didn't meet mine. She stood up so her ornament-weighted robe fell back off her shoulders, and looked at herself in the mirror as if alone.

"Honey," she said, turning to me in the dark hallway. Tendrils of jewelry hung off the side of her blank face. Her fingers could not bend from all the rings so she held them spread out and facing the ceiling like they'd been cast in bronze.

I turned and fled downstairs, taking three steps at a time. She was at the top flight by the time I slammed onto the first floor.

"Honey," she called. "Honey," she said, like she'd found the word she needed.

The manic energy and guilt that rose up in me made me want to sprint or mount some ten-legged chariot and fly over a sea of fire again. Stepping through the glass door into the backyard, I grabbed a shovel from the shed and started furiously scooping mounds of loose dirt back into the pit. I dug and dug, taking wild strikes into the dirt and flinging it until my arms burned and my whole body pulsed with one intention. There. There. There. That beat, beat, beat of a body doing the work of still living. I wanted to cry and weep and confess about Edwin, as if doing so would expunge my guilt. But I held it all in where it became something solid I've quietly carried with me until this day—a cancerous pearl.

When I was too tired to move, I leaned on the shovel's handle. Above me my mother's shadow filled her bedroom window. She'd been watching me. What must she have thought of me then? Her son. Her only son. It was very dark out when she stepped back from her window. I hoped she would sleep. It was strange to look up at the house. It seemed like I'd been buried and was only now working my way loose of the earth.

The next morning my father and Uncle Martin returned.

"There are Germans everywhere," Uncle Martin cursed as he walked into the door. "We have to get you out of here."

"We didn't find anything," my father told me.

My mother came down the stairs, heard him, and stopped. "Then I'm not going anywhere. Not until we're sure." She turned around and went back to her room.

"We'll go back. I'll keep looking," my father called after her. He walked past me like he was about to sink into the ottoman. "Hello, Jacob," he said. Then he saw the letter from Mr. Gunnelburg on the piano where I left it.

"Oh. Thank god," he sighed and picked up the envelope. "They paid."

His long fingers tore the seal back. With the paper folded back in front of him I saw a dark drawbridge slam shut over his face. He crumpled the letter and threw it across the room.

"They can't do this," he said. "Oh no. They can't do this."

He got up and went into his lab where I heard glass shattering against the walls. He spent the rest of the night at home wandering the house, in and out of his lab. He passed me a dozen times without noticing me or seemingly unaware, muttering to himself. When he was in the lab, I snuck up to the crumpled letter like a thief, smoothed it, and read.

Dear Mr. Koopman,

In light of recent events, we will be rescinding our initial payment and not placing any further orders. Thank you for your interest in working with Volkswagen.

Trevor Gunnelburg

I sensed that disappointment must have tipped my father then. I knew how hard he'd worked on the order, but didn't know then how much capital he'd invested in the project, or the practical, day-to-day stresses of the business that still required his attention despite our own family being shut down.

After that my father became immobilized by grief. Over the course of two days he emptied the brandy decanter and several other bottles of liquor in the house. Instead of careening room to room, he sat in his library alone and mumbled to the books. When he sobered up, he went days without eating and lost weight. During the darkest parts of the nights that he wasn't spooking through Rotterdam, the sound of his crying rose through the vents. It became as steady as one of the noises the house made: the wood settling, popping and cracking behind the walls, or the low groan of water flushing through the pipes. Waking to this sound sent a sadness through me that reached out from my chest and got lost in some unbearable emptiness.

When I did sleep, my dreams had become a frightening stranger that leaned against me and made me toss the covers off so the cold woke me. My trembling fingers felt for the edges of the blanket. Fergus rested his head on my bed. When I finished petting him, he'd go to Edwin's bed, sniff the sheets, then jump on the covers and curl himself into a ball. Until morning I would stare at the exquisite cobwebs tucked in the corner of my room and the shadows of tree branches that bent across the ceiling.

When the long days of summer came it was a blessing. It was easier to spend less time in or close to the house. The first tulip and forsythia blooms lining the front and sides of the house shriveled into dull little fists of petals from a lack of water and tending. But so much time off on my own or with Ludo and Hilda created the constant desire to talk to Edwin. When the need for this got too burdensome, I started talking to him in my head. At first, a short calling out of his name, then, slowly, as if Edwin became my own sounding board, I began to hear myself talk of my own grief. I wanted so terribly for some soft shiver of my brother's subterranean drifting song to find me.

At my loneliest moments, I walked around the outskirts and through the center of town, keeping Edwin's invisible presence next to me. I wondered what tragedies were held in each home on my street alone. One of the houses belonged to Liddy Robinson's family. Liddy and Edwin were in the same grade and she was the first girl to kiss Edwin. However, later she told Hilda that his breath smelled like cabbage cream soup and she didn't want to kiss him again.

Edwin had been gone for three months. He had missed two thunderstorms that shook the house. One storm came marching over our house on legs of lightning, dragging its heavy dark clouds overhead like a wet tarp. Each night after those storms, the clear sky of stars bloomed into sharp-angled shapes etched across the sky. Orion threw his leg over the horizon, climbed atop our world, and sat perched, steadily gazing upon everything we were losing.

Soon after they arrived, the Germans built a temporary tent city in the middle of town. More soldiers came by small boats along the water, and when their tent city was set up and the presence of the soldiers was ubiquitous, they sent men down to the Koopman Light Company's factory.

At first they just walked the factory floor. But one day, my father came home saying that they came in and stationed a soldier who wanted to go over all of the company's accounting. "All of your production will be going to Germany now," the soldier told my father. "You will operate as normal. We will have people here to help you load the trucks from now on and we will cover the distribution of your lights."

"What about payment?" he asked.

"'You will be maintained' is what he told me. Maintained. What does that mean? Most of our money was sunk into the Volkswagen order."

My mother didn't have much of a reaction. She listened from the couch, her blue bathrobe wrapped tightly around her.

"They've handcuffed me."

Still, my mother said nothing. For days after that my father came home and did not try to share his visible frustrations. In fact, whole days went by when I didn't hear either of their voices.

That silence I remember most. That silence spoke to me. We will not share these hurts. We will not voice this pain.

Then, one night, my father walked into my room with Fergus at his heels. "I'm going back to Rotterdam," he said.

The next morning, Uncle Martin and I walked my father to the train station.

"They're going to run the factory for you?" Uncle Martin asked.

"They asked me to repair a downed machine, but they can do that without me," my father said.

"That's not like you," I said.

"Well. They're doing the books. Everything. They only want me for repairs and as a consultant. They can manage without me for a spell."

When my father's train left, Uncle Martin and I walked to the harbor.

"Where else is there to look?" I asked Uncle Martin.

"I guess we look until we find," he said.

The soldiers set up large gun turrets to protect the troop transport boats that came in every day. Several soldiers smoked cigarettes by the tent city. More walked past the outdoor market booths, thumbed over the assorted seeds, coriander, beans, and potatoes Mr. Graaf sold. He was the only one selling anything outside that day.

There was a commotion up the road in front of the pharmacy. Above it were several floors of apartment houses. A woman screamed and then several soldiers ran up the street.

When we got closer we saw Patrice Mueller being propped up by two German soldiers. Her head had been shaved and slopped in heavy orange paint from a wide brush dragged across her scalp. Rivulets of orange paint ran off her forehead and cheeks and mixed in with a smudge of blood under her nostrils.

"What happened to her?" I asked Uncle Martin.

"She's been with a German man. Some of the locals didn't think too highly of it."

"My god. The townspeople did that to her?"

"Yes." Uncle Martin turned away from the commotion and started walking back.

The front of Patrice's gray wool skirt had splatters of orange paint on it. Her breasts visibly hung loose under her white blouse. They were wide apart and made it clear how large a woman she was. Little red blotches on her scalp bled where the knife had shorn off the hair too closely and cut the skin. To me, there was nothing sexual about her, and I had a hard time understanding how sex had put her in such a position. I turned away and caught up with Uncle Martin.

"But Father Heard said that was a sin." My uncle gave me a sideways look. "I mean, being with anyone before marriage." I wasn't sure what I was trying to say. I was confused and angry at Patrice Mueller, the German man she was with, and our own townspeople who had done this terrible thing to her.

"Don't be so certain of what Father Heard preaches. The good father's book doesn't bend enough to cater to its audience. I'll tell you something about being human. Captain Cook's bosun had to keep guard of his ship from his own crew, who traded nails for sex in Tahiti. The locals thought it an acceptable form of barter, and the bosun realized the men would have stripped the ship to a floating pile of loose logs at the rate they stole nails. And Columbus found the New World, discovered syphilis, and three years later it was an epidemic in Moscow. That ought to tell you all you need about how real people live, and to be wary of preaching that is so rigid and unforgiving of human nature."

I looked at him and started to speak, but couldn't think of anything to say. I felt an odd and welling sorrow, as if he'd peeled back the skin, red muscle, and porous bone of how I had constructed a part of the world in my mind. What was beneath all those teachings of Father Heard was a savage and raw pulsing heart, full of longing and lust and void of any ethereal or divine spark.

Late one evening, after my father returned yet again empty-handed from his trip to Rotterdam, Fergus barked at a car that came up the driveway. Two German soldiers got out, straightened their jackets, and marched to the house. One of them looked up and saw me in the window. He nodded and pointed at the front door.

"There are soldiers here," I yelled.

My father, Uncle Martin, and my mother came into the foyer as our buckle-shaped ironworks door knocker shook the whole frame.

"Open the door," my father said.

The two soldiers stood side by side in the doorway. Both men were very young, probably twenty at the oldest. Weapons bulged in their pockets. The sudden urge to salute them came over me.

Fergus strained against his collar to say hello to them, but my mother held him back.

"We are looking for Hans Koopman," one of the men in the doorway said.

"That's me," my father said.

"Come with us."

"What do you want with him?" my mother jumped in. The soldier seemed taken aback by the leap to urgency in her voice, her tone signaling a fierce protectiveness to keep the family together he couldn't have guessed at. He straightened up. The one closer to me stepped inside the frame of the house. My uncle eased closer to the men, but my mother reached out her hand and placed it on his forearm, a subtle touch that was not one of affection, but of a brief caution, telling him to wait, wait until she told him to act.

"You had orders to get a machine up and running. To get shipments of lights out."

"I had to go to Rotterdam to look for . . . " He didn't finish his sentence.

"You were given many opportunities to get that work done. Too many."

"I can still do it," my father said.

"No. We have something else for you now. We need you and your boat, Mr. Koopman," the soldier said. "We are commandeering all the boats in the harbor and we need people to run them for us. Seeing how you like to travel so much, you can travel for us now."

I was both scared my father had done something wrong and strangely proud they wanted him.

"Wait," Uncle Martin said. The crimson flush of blood painted his neck again, and I knew then it would be impossible to know the true topography of his inner life. "Hans runs the only factory in town. You need him for that."

"We will have someone look after that. Right now we need boats and pilots."

"Well, you don't want his piece-of-junk boat. That thing hasn't run for a long time. And he's a crappy pilot."

"We need Mr. Koopman."

"I've got the boat you need and I'd be happy to go instead."

"Oh, Martin," my mother whispered. Words meant for him alone.

"We came for Mr. Koopman," the soldier said.

"Yes, but look, he's got his nice family here, and you'll see that you need him for the factory. Besides, if you want boats, mine works. It's bigger, and I'm your man." Uncle Martin gave a full smile to the soldiers now. He had switched into his charming Dutchman mode of speaking. "Look at me, boys. I'm a bigger catch than this one anyway. Let me get my coat."

"We need Mr. Koopman," the soldier said.

"Well, you're getting one better," Uncle Martin said as he walked to the closet to get his coat. Fergus lurched to get close and sniff the men.

My mother reached up to my uncle and hugged him around the neck. "Thank you, Martin," she whispered.

I felt sick with uncertainty.

"Let's go, men," Uncle Martin said, moving his giant body into the door frame so both soldiers had to step back out of the house. By force of his will, the two men turned when he had their shoulders under each arm and they didn't turn back as he walked with them to their car.

My uncle, without hesitation, sacrificed himself so my father wouldn't have to go. Part of me wanted my father to go with them though, wanted him to be needed. Then the soldiers pulled down the driveway and the back of my uncle's head rocked back and forth in the car, still talking to the two men in the front, like they were now the best of friends. When the car rounded the corner, the quick flash of the headlights blinked along the trees as they pushed down the road and out of sight.

THE *LIGHTHOUSE LADY*

7

Father Heard came to our house one Sunday night.

When my father opened the door, the two men hugged in the vestibule.

"Come in. Come in," my father said.

They stepped into the living room, where I sat with my mother. She stood, pinched the blue bathrobe tight around her neck, waved, and walked out of the room. Several minutes later she came back in after changing into black slacks and a loose, button-up gray sweater that she held tight at her waist. Her hair was still tangled and flattened from lying on the couch. She held a plate with a cut-up pear and cheese slices.

"I need to speak with you, Hans," Father Heard said.

He had received a letter that the Dutch archbishop had sent to all the priests in the country with the order to read it aloud to their parish congregation that Tuesday. Father Heard placed the letter on the coffee table next to the untouched plate of cheese and the pear slices, already browning.

The simultaneous reading of the letter was meant to inspire a general strike of workers in Amsterdam. The news from the rest of Holland, funneled in by commuting workers, said the encroaching Germans had removed Jews from all public functions, including universities. Protests had begun in Leiden and spread throughout the country. The Germans sought control and were met with violence. Jewish sections of Amsterdam had been fenced off and non-Jews were blocked from entering. They rounded up over four hundred Jewish men and took them away, to where we didn't know.

"Jacob should go upstairs," my mother said.

"No, he needs to hear this," my father said.

Some part of me thought those missing young men had been taken to the training camps in Germany, that they would be shown movies and taught songs, and be returned champions. But I soon learned that the Germans had stationed machine-gun nests around the Jewish quarter, a fact that couldn't fit into my understanding of things.

The archbishop's response to the current unrest was this letter. Father Heard said it contested the alleged mistreatment of the Jewish population by the Germans in the country. Though, of course, there was never any mention of it in the new German newspapers, which had started circulating in the town the previous fall, the archbishop had ordered the Catholic Church to voice its concern to the congregation, to draw light to what was happening.

"I'm going to read it. I came to tell you because we're friends, and I know it may complicate your relationship with the Germans in your factory."

"But, Father, this might not be safe for you," my father said. "Let's think about this. We can play it safer, I'm sure."

"Hans. I am going to call the congregation together. My mind is made up. Like I said, I'm trying to be respectful and give you fair warning."

"This sounds bad to me," my father said, and I heard the tremulousness in his voice. For years, my mind would crawl back to this revelation, and I would blame my own timidity on the intense shadow he cast over my childhood. I come back to this conversation as the one that illuminated my father's cautious and scared nature, which felt to me like my unfortunate birthright. It had slipped right past Edwin, who was certain about his life and how to carry himself, while it struck me clean on.

"They're trying to silence us," Father Heard said. His upper lip rose over the jumbled line of his yellowed teeth. The whites of his eyes engulfed the dark iris. Blood pumped to his large ears.

"But we don't want to stir up trouble. Make things worse."

"Hans. How is the status quo working for you? How has that been going?"

"I don't want to risk anything else."

"We have to. Look around you, Hans," Father Heard spoke in his booming sermon voice. Then he lowered his tone. "Look around. Edwin's gone. Look at Drika here." He held his hand out to my mourning mother. "Your factory. And for heaven's sake, Martin has now taken up with them. Seemingly in spirit as much as in body."

"Leave him out of this," my mother spit out.

Father Heard took a moment. "Security is off the table. Nothing is safe, and that's why I have to do this."

My mother picked up a pillow, cradled it in her lap, and sunk her face into it. My father turned to look out the window.

"I'm sorry to be so harsh," Father Heard said. "But the archbishop's letter is the voice of reason. The voice of pacifism in the face of all of this aggression."

My father held up his hand to stop him from talking. "Jacob. See Father Heard to the door please."

Father Heard picked up his letter and let me lead him out.

"I'll see you on Tuesday, I'm sure," he said as he left the room.

That Tuesday afternoon, when Father Heard had called everyone in his congregation together, my father and I were the last two people to arrive. Inside the church, the windows had not been repaired since that first dusting of bombs dropped over Delfzijl. The large stained-glass window above the altar of three dark crosses on a jade green hill was now a yawning hole with glass-shard teeth, jagged and translucent. The smell of incense and smoky wool rose off the congregation as we joined them, huddled together in wet coats and hats. Steam rose off their heads as they tucked themselves further into their clothes.

A wave of chills rolled down my spine. I was always cold then, always breathing into cupped hands to warm them. Father Heard had swept all the glass debris off the floor, but there were still pieces lodged in the organ pipes, shifting inside them as my mother played. It was a subtle sound the other people in church would not have picked up on, but I'd been listening to the smallest nuances of her playing for years, ever since my father donated the money to Father Heard to first install the organ. In the front of the church, the organ pipes now seemed like they lifted out of my mother's body, like it was her breath that set the timbre of each wailing tube of alloy. Since we lost Edwin, the songs she played had been slower, more morbid. Even the standards she played during the Mass had a different tone to them. They were the same songs everyone knew, but it lacked her clarity of rhythm, as if she had plunged her hands into a clear stream but her fingers mucked up a cloud of silt and dirtied the water. Her mournful sound made its way out from under the rafters into the immense, open sky, where the dark essence of her dirge drifted over all of Holland.

My father and I stepped to the side of the back door and listened to my mother play. Father Heard walked out from the door off to the side of the altar, keeping his shoulder to the wall. He walked to the back of the church and leaned in close to my father.

"Please don't do this," my father said.

"Hans, Samuel is missing," Father Heard said.

The news made no sense to me. Samuel, the air-writer, had been a fixture of our town my whole life, furiously scribbling out his thoughts above his head. I could close my eyes and see him feeding pigeons, hear Ludo mocking his spasms.

"The vendors who provide him with food spoke to one another after the bags went unclaimed. This was yesterday. They let me know this morning, and he wasn't in his apartment."

I imagined Father Heard trying to find a trace of Samuel, wanting to read the writing that must have filled the air between those apartment walls.

"Should we go look for him?" my father asked.

"I had people out all morning. He's gone."

"What do you think happened?" my father said.

"What do you think happened!" Father Heard spit back.

The people in the back rows all watched the priest and my father exchange animated whispers.

"You both can help me look after I read this letter. You see why I need to read it now, don't you?"

My father blankly nodded to Father Heard.

"Okay," my father said. "Okay." He leaned in to hug Father Heard. "We'll look for him."

Father Heard returned the embrace, then walked down the center aisle to the altar. My mother stopped playing. As Father Heard read the letter, his voice was calm and steady. His deep-set eyes narrowed and scanned the room to single each of us out. His right hand wrapped around the podium, his knuckles were white where he gripped the edge, and his left hand chopped the air in front of him in rhythm with the enunciation of his words. He was once again the familiar authority figure our little church knew him to be.

"We must protest this abominable persecution." His voice boomed out over the room. The shoulders of the men in front of me scrunched up beneath their heavy jackets each time he uttered the word *strike*.

My mother turned on her bench to face Father Heard. The organ pipes rose up behind her to the exposed wooden rafters of the A-frame roof. My father sat in the back row of varnished pine pews. Ludo and Hilda were sitting in the front with their parents. Men from the factory and their children filled the rest of the pews. A random smattering of fishermen sat among them. From behind, the whole congregation looked like rodents peeking out of holes. Their spines arched forward, their bodies doubled over either for warmth or to hide, perhaps, from the call for ethical action to be taken.

"Lord, please keep your finger on our shoulder to protect us during these trying times," Father Heard concluded.

Then the children in the church walked out of their pews and gathered in the back corner, like it was a regular Sunday Mass. They all looked at my father. It was striking to not see Samuel sitting among them. Once my father stood up, the children sat in a half circle. He walked by me and put a hand on my shoulder. He chewed the inside of his lip, causing his left cheek to suction in and out.

He walked to where the children waited, sat in the chair one of the little boys put out for him, and started telling us a story.

"Behind Thump-Drag's cabin in the woods there was a giant open pit that he could not see the bottom of," my father began. "When he walked to the side he looked down and saw only a pool of darkness. Every morning when he woke, he walked to the lip of the pit and peered inside, tossing pebbles and stones down and listening for them to land. Townspeople knew of the pit too, and they brought their wagons full of trash, dead cows, and piles of stones they unearthed from their fields, and they dumped everything off the edge and were happy to be rid of it.

"'We have never had to dig a hole to bury our dead or to dispose of our waste because of this pit,' an old woman told Thump-Drag.

"Thump-Drag could not keep from thinking of the bottom of the hole and all the mess people had let fall down there. He stood beside it late into the evening, peering into the dark and seeking out the bottom. He did this until he imagined himself sinking into the mouth of the hole, weightless and descending into the cup of earth, sinking away from the surface of the world. When he could no longer withstand not knowing where the hole ended, he built himself a chariot out of ropes and an old claw-footed bathtub. He stood in the tub and held a torch with several unlit torches at his feet. He had the town's people help him by lowering the tub with him into the pit.

"The pit's walls twitched with shadows in the light of his torch as he descended, deeper and deeper, until the last of the rope pulled tight and he still had not yet reached the end. He dipped a torch into the pit and watched it fall, then fade into an orange pinprick until it disappeared altogether. He swung there in his tub and cursed the dark abyss. So he got out his knife and yelled good-bye to the people above, and he cut loose the rope and fell down the hole.

"And still, he is falling, being swallowed by the slow darkness and beginning to fear that it is, in fact, a bottomless hole."

I was choked with sudden emotion. It was clear that my father was saddled with the endless burden of wondering where his other son was, a burden that bubbled up through his stories, and I felt it too, the pressure of being responsible for Edwin, for the loss of him.

The children leaned in close to my father, expecting the rest of the story, what was at the bottom, what adventures were to be had down there, and how Thump-Drag gets out. But my father stood up. It was the first time in all the years of telling stories he got up from his chair before the children around him did, before they were satisfied with the experience he'd given them.

"Dear god, Hans," my mother said as we left the church together. Her face was red and grimy. She'd been crying. "You'll give them all nightmares."

"A taste of darkness won't kill them," he said.

After a fruitless night of searching for Samuel, my father looked very near collapse. But instead of getting some rest, he holed himself up in his lab again. When I went there to see him, he called out, "Not now," so I left him alone.

Three days later, my family and Ludo and Hilda went to the harbor. Soldiers stood nearby around a fire they'd made in a steel drum. They'd punched holes at the base of the drum for air to get in, and the flames looked like fiery eyeballs and reflected off the snow and all the polished, black boots. It was still strange to hear the guttural German language spoken everywhere in my own village. Other soldiers loaded and unloaded boats on the dock. They pushed little lorries and wobbly wheelbarrows up the icy path toward waiting trucks.

There was a loud roar from planes flying overhead. The hum of German planes on maneuver sounded like a quickened thunderhead from a great distance, and was followed by the high whine of their propellers sucking the air off the ground as they hammered across the sky.

"Heinkels?" Ludo asked.

"I think they're Messerschmitts," I said. "They have a deeper growl when they fly at those altitudes."

Most of the fishing boats in the harbor were iced over and looked like they hadn't been used in a long time. Three kids skated on the frozen canal, but the channel itself was open and clear of ice as the Germans used the port. A constant, streamlined movement of soldiers cleaned and painted the military boats in the harbor, loading and unloading even more soldiers and supplies from the pontoon dock.

Before the Germans' arrival, when the cold came and froze the water, everyone would sharpen their skates on their whetstones. They'd skate the canal, carving looping alphabets across the ice, some of the adults and older kids going on for dozens of kilometers.

"People drown under the ice every year," our mother would say. "Don't trust any patch of ice unless there are already many people on it. Be careful at the edges and under bridges. Those don't freeze properly."

But on the occasions she went out herself, she enjoyed gliding over the ice as much as we did and took long, graceful strides that appeared effortless as she cut down the canal, past the row of hollow post windmills, calling after us, "Keep up boys, keep up if you can!"

It had been six months since the soldiers had come to my house and left with Uncle Martin. They had him operating as a ferryman since then, and it turned out he was often back in Delfzijl, navigating his own boat across the water, delivering soldiers, equipment, and supplies. He was due back again that afternoon, and as we got to the docks we could already see the *Lighthouse Lady* off in the distance narrowing in on the shore. The boat cut straight toward us and shone in the sun like a jewel. We waited, tucked into our clothing, surrounded by little clouds of our own breath until the boat crossed the break wall.

We could see Uncle Martin on the steering station on top of the wheelhouse. He wore a long dark jacket and a twin-peaked hat with the red and black German insignia on it. Once he tossed mooring lines to the shore man and the boat was cleated to its berthing spot, he cut the engines. He hadn't seen us yet when he stepped off the ship with a duffel bag slung over his shoulder and a giant wooden bucket in one hand. He patted the man who tied off the lines of his boat and said something to him, and the man smiled and sort of shrank away from my uncle's giant presence. Martin spotted us and walked over. It seemed everyone knew his name and he smiled or winked at them all as he passed, tall, wide, lumbering back home.

"You've gone native," my father said when they shook hands on the shore.

"Playing along," he said.

He put his bag and bucket down and hugged my mother, picking her up and giving her a full-circle swing. Then he did the same thing to me. I was sixteen then, and embarrassed to be engulfed in front of Hilda. He took a swat at Ludo's head and shoulders and then rustled his hair.

"Hello, Martin," Ludo said, making a show of straightening his hair back down.

"Little lady," Uncle Martin said and bent down to kiss Hilda's hand, which made her blush.

Inside the bucket was a commotion of leaf-sized crabs with shimmery blue-brown alligator spiked shells jostling on top of one another. Beady black eyes were set wide across the ridge of their broken shale backs. Every time one tried climbing up the side, the others pinched onto it and pulled it down into the clump of shells.

"You think you can boil these up for our dinner, Drika?" Martin asked.

"I'm not sure I want to touch those."

"I wouldn't either," Hilda said.

"Come on. Boiling water isn't beyond you, is it?

My mother tucked her body into him for another giant hug.

Martin had been told to stay on his boat or in the soldiers' bunks when on shore, but by that winter he'd worked with the Germans long enough that they trusted him to do his own paperwork, run his ship by himself, and come home for a meal with our family. My father had made bread the night before because he couldn't sleep. He was nervous about the repercussions of Father Heard's reading. He didn't even bother going into the factory that day. The Germans were maintaining all of it by then anyway.

We walked up our road without speaking. The bucket of crabs swung at my side and Ludo held Martin's duffel bag slung over his shoulder. The familiar blaze of blue ink rose up from Martin's collar just below his left ear. The briny scent of gasoline fumes fell off his coat, which was so long he looked like a giant bat from behind. When we got home, everyone, even Ludo and Hilda, started asking him questions about what was happening in Germany and what they had him doing.

"There's a complete naval blockade around the country," Martin answered, "so there's no escaping by sea."

My parents wanted us to leave as soon as possible, and I'd convinced them to at least talk to Ludo and Hilda's parents about letting Ludo and Hilda come with us if it came to that, but my mother could not bring herself to imagine leaving without final news of Edwin.

"You and Ludo will get drafted when you're eighteen," my father told us. He and my mother were anxious to think of ways to get us clear of that.

"Why is that so bad?" I asked.

"Wake up, son," my father said. "Ludo's arm will ensure he's sent to a work camp. God knows what will happen to you."

"We were there. We know," I said, my feelings hurt. I was trying to act smart in front of Hilda.

"You weren't really there, and you don't know. We've kept you from knowing what's really happening."

"Well, you did send them to camp, Hans," my mother said.

"Not now, Drika."

My mother curled over on her side on the couch, the wind taken out of her questioning. She reached over and took my hand in hers. "You have to carry your family in your heart, all of your family," she said, "and make it out of this nightmare."

That Sunday, when we prepared for Mass, my father made more loaves of bread to bring to Father Heard and several other families in town. Food was becoming harder to come by, but because we still had a full larder, my father wanted to share. My mother had stopped cooking since Edwin was lost. The only thing she continued to do was play the organ at church. It was the only time she wasn't in her blue bathrobe.

I had been working in my father's factory after school every day since the German occupation, and the floor was buzzing that week with talk about Father Heard's letter. Everyone at the factory wanted to know what Father Heard was going to follow up with during his Sunday Mass; we expected his next service to be more crowded than usual.

We got there early and my mother let us in with her key. She unlocked the door that opened below where the windows used to be; Ludo's father had finally covered the holes with plywood the day before. My father and I sat in the back row, as we usually did, while my mother went to the organ and started to warm up. She struck each key once and let it dole out and fade. Across the ivory keys, the pitch of each note changed ever so slightly, so that listening to her warming up taught my ear how to detect deviations of noise. Ludo could never guess the exact type of plane soaring overhead, but I always knew not only what it was, but which country it belonged to, and thereby what level of threat it posed, all by the pitch of its engines.

By the time she'd gone through the whole keyboard, and played a few partial songs to warm up, the church was already half full. She walked to the church's back room, where Father Heard would get ready.

Sitting with my father, I felt an overwhelming need to call out to Edwin. To speak his name and never stop calling out to him.

"Dad," I said.

"Yes."

"I'm sorry."

"What for?" he said. His mind had been elsewhere.

"I'm sorry," I started. I needed to tell him how sorry I was for Edwin. To let those words reach his ears. To confess how Edwin wanted to stay put. That I had forced the one person with the most potential to do something great with his life to his death.

But then my mother came back out and jogged to the back pew, passed me, and sat next to my father.

"He's not in back," she said. There was a quick tremor of nervousness in her voice. "He's always here by now."

"Play some music for a bit then," my father whispered. "Jacob, go to his house. See if he's all right. Hurry."

Outside all the windows of the apartment buildings in the village were iced over. Several Heinkels zoomed in from over the North Sea. They echoed off the buildings as they crossed overhead. Father Heard's small home sat several houses past the apartment buildings, a one-level cottage with an angled roof that helped the snow slide off. I wished Edwin were with me as I knocked on the door and waited. When he didn't answer, I knocked again, then tried the doorknob. It was unlocked and opened into the foyer.

"Father Heard. Hello. Father Heard?"

The kitchen smelled like stale tea and sage. The living room had a bookshelf and a simple wooden crucifix nailed to the wall next to the large window that overlooked the street. I remembered the word *garçonniére*, a bachelor's quarters. The faint scent of church incense and an older man's musk filled the bedroom. The blankets on the bed were unmade. A comforter was crumpled and hanging off the side like it had been tossed in a hurry.

"Father Heard," I called out one last time before leaving.

As I walked back across the center of town, I passed my uncle standing around a garbage can fire with several soldiers. One of the soldiers, with a charcoal-colored rain cape, spread his arms out to capture the warmth like a giant vulture. He breathed little white clouds into the billowing smoke. They all laughed at something Uncle Martin had said. Then Uncle Martin saw me and walked over.

His heavy black boots left tremendous prints in the snow. His jacket was buttoned up to his neck and hung down below his knees. He had leather work gloves, worn black and smooth at the fingertips. "What are you up to?"

"Seeing if Father Heard was at home. Have you seen him?"

"No," Uncle Martin said, falling in step with me.

When we were close to the church, I could hear my mother playing J. P. Sweelinck's "Polyphonic Psalms," which was something she never played during Mass, which meant Father Heard was still not inside the church.

I opened the door and everyone turned and looked at us. Hilda sat in the front pew with her parents. She gave me a small wave and I wanted to swim through the air to be beside her. Others let their eyes linger on Uncle Martin's uniform. My mother kept playing. Uncle Martin shut the door behind him. People looked like they either were terrified of him or wanted to stab him. I sat back down next to my father and listened to the people in the pews around us, wondering where Father Heard could be.

"I couldn't find him."

My father bent over with his hands on his knees. "I feel sick." He looked at Uncle Martin. "What if they took him? What can we do?"

People whispered to one another. They began to speculate that Father Heard had been taken, and then they started to worry it was because he read the letter. Someone in the room must have told the Germans. People started looking at my father and me. We owned the factory. We owned the big house. Then they stared at Uncle Martin in his Nazi uniform. There was a feeling of shifting, uncertain loyalties. When several other dispatches came back without the missing priest, the entire congregation fell silent beneath my mother's playing. The music had burrowed itself into the spaces between everyone and was now the common voice of worry. When she let her song fade, and then go to nothing, the silence in the room was absolute.

"I have to do something," my father said.

Then he stood up, took the small chair that was always set out for him to sit and tell stories to the children, and carried it down the main aisle of the church, up the altar steps, and sat it down next to the lectern.

"Maybe we'll have story time at the front of church today," he said. "Come on up, children, come on." The bundled children came and sat on the floor around him.

"Where is Father Heard?" someone in front called out.

"He probably knows," a woman named Anneke Gelen said and pointed to Uncle Martin.

"He probably took him," Edward Fass said.

I wanted to step into the aisle between the congregation and my uncle, but Uncle Martin straightened his head up, and looked even more menacing in his long German overcoat. Something in him seemed to harden.

"Let me tell everyone a story about the old goat, her seven kids, and the wolf," my father said. This time he spoke to everyone, and we all listened like his was the only voice in the world.

"The old goat went to the forest to get some food, so she called all seven of her kids and said, 'Now, children, be on guard against the wolf. He often disguises himself, but you will know if it's him by his rough voice and black feet. And remember that if he comes in here, he will devour you—skin, hair, and all.'

"It was not long after that a knock came at the door, and a voice said, 'Open up, dear children, it is your mother, and I have a treat for each and every one of you.'

"But the kids said, 'You are not our mother because your voice is too rough and we see your dark feet leaning against the window. We will not let you in.'

"So, the wolf went into town and bought a big lump of chalk and ate it and made his voice soft. Then he went to the baker and had him rub his feet in dough. Then the wolf went to the miller and said, 'Put white meal over my feet for me.' The miller thought the wolf was up to no good and trying to deceive someone so he said he would not help the wolf. But the wolf threatened to devour him. Then the miller was afraid and made the wolf's paws white."

My father paused there. He looked over the children's heads and around the room and said, "Some men are like this."

"So, the wolf went back to the kids' house and tricked them into opening the door.

"Soon afterward, the old goat came home from the forest and saw that her house had been torn apart and her children were gone. She called each of them by name, but only the youngest child who was still hiding said, 'Dear Mother, I am in the clock-case.' When the mother found her child, she wept hysterically for her other lost children. In her grief, she wandered out of the house and her only remaining child followed her. That is how she came across the sleeping wolf in the meadow.

"She looked at the wolf and saw something struggling in his gorged belly. 'Oh my heavens,' she said, then she sent her youngest child home to get her scissors, a needle, and thread. The mother goat snuck up on the sleeping wolf and cut open its stomach. Then all six of her lost children sprang out, and each was still alive and had suffered no injury at all. In his greediness, the wolf had swallowed them whole.

"The mother goat sent them each off into the woods to get a large stone. When the children came back she placed all the stones inside the wolf's open stomach while he was still sleeping, and then the mother sewed him up as fast as she could.

"The wolf woke up because the stones settling into his stomach made him very thirsty. So he stood up to go to the well for a drink, but when he began to move about, the stones in his stomach knocked against one another and rattled. Then he cried out,

'What rumbles and tumbles
Against my poor bones?
I thought it six kids,
But naught it's big stones.'

"And when the wolf stooped over at the well for a drink, the heavy stones made him fall in, and there was no one to help him from drowning miserably. When the seven children saw that, they came running to the spot and cried aloud, 'The wolf is dead! The wolf is dead!' and they danced for joy around the well with their mother because evil, in its most cruel form, no longer belonged to the world."

8

By that March we'd gone through all the supplies in our larder, and it became my job to do the shopping as my mother still very rarely left the house. Bacon, sugar, tea, butter, and meat had already been rationed, and by the end of the month the ration on eggs was one per person per week. There were no more bananas. When shopping, there was little talk. We had to use our ration cards if we needed clothes as everything was directed to the war effort—everything. My mother made me darn my own socks and sew rags together into heavy blankets that we slept under at night. Paper, petrol, and washing powder were now limited, and only one bar of soap was allowed a month, so when we used a bar down to a nub, we squeezed it together in our fists with the previous month's nub to get a few extra washes out of it.

On the night of April 20, despite the blackouts, several stores placed lit red wax candles beneath new oil paintings of Hitler's face behind their windows, as they had the year before.

"Christ. Will you look at that," my father whispered when he saw them in town.

When he told my mother, she took all her handmade red candles and tossed them in the trash.

Sometimes Uncle Martin showed up with a net of fish he caught by dropping a line off the edge of his boat as he ferried the Germans, and he had me trade the fish for extras.

Before Mass on Sunday, everyone in the congregation spoke of what supplies they had and what was going to arrive soon. If some new shipment was expected, I'd stop by that shop before reporting to the factory to see if anything had arrived, which was clear by whether or not people lined up out the door.

On Sunday, children huddled outside the main church doors before being called in. They showed one another shrapnel they collected from bombs or dogfights between planes that had fallen near their homes. They held each little jagged scrap up to the light and ran their tiny fingers along the uneven teeth of the edges. One little boy bit down on a charred hunk between his molars. The children swapped shrapnel like the adults traded ration cards inside the building.

We had not had a Mass service since Father Heard disappeared in February, but we still met at the same time each week. My mother played the organ and the sounds rose out of the gaps in the plywood where the windows had been. People traded warnings, ration cards, and finally, the children would gather around my father so he could tell them a story. Except now they gathered around the front of the altar where Father Heard would have stood, and the adults listened too.

My father doubled his efforts in the lab after Father Heard disappeared and also spent several hours each night in his library reading Bavarian fairy tales, Aesop's fables, and the newspapers for story ideas; since he'd become the voice of the parish, his stories to the children had become more complex, more nuanced, and as he spoke, his voice washed over the pews, beneath the rafters, and into the cold, fearful center of the congregation's heart. The tiny vibrations reminded them they were still living their lives, even if those lives were full of uncertainty.

That day, my father made Thump-Drag a stand-in for Solomon in the story of the two mothers.

I'd been feeling numb and wrung out in a way, which was beginning to feel normal, and then this giant wave of hurt would rise out of something as small as a music note. Or the scent of burnt sugar, or the feel of chalk dust on my fingers. And I'd suddenly miss my brother so deeply that I would have done anything in that moment if I could touch the top of his foot, long enough to remember he had been real. I would fold into myself at those times and imagine who I would have been if he had not been lost. If he had been around to sketch our futures. I felt the great weight of responsibility settle over me. To not only make my life worthy, but to do so twofold to make up for the potential life I had taken from my brother.

By late April, the Germans had forced my father's factory into making lightbulbs exclusively for their war effort. They'd taken over procurement of materials and shipments of finished products. They kept my father on to help when needed, but no longer let him look at the books or profit margins. He had been told he'd be maintained but received no payment for the use of his factory. No money ever came in for the Volkswagen shipment, though confirmation of delivery was received by the transportation company. The workers he employed were required to continue to work in order to get their food ration cards, and as anyone who could have escaped by then already had, the workers showed up out of habit, need, and fear.

By May, the Germans had installed covers on every external light-bulb in the factory and surrounding buildings, and had the windows covered with dark, heavy sheets to obscure them during air raid threats. The factory took on the shadow of night all day long. I worked on the assembly lines, feeding the glass bulbs into the machine that screwed them into the finished brass fixtures. The work was intolerably boring, but depending on the schedules, I often got to work alongside or near Hilda, who had been called into mandatory service as well.

I longed to be out on the water with my uncle, for his boat to take us to all the wild places he'd been and I'd read about. We could fish the world and when we came back, Europe would be unified. My father would have his factory back. The Germans would control Portugal to Siberia. Edwin could find his way home. But instead I was stuck on the assembly line.

Ludo began working at the factory alongside his mother several months earlier so he could get a ration card. Years before, I had over-heard my parents talking about how Ludo's mother had lost nine babies in the womb before having Ludo, and that was why she coddled him. She poured springs into the hopper so they could be parceled out down the line, and it amazed me how attentive she was in her repetitive motions. The fear of spending the rest of my life at such work flooded me.

Once a day, a guard of four German soldiers walked through the factory eyeballing the workers.

"Here come the uptight boys," Edward Fass said.

"Be quiet when they're near," Silvers, the man next to him, said.

Their heavy heels click-clopped on the tile floors in a big circle around the building. If it rained outside, they stayed longer, but for the most part, they came in, walked their loop, and continued their lap of the town.

By June the Germans implemented a new assembly line to produce a different shape of lightbulb for their new line of U-boats. The lights had to account for flux in the steel sides of the boats from the increase of water pressure. Several engineers and German military officers had my father show them the entirety of his factory. Hilda and I were working with glass orbs on the assembly line as the men walked past. My father nodded at me. The Germans were silent on their tour. Several of them wrote notes as they walked. The next week the same men came back with a truck full of equipment and designs for a new assembly line. They had my father and several of his workers build it, exactly where the line my father created for the Volkswagen order had been.

It was after the first full day the new assembly line was in production that we had three nights of light bombing. Air raid sirens wailed each night as everyone in town sought the shelter of basements or scrambled to get away from the harbor, where the bombs tended to fall. The sirens made all the dogs in town bark, howl, and run circles around their enclosures. Fergus went mad with fear. Then came the high, sharp, whistling followed by the walloping crash of bombs blasting into the ground.

On the fourth night, the sirens sounded and there was a large rumble of planes high overhead. This time though they didn't turn over us; they kept going toward Germany. The sprinkling of bombs that randomly fell on Delfzijl that night rocked a tenement building, blew the harbor ramp away, and sunk a few transport boats. Uncle Martin kept his boat docked offshore with his navigation lights off and shielded by black lightbulb covers.

By early July, my father worked every night when he got home from the factory. He went to his lab to march in small, tight circles around a hanging bulb socket. He skirted the pocket of pale light, and his shadow bent at the corners of the room, draped over his workbenches that were covered in burnt fuses, soldering irons, screw caps, filaments, needle-nose pliers, clamps, coils of thin wire that burned hot orange, and gas containers of argon he had delivered from Hungary. Broken glass piled in the corners. Rectangular and triangular cuts of mirrors sat on workbenches that were all lit, making the work space look like a diamond-studded mine.

He marked the time when he left the room on a large lined piece of paper he'd nailed to the doorway. How long would the bulb burn for? How long would it hold its brilliance? How could he improve upon such a thing? Often, in the middle of the night, he'd walk through the house to his workroom to pace more circles around the dangling bulbs. Perhaps he walked a million kilometers in his own home in trying to capture the light.

One night, in an attempt to feel like I did as a kid again, and wanting to feel closer to my father and his obsession, I snuck into his lab. I hit the grimy switch and then fumbled to screw a bulb into the exposed socket. My finger and thumb brushed the metal linkage and I felt coursing volts scream through my hand, rushing up my arm to my shoulder, and spread needles over my scalp. It felt like muscle and tendon were pulling apart. Bolts of energy manically vibrated deeper into my chest like plucked cello strings before I shook myself loose. For a moment my arm hung limp, a feeling of paralysis, and that shocking sensation lingered. Even as I left the lab and snuck back to my bed, it felt like a space in my body had been cleared and laid with new chords of nerve that bristled and sparked.

I never told anyone about that incident as I felt foolish. Though afterward I had electrocution dreams. A silent gushing of force would fill me up, make my muscles quiver, and the linkage of my bones hum. In sleep I was a container for that light, which lifted me away from my body in white starbursts.

The morning after, my father called me into his lab. I thought he knew I disturbed his work.

"Jacob, come in here, please. Put your glasses on, and stand back there against the wall."

My safety glasses were on the hook hanging next to Edwin's pair. My father couldn't bring himself to throw them out. I saw my brother's glasses and didn't care if I was going to get in trouble or not. I felt a compulsion to stomp on Edwin's glasses so I didn't have to look at them.

"I need some help," my father said.

No accusations came, so I set the cloth strap against the back of my skull and pulled the glasses down over my eyes. Large shards of glass and metal crunched into the floor. Fergus knew not to come into the room and I heard him lay down outside the door.

My father called out times for me to write on the paper. Often I'd watch him walk in those tight circles while talking about how to pressurize inert gases, how to set the stem so the contact wires sit properly, and how to best insulate the cap around the electrical contact points. There was a different language used altogether in that room. We spoke of science, using the language of chemistry and the periodic chart. There was also the language of the countries he ordered supplies from and the strange writing on the crates and gas canisters that arrived at the factory, which were skimmed from and brought home.

"Mark every minute on your paper there," he told me.

"How long are we going to time this one?" I asked.

"Just mark them."

"Nine thirty-seven," I said.

"Nine thirty-eight."

"Nine thirty-nine."

"Nine forty." My father seemed as multifaceted, unknowable as the hundreds of glass fragments scattered around the room.

As I was calling out "nine forty-one," there was a quick pop, and the lightbulb shattered in a small explosion of radiant orange dust. Glass rubble holding the last touches of light rained onto the floor. Little white after-burn spots floated across my eyes. Then the room went dark. The smell of burnt filament with an aftertaste of some chemical I didn't recognize floated around us as our eyes adjusted to the thick shadow we stood in.

"Ah-*ha*!" he yelled out.

The outline of his posture changed from that of a wounded person to someone who had just been healed and was starting to stand taller.

"It's the smallest details that matter most," he said.

"Are those smallest details why they keep exploding?" I asked.

"Yes," he said. "Precisely."

———————

The next day, while I was working on the assembly line, my father came down to the floor and started working on the new line the Germans had set up. He often poked around with the lines so no one else paid any mind to what he was doing. The workers instead focused closer to their jobs since the boss was nearby. But I watched him as he installed a small mechanical pump behind the metal side panel of the base assemblage. The tip of the pump looked like a homemade baster, similar to what he'd been experimenting with in his workroom at home. It dropped little dollops of thick, dark liquid onto the coil. He checked a few of the lights that the line put out, put the panel back on the machine, and went back to his office. He looked at me and raised a long finger to his lips. Then the four soldiers on their daily lap of the factory opened the door.

I didn't have the inherent interest my father had in the science behind harnessing light. There was a time when my father told Edwin and me that the factory would be our inheritance. Now that Edwin was gone, I didn't care if the Germans had it. They were moving west. Taking everything. At the time, I thought I understood why. At camp they had pumped us full with their reasons. They told us how the Treaty of Versailles had crippled them after the Great War. Though I didn't know this was the talk that gave Hitler his foothold. That the plan I happily lapped up of taking over Europe was far more severe than imaginable. At the time, at some misunderstood level, I was also furious at my government for flooding Rotterdam and secretly blamed them for the loss of Edwin. I didn't care what the Germans did, despite the rumblings of my father and Uncle Martin about them taking everything over. I was locked in grief over the loss of my brother. It no longer froze my days like it did my mother's, but it froze something inside of me that I didn't think would ever warm.

9

A gristly half kilo of ground pork sausage was the first piece of meat we had in months. My mother inspected it on the counter. She wore her ever present blue bathrobe. Her pant legs and thick wool socks stuck out beneath the hem and glided over the floor. She brought out two yellow globe onions and a dark cast-iron pan from the cupboard, and it clanked against the large pot in which she had boiled the crabs Uncle Martin had brought over. The noise of her cooking lifted me for the moment, as I had become used to her living like a ghost in our house. She took one of the onions in her hand and started rubbing off the skin between her palms, making sure we'd have as much of it as possible. When both onions were bald, she chopped them and put one into the skillet and the other into a pot of water with several carrots and a pinch of salt from the glass spice jar. She turned on the burners and when the coils pulsed orange she put the frying pan with the onion and the full pot on the heat.

The front door swung open and smashed against the wall before being slammed shut. Fergus jumped up from the corner of the kitchen and started barking.

"Drika," my father yelled from the doorway. "Drika."

He ran into the kitchen, frantic, beads of sweat on his hairline. "They found out," he said.

"What happened?" my mother asked.

"They found out," he said again. He leaned on the kitchen counter-top to steady himself and knocked the empty milk pot over. His face was flushed red from running, something I'd only seen him do once before, under the bridge in Rotterdam. "The engineers came back to the factory and found out what I'd done."

"What'd you do?" I asked.

"What have you done?" my mother mouthed. She walked up to him and hit him on the chest and yelled this time, "What have you done?"

"I sabotaged the assembly lines to make all the lights we've been sending blow out or explode."

"What the hell is wrong with you?" she asked.

"After they took Father Heard, I had to do something."

"Not this. No, let others fight this war, but not this. Now what will you do?" she asked.

"Let them build this nightmare of theirs in the dark."

The heat of his words silenced us. We all stood there for a moment. He was still panting, his chest swelling and sinking. The water on the stove rose to a boil. The image of the lightbulbs shipped from Koopman Light exploding all over Germany came into my mind—a hundred thousand lightbulbs, all over the continent popping and raining little shards of glass onto German soldiers.

"What happened?" my mother asked.

"They figured it out. I went to the factory and the engineers were back and working on the assembly line they had me install. When they pulled out my addition, I ran off. They'll know to find me here. They'll be here soon."

The smell of wet, boiling onions hit me. "Our food cards," I said, immediately ashamed that this was my first reaction, fear of where my next meal would come from. "They'll take away our food cards."

"They'll take away your father first."

He ran from the room and up the stairs to his bedroom. Fergus followed. A moment later he came down with a satchel and was stuffing a shirt and a pair of pants into it. In the corner of his library he fished through a file cabinet for papers that he started shoving in his bag. He held up his passport and then he shoved it into the satchel.

"Where are you going?" my mother asked.

"You can't go," I said.

"Jacob. Come here." He put his hands on my shoulders and bent down and kissed me on the forehead. "Meet me later tonight by the tree fort you boys built in the woods." He pulled his pocket watch loose, flipped the worn lid open and checked the time. "Ten tonight, okay? If I'm not there by twelve, don't wait any longer. Okay. Okay?"

"Aren't we coming with you?"

He squeezed my shoulders and looked me square in the eye. Then there was a loud pounding on the door. Behind it words, stern and brutal. Hearing the voices without having heard a car pull up arrested us all for a moment.

"Open up, now," a voice said. The pounding on the door started again, with greater force. We looked at each other without moving. My parents' whispered conversations late at night over the past several years—their hushed words and careful planning—had all been to avoid this moment.

Fergus barked at the door. The doorknob turned and pushed open.

My father sidestepped out of the hallway into the shadowy interior of his workroom. I had heard the same things everyone else had. That there were places the Germans sent Jews, nonconformists, and people like Samuel the air-writer—camps.

Camp. The word whistled through my mind as our front door swung open. My mother put her hands up to her pale face and stood frozen. Two men in knee-length, shiny, black leather jackets and padded field-gray hats with the red and black Nazi crosses above the eyes walked into the foyer. Each had a Luger pistol in his hand, leveled at his hip. From the corner of my eye, I could see into my father's workroom, where he knelt, lay down on the floor, and began crawling across all that glass on his belly toward the outside door. His pocket watch dragged beside him by its thin, gold chain. He pulled himself by his bare forearms.

"Where is Hans Koopman?" one of the officers asked.

Fergus jumped up on the man who spoke and rested his paws on his jacket and barked. The man jerked his knee up into the center of the dog's chest. Fergus collapsed. With a gasping exhale he kicked on the ground as his stomach shuddered. He dug into the carpet and writhed for air, making a dry swallowing sound, then stood up and limped out of the room.

"Where is Hans Koopman?" the man asked again and stepped forward.

"He's at work," my mother said and stepped closer to him to block his view of the workroom. Her fingers trembled.

The shadow of my father slithered over the floor.

One twitch of my eye, one tremble of the wood boards beneath him, and he'd be given away. His knees parted the layers of glass beneath him and his long body looked unnatural sprawled out on the ground. He swung open the door of his workroom to the snow-dusted yard and snaked out. Natural light flooded into his dark work space before he pushed the door shut with his foot. Part of me wanted to grab him and stand him up, make him face these men. I wanted him to be brave enough for all of us, for him to show me that there was no real threat to be scared of. To look these men in the eye the way I wanted to but still could not.

"Check upstairs," the German who kneed Fergus said to the other.

Fergus cautiously followed the man through the house.

"You two, come over here," the man in the foyer motioned with the gun.

My mother stepped in front of me and didn't move. The heavy, heel-toe, heel-toe footsteps from room to room upstairs was followed by the tap and scratch of Fergus's nails.

"We want to talk with Mr. Koopman right now."

The soldier upstairs came down and searched the basement. He came up and walked by me, trailing the scent of cool leather. He stepped into my father's workroom. Time stopped. He pulled something from his deep side pocket. Then he scratched a match across the box and held the flame out in front of him. The match made an outline of the rounded features of his hat. He stepped farther into the workroom. The match lit a path several feet ahead of him, and if he saw the door, he'd see the path my father made in the snow. I tried to say something, even reached my hands out toward the man to touch him, but there was such a knot in my throat that no words came. As he got to the end of the room, he waved the match in front of him, then turned back to me. He stood in the back part of the room for a moment. Then scraped something off the shelf. Small copper fixtures chimed on the floor as they landed. Each little, metallic note echoed in the air. Then the man shook the match out, and the smell of smoke drifted into the air as he walked back out of the room and into the kitchen.

When he came back, he held the skillet of caramelized onion.

"When does he come home for dinner?"

"Right after work," my mother said. The officer tilted the skillet so the hot onion fell in one glop to the floor. They stood over it, huge, menacing. Fergus slinked up, sniffed, and then ate all of the sizzling onion in several giant gulps.

The soldiers confiscated our ration cards and left, leaving the front door open. Fergus followed them outside and retched up the steaming onion.

When their car was gone, I went to the window that looked out on the side yard and saw the wide track of snow my father had belly-crawled over to reach the far woods. There were no footprints—only the indent of his dragged body, a giant slug's slime trail. I called Fergus inside when he started to eat the snow he'd thrown up on. Once he came in, he wagged his tail and sat next to my mother who dug her fingers into his coat. Her wet, red-wrecked eyes focused on me as if I were the only thing she had left in the world. I didn't know if I could withstand that weight.

<hr />

When it was 10 P.M. that night, I slipped out the side door with a backpack of clothing and what limited dry foods we could muster. My mother put a small roll of cash into the pack's smallest pocket with a note I didn't read. It felt too private, like a good-bye between them I didn't want to acknowledge.

Outside, narrow pillars of trees shot up into the surrounding darkness, and the naked branches formed a canopy of thousands of interlocked, arthritic fingers. Beyond that was a fury of stars, each some bright splinter of shrapnel whose purpose was to explode and rain down until everything remained jet.

I waited for two hours at the fort while the wind picked up and my fingertips and toes throbbed with hurt and then went numb. Wherever he had gone in the woods, my father's footprints were covered by the wind.

Well past midnight, I left the backpack inside the walls of the fort and went back to the house. My mother's shadow was framed in the kitchen window. Her figure shifted back and forth on her heels, her fingers manically twirling the ends of her hair. The snow crunched under my feet. In the middle of the open side yard, I stopped. Something felt off as I looked into the woods to the front of the house. A quick red dot of ash breathed to life. I froze. The cigarette's cherry rose up and brightened with fire again. That same deep fear that coursed through me earlier when the soldiers opened the door to our house surged again. I wished myself a shade, a shadow of a tree that could blend in among the natural world.

Still holding my breath, I walked inside the house to where my mother sat by the window with her knees drawn up into her chest. The combination of tenderness and desperation with which she looked at me was jarring. Her face split in three directions. "Did you see him?"

"No."

"Did you look everywhere?"

"He wasn't there."

"Well. Maybe." She opened her mouth as if to speak but fell silent, close to tears, not trusting herself.

In the morning, before the sun came up, I snuck out the back door of the house and into the woods, approaching the fort from another angle. There, I saw the backpack had been riffled through. The money, my mother's note, and the food were gone. The clothes were strewn about. Next to the last traces of my footprints from hours before were two other sets. Each print was set deep into the snow, with a heavy heel and toe section divided by the indent from the heel's lift. There were no signs of my father since he had taken to moving on his stomach, an image that inexplicably made me ashamed.

Fingers of light poked sideways between the tree trunks, the slanting beams each a welcoming arm of ghosts. At that moment the forest was full of ghosts—the ghost of my younger self who built the fort with Edwin. Edwin, whose makeshift gravestone rested on its side not ten meters away. And now, the ghost of my father joining the others, and I was suddenly paralyzed by the tally of these losses.

I returned to the house, slipped past the crater the bomb had left in the backyard and into the kitchen, where my mother sat at the table.

"What'd you find?"

"Those men ripped through the pack."

"The letter?"

"It's all gone."

Her face looked different, her hurt was transparent and it seemed like the real tragedy was having lost whatever those words were she had written him.

I desperately wanted time to reverse. I'd pick my father off the floor, hose the chemical smell from him, and tell him I was proud of Koopman Light Company. I wanted the time I spent mourning to go backward so I could step out and chip all the russet green peels of paint from our house that had gone untended once Edwin was lost. I'd sand it away and coat it fresh with layer after layer of white primer, then change the color of the place altogether. Soft blue trim at the shutters, true the edges. Given the chance I'd go back to when my mother still had the energy of a young woman and gracefully swayed through her day, gesturing freely with her hands as she talked, pressing her clasped hands to her lips when we made her laugh. I'd go back and make a fresh start of it all. I'd nestle Edwin and me as boys into the wedge of the twin-trunked sessile oak and make a fresh start of it all. I wanted time to go back so I could have kissed Hilda, and perhaps more, wanting the experience of exploring her. I would touch upon every embarrassing moment and say no, no, no, this is not the way, and stage-direct every instance back into proper order. Whitewash each with primer. My mother finding me masturbating in the laundry room. More primer. Throwing rocks at spotlit rats. Gone. My brother dropping beneath the water. Dear god. Never happened. My father dropping to his stomach on glass that I knew pierced the flesh. My mother's slow and painful breaking apart in front of my eyes. Whitewash it all, paint it away, gone from the world and any memory of it.

————————

My mother stood up, walked over, and hugged me. "Okay. We're going to the factory today then. I'll work for your father. First, we'll tell Martin. Martin will be furious."

When she let me go, she walked out of the room while peeling off her blue bathrobe. Several moments later, the shower began running, and within a half hour, my mother stood in front of me in her gray winter slacks, a heavy sweater, and her jacket, hat, and gloves. She looked nothing like the woman we had left behind when we went to Rotterdam and lost Edwin. Her face was gaunt, her cheeks sunken and ruddy. Deep furrows ran from midway down her nose to the corners of her mouth. Though somehow it was her standing in front of me—her brief luxury of mourning now stripped away without food rations. She placed her hands on my shoulders and smoothed out the wrinkles in my coat, then looked at me the way she had when I was a child.

Together we walked to the factory, the product of my father's life's work. Two German guards had been assigned to check off workers' names as they arrived, to make sure everyone contributed as expected. Those men stood by the entrance to the assembly plant and the sight of them left a burning resentment in my chest. But my mother led me to the office entrance. Inside the room was bright, too hot, full with lamps and file cabinets. Several of the German engineers my father had shown around were at the desks.

"The workers' entrance is around the back," one of the officers said to us in Dutch as we walked in.

"I'm Mrs. Koopman," my mother said.

"Ah, *goedemiddag*, Mrs. Koopman. Where is your husband?" the officer asked.

"I don't know. Several soldiers came last night to our home to look for him, but he has not come home, and they took our ration cards."

"Well, that is because we need to speak to him immediately."

My heart jumped. They hadn't caught him yet. Maybe he'd gotten away.

"We would like to know where he is too, but since he is not here, and we have no ration cards, I would like to work instead of him and have his ration card."

"Ah, I see. The good Mrs. Koopman has arrived to make claims on us," the officer said, loud enough so the engineers would hear. "Well,

well. Why don't you start working on the lines starting this morning, and you can have your son's card back. I presume this is your son."

"Yes," she said.

"Well, you can have his for your working. But we would like you, young man"—the officer pointed at me; I didn't look at him but at the glowing thread of his typewriter ribbon—"not to come back unless you have your father. We know what that slippery bastard was up to."

10

My mother went to work at the factory every day that winter after my father left. That first Sunday, she showed up to church and played her organ for the people who came. In my father's absence, she played louder and harder, and for once since Edwin left, she was animated, and wailed on the keys and pedal, giving a wild concert. Her song trailed off into its last echoes, each note coming to silence like a dark bird piercing a silver cloud. Week after week she showed up to play the organ, letting the voice of those pipes clear and sing whatever mourning or worry she had locked in her, but fewer and fewer people came.

During the rest of the time she was frantic with worry, pestering me about where I was going and when I'd be back, pacing around the house, saying, "I can do this. I can do this." She did this until she crested some new height of fear, and then in an act I will always be proud of, she got herself dressed.

"I can't stand it anymore. I can't wait," she said. "Martin is doing everything he can, but I can't wait." She decided she was going to go find my father. She bundled herself in three sweaters and an overcoat and marched from house to house all through the town and looked into the eyes of the people who lived there.

"Please. Have you seen or heard from my husband?"

I accompanied her on the first several rounds through town.

For me, my brother was always present, floating in a blue underground river. I imagined my father, who belly-crawled through the frozen woods with his cheek to the ground, had heard some trace of that current, that he was rubbing his body over it to understand where to go next. I glommed onto that image of my father, driven by a purpose and not merely a deserter. Though how I thought of him shifted and spun like the Devil in his story, coming out of each dance turn in a new disguise. The businessman. Storyteller. Drinker. Inventor. Coward. Saboteur. Runaway. The Missing. The Gone.

Sadly, my mother, who was very much present, I tried to dismiss as a stranger. Her worry poisoned me. It compounded my hurt and anger. I was angry with my people for releasing the dams and flooding my brother away, with the Germans for pushing forward with their wild expansion, and most with my father for breaking the rules and being forced to run away. For my mother, I was angry with her for her obvious and glaring pain, as it kept me from going numb.

At home, rock piles by the pit in our backyard looked like they were placed in the forms of arrows, pointing toward my father's hiding spot. Everything became some indecipherable clue. Because of this, I avoided going home as much as possible. I started going to the woods behind Hilda's house to watch for movement behind lit windows or to the docks to help Uncle Martin on his boat. My options were very limited. After my eighteenth birthday, the Germans would make me join a labor crew in the German factories, the Heer, or the Waffen SS, and probably send me to the eastern front. For a while that winter, I was actually eager to leave.

On a warm morning, Hilda came by our house.

"Will you come watch me ride?"

"Sure."

We walked up the road between our houses.

"Thank you," she said and reached over and held my hand.

My body felt so tight I didn't dare turn and look at her. For a moment I thought things might begin to get better.

I climbed and sat on a wood split-rail fence as she saddled and led a black-and-white quarter horse into the paddock.

"Here we go," she said. "You ready?"

"I'm watching."

She eased the horse in a circle close to me and then picked up speed and started doing fast jaunts about the field. I tried to memorize the way her body moved on the horse's back through that beautiful wooded meadow.

When we were children, Hilda's father had a white horse that he let be used by whomever in town dressed up as St. Nicholas that year. So on St. Nicholas Day, December 5, the parade started from Hilda's house and worked its way down our road into town. When we still believed, we waited in our driveway and joined the procession of St. Nicholas and his gang of boys in blackface called Black Peters. When we were old enough to understand what was happening, we went to Hilda's first thing in the morning every December 5. Hilda's mother, a redheaded woman who smelled like dried flowers, painted all of the kids' faces black with shoe polish, and gave us bags of candies and gingersnaps to throw at people once we got into town.

"Don't eat all of this yourself," she'd say, giving us a soft smile, knowing we would eat our fair share.

One year, when Hilda was nine and we were dressed, and our skin blackened, we ran around half wild until the adults readied the horse and St. Nicholas. It was during that intermission some of the kids knocked over Hilda's wooden dollhouse. She dropped her bag of candy and knelt next to the large house and picked up the far wall that had broken off.

"Don't worry, Hilda," Ludo said, "We'll get my dad to fix it."

"I can help. My dad can help too," I said, wanting to be the one to do it.

The next afternoon my brother and I carried the dollhouse on a cart to my father's lab.

"What do we have here, Jacob?" he said, looking at the dollhouse, then at me. "Think we can get it back together?"

"I hope so," I said.

"Sure we can."

He used industrial glue and tiny clamps to repair the broken wall, and when that was done, he bent down with his hands on his knees and peered into the house.

"You know what. I think we should spruce up the old place for your special friend, Hilda."

"How?"

"I've got some ideas."

He spent the next three hours installing tiny lights, wiring, and a light switch, which Hilda flipped on when we brought it back to her. She stood at the front door laughing as the tiny rooms became illuminated.

Each room of the dollhouse had miniature polished pine furniture. Beds with headboards, rocking chairs, and coffee tables. From one of the bedrooms, I stole a small chest of drawers and kept it hidden under my mattress. At night I'd open and shut the little drawers and imagine Hilda in her house. I'd see her walking from room to room. Taking a snack from the pantry. Reading by a window. Her feet tucked under her legs. Nothing special. Just her going about her day.

I was thinking about the dollhouse while Hilda rode the black-and-white mare, nearing to where I was on the railing. The sun caught her eyes, which were wet from crying.

Without wiping her face, she swung off the horse, removed her helmet, led the horse to the fence I sat on, and tied the rope to the post next to me. I sprang down to stand in front of her.

"Are you okay?"

"We have to sell her," she said. "The food's getting too expensive."

Her cheeks were blotched as crushed roses. The light silvered her upper lip, where tears and snot slicked her skin. She walked up to me, like she was trying to walk through me and tucked her body into mine. I hugged her. She smelled like horse sweat, hay, and Hilda. She always had her own scent, which came off her in waves. Crushed flowers. Soaped hair. The sun. Hilda.

Her shoulders heaved up and down and her hands made one fist at the small of my back.

"I'm sorry," I said. Of course I did. My mantra.

Before she finished crying she tilted her head up, closed her eyes, squeezed me closer, and kissed me on the lips. Her tongue jammed inside my mouth and surprised me. I pushed myself into her. I did not shut my eyes but she did. She kept hers shut as we kissed, even as she loosened her hands from behind my back and pressed her palms and fingers downward flat against my stomach and slid them into my pants.

It was the middle of the day. The sun was on us and I thought, Sweet merciful Christ, finally. She must have felt me swelling when she leaned against me, which was more a bodily reaction than a courageous act on my part, but before I dropped my arms from holding her she had her hand on my half-erect penis. She leaned her forehead into my chest and I looked up at the sky.

There was nothing gentle about what she was doing, and I kept thinking about putting my hands down her pants. Do it. Reach down. Reach down. Grab her there, now, but before I was fully hard, I crumpled over and came into her hand. She still had not opened her eyes or looked up at me.

The sun was on us still. It was the first time a girl had made me come. Though it hurt enough to feel like she'd dismembered me, the whole moment bloomed into a vivid flame and seared itself intact onto the underside of my skull. Always afterward, when the thought of touching anyone arises, it's Hilda's hands reaching into my pants. The promise of her touch.

The light caught Hilda's hands and the pearly sheen on her palm and fingers as she pulled them free. She bent down and wiped her hand on the grass. Then stood up, and still, without looking at me, leaned in again.

I walked her to the barn and held the hand she hadn't wiped in the grass and rubbed my thumb against her knuckles, noticing how soft her skin was. Back and forth. Back and forth, like I was making sure she was real. In the barn I watched her take off the horse's saddle and scrub its back and along the sides with a large sponge like it were a final ceremony. I do not recall talking as she did this. I was looking at the corner of the barn as a place for Hilda and me to fall together again. I imagined her bed. My bed with her in it. Us crashing into each other and toppling over again and again. Her hands all over my body. Mine all over hers. The whole world was now a place to be with a girl. The whole world hammered with potential.

Now, I see that what I was witnessing was a sad girl who had to give her horse away. I did not take that in at the time. I did not take in the hurt that made her reach for me.

11

Uncle Martin had arranged for me to help him out on the docks for my own ration card. And he kept appearing with food, money, and supplies that he traded fish for. He started taking me out on his ferry trips between Germany and Holland. Before that, the periphery of my world had been edged by the bend of the ocean in the harbor and the egg-shaped border of the town. Everything beyond that had been too enormous and threatening.

On the docks the wood boards creaked beneath my feet, and guilder-sized wharf spiders climbed up from between the cracks and disappeared between other planks. Uncle Martin taught me how to tie bosun's and bowline knots. I enjoyed the fresh air from being out on the water. Out there, my mind opened to the grace of seabirds gliding over the rolling water and beating their wings back slightly to rise on the wind. I'd see a glimmer of silver scales tuck and dive headlong beneath the surface.

Thinking I was alone on the deck, I reached for a fish from the aft hold. I pulled out a giant sturgeon by the gills and ran my hand over its rounded nose and down its markings, which looked like fallen leaves and tiny chevrons bleeding into one another.

"Find that one attractive, do ya?" Uncle Martin said.

"What? No. No." I dropped it back in and he must have known he embarrassed me.

"I'm teasing. I used to do the same thing. Stare at them like that. I'd take them apart too."

"Filet them?"

"No, like peel the scales off. Carve away the skin and muscle. Try to figure out the bones like I were a surgeon. Teaches you about them. Makes you better at cleaning them." He knelt down and pulled the sturgeon back out. "Let's do it to this one."

He handed me his scrimshaw blade.

"I have my own," I said and pulled out my camp dagger.

"Go against the grain to take the scales off."

"Why do you take the scales off?"

"No practical reason. But if you're a fisherman you should know fish. That's what I think. My dad once caught me doing this when I was younger than you and smacked me across the deck for wasting a fish. The knife I was using slit my fingertip apart like a snake's tongue. Look at this." He held out the tip of his pointer finger and there was a white wedge-shaped scar I'd never noticed before.

"Start down by the tail," he said. "Do it like short strokes of a comb."

I started shaving off the bronzed scales. "What did you do when your dad hit you?" I asked, not taking my eyes off the fish, and feeling like my words were each a finger, reaching into a fire.

"I balled up like a runt," Uncle Martin said. "But I ran off soon after that."

"That's when you went to sea?"

"Yeah. Now I wish I'd have stood up and popped the old bastard. But he passed away soon after I left and I never got the chance. Would have done me a world of good if I'd have done that though."

"Why?"

"I don't know. He was mean but had a hard life so I sort of understand him now. Though then, he used to tell me what to do and when to do it. Drove me batty. Couldn't handle that. Still can't."

We took the fish apart and when he had the steaks cut off, he cubed them and put them aside to fry for dinner that night.

"Why do you think your father was the way he was?" I asked.

Uncle Martin took a small translucent bone and used it to pick his teeth, then flicked it away like a butt. "Who knows," he said, then went back to the wheelhouse.

Uncle Martin had gained the Germans' trust by doing whatever he was told and by entertaining them whenever he was around. He was somehow casual, despite the recent losses of his own family members. Though at night on the ship he was solemn, and drank Bols from a brown clay bottle and studied his navigational charts.

At night on the *Lighthouse Lady*, I'd lie in my bunk and think of Hilda. The high arch of her eye sockets, her cheekbones, which capped off at her rounded chin, her freckles, her soft lips, her strawberry hair, and how everything about her had the look of being from the coast. She gave off a sense that the ocean would precede and follow her everywhere she went.

When it was only Uncle Martin and me onboard, I'd ask him where he thought my father was.

"I don't know," he said. "I've asked about him everywhere." He ran his hands over the top of his head as if scrubbing his hair. "I can't stop thinking about him either. It's making me a bit crazy."

We sat until we heard a dogfight over the Ems River. The German fighter planes sounded like the steady hammering of a typewriter.

Uncle Martin had me load a cart full of cinder blocks and about forty two-meter lengths of thin mooring lines. I carried the ropes to the boat and stacked them along the stern like a tangle of giant hemp snakes.

"What do we need all this for?" I asked.

"Someone on the other side wants them."

When everything was loaded, I untied the mooring lines from the pier and jumped aboard the stern. Martin aimed the bow toward the open channel and set out to cross the Ems over to the German side. The water was calm, and there were no other boats once land was out of sight.

On the German side there was a large base along both sides of the river mouth where the Ems cut south through Emden. The soldiers waiting there were the young men who had commandeered Martin and the *Lighthouse Lady*. They stood on the dock.

"*Guten Abend*," Martin yelled to them. The men waved back and watched me jump off and tie the boat to a cleat on the dock. They looked happy to see us. Martin was the jovial ferryman to them, this giant man full of sea stories, who could barter for things from across the water. He had worked well for them so they started letting him work the logistics of transfers across the Ems, sign the papers on both sides of the water, be in charge of who was coming and going, and they stopped sending a supervisor along.

"What do you think about this?" Martin said to one of the men. Martin handed the man a small cigar box, patted his shoulder, and smiled. "You boys will like these, I bet."

"Very good. Thank you," the soldier said. "But how'd you get your hands on these?"

"Ah. I have a habit of losing property. Tricky paperwork. Faulty radio calls."

"Huh. Thank you. But you'll want to be careful with that sort of thing from now on."

"Why's that?"

"All kinds of havoc was happening with the supply chain in Delfzijl. We're sending new management over."

My uncle's face reddened. "Are you still going to be in charge?"

"No. General Halder."

"Oh."

"Yes. He travels with a whole platoon. I imagine you'll be very busy."

"He's going to bring all those people to our port?" Uncle Martin asked.

"We have to get everything running smoothly."

"I see," my uncle said.

That my uncle could work so well for these men signaled an ability to segment parts of his life, keeping each separated by unknowable chasms.

"Stay here, Jacob. I'll be back." He followed the soldiers to a building on shore. There were triangular cement pillboxes along the river to station big guns. Stiff-looking soldiers scurried about the base. Large red ribbon flags with swastikas on them hung limp from flagpoles. More flags stretched taut on the sides of the buildings. The soldiers working on the docks all looked official, stood straight, and seemed to work with purpose. There was something inspiring about their efficiency and productivity. The image left me no doubt that the Germans would win their war.

When Martin came back, he led twenty soldiers. Each soldier had a flailed-out metal helmet that covered his ears, knee-high black boots, and a thick black belt cinched above his hips that wrapped his wool jacket shut. On the shoulders of each jacket were lapel buckles, and down the chest line were a line of coin-sized buttons. They were armed with truncheon-shaped potato masher grenades dangling off of backpacks, and carried either Karabiner 98ks, five shot bolt-action rifles, or chrome black MP40 submachine guns. A few had Great War Lugers or Walther P38s.

"This is my nephew, he'll help us across," Martin said to the soldiers, who climbed on the boat from the stern. They swaggered aboard and spread out on the decks. Half of them sat on the cinder blocks and half went up and rested on the bow. They leaned against their own packs or rested on the mounds of fishing nets to get warm. The SS officer to whom Martin had given the cigar box jumped onboard as well.

"Jacob, this is Aldrich. He'll be taking the trip with us tonight," Martin said, pointing to a flat-headed man with a croupy laugh. "Will you go west with them tonight?"

"Yes. I'll have you drop us off after dark at Delfzijl and we'll move out together from there," Aldrich said.

The soldiers on the boat sat among the scatter of lines and nets. By the time the boat was out of sight from land, it was dark, cold, and overcast, with enough cloud cover to keep out any moonlight.

Some of the soldiers looked domestic—soft faces, clean hands, alert, scared eyes. Even the calm seas shook their stomachs as the pallor of their cheeks altered from bright red to dark moss green. Others had clearly been on boats, crossed borders, and fought battles before. They let their bodies move with the motion of the water. Their uniforms had patches over frays on the knees and elbows, their packs were lighter, but wrapped in more ammunition rounds. They seemed content and impatient all at once.

One of the soldiers closest to me had a knife attached to his belt. The knife was the size and shape of the Hitler Youth dagger.

"Do you know what this is?" the soldier asked me when he caught me looking at it.

"I think so. I have one like it," I said.

"That's good. You've been through the trainings."

And there was the truth of it—of what my summer in Germany with Ludo and Edwin almost three years before had really been. These soldiers were not that much older than me, and it was clear to me then that the whole camp system must have been one of the most cunning military maneuvers in history. The camps took every boy in a nation, filled them with a passion for their country, the ideas of what their unified country stood for, and under the guise of games, taught them how to become an army. An army that believed wholeheartedly in the Fatherland—an army that worked its way across the channel and encamped on Dutch soil.

Two of the soldiers we were transporting sat on the stern of the boat. One lay on his side and let the other one light a paper candle and hold it up to his ear. The stick of fire burned in a smoky pillar rising from his head.

"What are those two doing, Uncle Martin?" I asked.

"The fire culls the ear wax out and wood ticks if you have them so you can use tweezers to yank them free," he said.

I felt sorry for these men then. All of them were shipping out to join patrol parties or fortify the western front. I scanned the dark water around the boat and imagined myself in the Nazi uniform, the warm straight wool, the canvas loop of my rifle slung around me, rubbing into my shoulder like some hero running into battle.

"Hello, gentlemen," Martin yelled in German to the men over the engine noise. "I need you guys to get in the stern for a few minutes while we pass this section. We need to weigh down the back to ride smoothly over the sandbar up here."

"What is this about?" Aldrich asked.

"There's a shallow sandbar up ahead. It's better if there's more weight in the stern. That's why all those cinder blocks are there. You too, old Aldrich," Martin said. When Aldrich and all the soldiers were in the stern of the boat, their flailed helmets in the dark looked like a fistful of obsidian steel balloons. Martin called for me. "Go down in the forward holds and check the manual steering gauges. Watch them until I yell for you to come up."

I crawled into the holds, undid the floorboard latch, and lifted it off to lower myself into the forward cubby with the steering column axles. The sides of the holds were filled with backpacks similar to the ones the soldiers above decks had. Above the vibration of the engines, Martin yelled to all the Germans, "Now, I'm going to slow down here and you need to look over the aft sides in the back and tell me when you can see the bottom or any sand. It will look light yellow or white. Just call out when you know how much clearance we have. Jacob, are you down in the hold?"

"Yes."

The mechanical shift of gears changed as the boat slowed down and settled into the soft hum of the lowest gear. I'd been hearing the music of boat engines my whole life and knew the speeds we were going, the weather, and current conditions by the sound of the engines and the hull against the water. Uncle Martin had told Edwin and me when we were younger that we came from a long line of North Sea men. *"It's in your blood, boys. Light and the sea are in your blood. Your ancestors have crawled through the golden guts of fish to give you their seed."* The slowing hum of the engines tucked inside the vibrating steel womb felt comforting to me. But there was no sandbar.

What peace I felt was shattered by the chaotic percussion of automatic gun fire echoing through the hull of the ship. There were two long spurts of a weapon being fired that moved from port to starboard and then back to port. After I ducked down farther inside, there was a brief but heavy flopping of something on the deck above my head. The water lapped at the side of the boat. There was the quick crack of several more lone shots, then the sound of the boat's engines shifting into neutral. Not knowing what had happen terrified me. I had to do something, so climbed up and stuck my head out of the forward hatch and saw my uncle on the steering deck. He held a long gun out in front of him in his outstretched hands and waved it at the back of the boat. His posture was erect as he fired off another round. The action of the gun shook the muscles of his forearm and bicep, and he was strangely beautiful with the orange flashes shooting from the muzzle. He looked natural up there, as if he'd been practicing his whole life for this uncertain world.

Then Uncle Martin called to me, "Jacob, you can come up now."

On deck, Martin grabbed the thick black belts of dead soldiers who hung slack over the gunwales and pulled them back to where they collapsed into a heap with the other dead. Aldrich's head was at my feet, half of it missing, leaving a bright red cleft like a split watermelon rind. Thick bluish red blood poured down his temples and disappeared into his hairline. I kept looking from one body to the next without any real connection in my mind as to what happened.

When Uncle Martin had all of the bodies on the deck of the boat he turned to me. A German magazine-fed MP 40 submachine gun hung from his shoulder. Everything about him seemed electric as he stood above the large pile of bodies. Dead men were draped over the pile of cinder blocks. Several cinder blocks had shattered and dusted the soldiers' clothing. Martin grabbed me by the shoulders and looked me right in the eye.

"Jacob." He slapped at my cheek. "Jacob, here's what I need you to do. Listen very closely. Can you do that?" He touched the side of my face again, "Can you do that?

"Go to the wheel and scan the water for any lights." When there were none, he called me down to the stern. "Take all the backpacks and weapons off these men and put them below deck, down in the hold with the steering column. Did you see the other packs down there?"

I nodded.

"Good. Put them there," he said. The quiet, easy control he had over his tone was frightening. "Then, help me go through all their pockets. Get any papers and money that they have, keep anything you think could be valuable or edible. Check to see if they stitched anything extra into the lining of their clothing."

"There is no sandbar out here," I mumbled.

"Hans wasn't the only storyteller in the family," Uncle Martin said.

The *Lighthouse Lady*'s stern had bullet holes fanned out across the bulkhead. Martin kept the engines in idle, and we drifted as we set to work. The weapons were piled in the ship's lowest hold, the muzzle of the rifles faced forward, and potato masher grenades were stuffed between backpacks so they wouldn't roll.

"What happens when we get to shore without them?"

"No one's expecting them. I did the paperwork. The people in Emden think these guys were headed for a patrol for a month along the North Sea shore. And no one at home knows they were supposed to be coming. It's all taken care of."

On the deck, the soldier I had spoken with was on his side, and his scalp hung off his head like a ghastly lid. His Hitler Youth dagger had the same inscription as my own, *Blut und Ehre*. My eyes snapped to the RZM number. The dagger felt weighty as my fingers wrapped around the handle. It could sink into flesh—slip between rib bones, pierce a lung, or slice a kidney.

When the last of the backpacks were loaded into the hull, I didn't want to go back on the deck to see what Uncle Martin would have me do next. The boat was still in idle. Martin had maneuvered all those men to the back of the ship so he could gun them down when they weren't looking. My hands shook.

On deck I stood above him and looked into the pit above Aldrich's eye.

"That's the man that tried to take your father away," Martin said. "He's part of the reason he's gone. Do you get that? Do you get what they've done to your father?"

Until that day, to me, the soldiers were untouchable. It seemed only a matter of time before they would take over all of Europe. It had never occurred to me that their authority could be anything but absolute, unwavering.

"Help me with the pockets. Get the papers, the papers are the most important part," Martin said. "These are what we want. *Soldburchs*." He held up a little paper booklet. Each soldier carried the ID booklet with their unit information, orders, and equipment issued to them.

We sifted out the papers, money, and food and stashed it all in a large burlap sack. When we were done, we put the bag below deck. We took their oilskin jackets and playing cards with naked women on them. One of the men had a typing machine exchange element, an acorn-sized metal ball with the German alphabet stamped across the surface of the sphere. I cupped it, all the possibility of their language contained in my hand for a moment. The pads of my fingers ran over each letter, each the start of some grand story. I put it back in the dead man's pocket as it seemed too personal a talisman to take from him.

Martin stripped the unsoiled uniforms off several of the soldiers killed by shots to the head. Their pale white skin scratched against the sand painted into the deck for traction. Martin took the uniforms below deck.

"Now, here's what we do with those cinder blocks and sections of rope you brought aboard." He dragged one of the soldiers he'd stripped off the pile of dead and laid the man straight out. With one of the six-foot-long sections of mooring lines he tied a harness around the man's shoulders that also looped his neck. He tied the extra rope of the harness through two cinder blocks.

"Are you watching?"

"Yes," I said, but I meant Yes, I am always watching. It felt like my eyes would never close.

When he pulled the corpse up to a sitting position, it looked like a pale flesh puppet with a messy borehole in his forehead wearing a cinder-block backpack. Uncle Martin draped a large rubber mat over the port gunwale of the ship, then lifted each of the blocks and tossed them over the rubber mat so they dangled off the side without scraping the paint.

"Grab an arm," Uncle Martin said.

We picked up the stripped-down soldier from the deck and slid him over the rubber mat where the weight of the blocks pulled him down into a white roil of water. The shape of the body sunk away. The chest was concave as the blocks pulled it downward and the soldier's rubber-stamped boot soles sank anonymously out of sight. I thought of my father's story, about the drowning wolf with a belly full of stones, with all the little goats dancing on their hind legs, standing erect like animal spirits.

"Twenty more to go," Martin said.

"What have we done?" I managed to ask, watching as my uncle dragged another soldier over.

"Look at them, Jacob. They swarm like locust. They'll spread out and chew on everything, leaving only the pulp of their dark shit behind them. I'd shoot all of them if I could." Martin cupped my face again. "I'll drag the body over, and you bring me two blocks and a length of rope for each, then we'll toss them over together, okay? That way the knots are tied right and none of these buggers come floating up to talk about what happened."

"They'll know."

"No one will know. No one is expecting them."

"What will happen when the new German troops arrive?"

"I'll take care of it."

Martin worked with a content silence, as if we were skinning fish on the foredeck. Body after body went over in the darkness and disappeared. It took us a couple of hours to dump them all. I pictured the bottom of the Ems with twenty-one full-grown men anchored upside down at the depths, all their bodies moving with the current and swaying together like seaweed. Fish would eat away at them. At their eyes. The open skin around their wounds. I couldn't help but wonder if I had eaten such fattened fish.

Martin handed me a bucket on a rope. "Start washing down the back deck."

I dipped the bucket overboard, hauled it up by pulling at the line hand over hand, and splashed the water on the deck. When Martin came back up he had a bucket of paint and small welding patches. As I scrubbed the run-off gutters, he started to caulk the bullet holes. When he finished with that, he pulled out his welding tanks and a torch. He put an arc welding helmet on, started welding patches over the holes, and bent into the shower of molten orange sparks bouncing off the dark faceplate.

"When you're done with that start painting over what I'm doing," Martin told me. "But don't touch the metal. It's still too hot to touch. Do a coat over each patch and then do the whole bulkhead."

Whatever he asked, I did, as if I'd lost any free will I had. The bulkhead was pocked with little circular scars like chicken pox scabs that had been picked off. There were already welding patches all over the sides of the ship that had been painted over before. Each joint of the beaded melding points of the patches somehow melted into the bulkhead in rough but intricate curves.

Martin checked my work, then ran his hand over the outside of the boat to see if there were any puncture holes from his wild spray of bullets. He swept up the shell casings scattered around the wheelhouse and ladder to the back deck.

"Make sure you check the drainage grates too. Hair gets caught inside those."

A tuft of dark blond hair attached to a chunk of wet bloody scalp was stuck in the grate. I held it up by a strand and flung it overboard. When the boat looked clear of any atrocity, Martin started back toward Delfzijl. I sat on my knees and watched the back of my uncle's head as he drove the boat.

"I've taken on the job of thinning the herd," he said. "Let the fuckers get a bit nervous when their peers start disappearing." It was clear he was a master at hiding his apoplectic rage, and muting that other language that was written now all over his body—something instinctual, submammalian.

We didn't talk the rest of the way back to the Dutch side.

Martin pulled the boat to a pier jutting out of the woods adjacent to my house and let me off there. He tossed a pillowcase he'd tied off on the dock at my feet.

"You did good tonight, Jacob. Take that bag home to your mother. Don't tell her or anyone else about tonight, and meet me at the docks in the morning, okay?"

I watched his boat pull away. The shore was calm and I wanted to lie down in the surf and let it pack me into the land where I could be alone and quietly whole.

Inside the sack was a large loaf of dense, black bread, a small pile of chocolate bars, canned meats, crackers, and a wad of both Dutch guilders and German marks. It would be enough money to feed me and my mother for two months, but seeing the food made me nauseated. I was caught in my own silent tragedy, not understanding my place in all of it. The tide washed ashore shards of glass and seashells that scattered and caught the moonlight so it looked like the coast had a thousand sets of beautiful eyes. That must be how the dead see us, I thought, that's why we feel their presence so near.

I ducked into the trees and ran north past my home to Hilda's house. In the dark, I crossed over the spot in the pasture where she had touched me and felt the soft pull of the soil. I stashed my bag and snuck up to her home with a stack of chocolate bars to give to her.

At her house I walked around the side to be below her window. I tossed pebbles up at the glass. Whispered her name. I wanted to tell her everything, feelings I'd never given voice to. I wanted to lie down next to her. After several tries, I walked around the dark house to see if I could find her sleeping on a couch. But there was no open curtain to peer through, so I went and got my bag and headed home, walking beneath the cracked branches of elms and rankled old clouds outlined by a sliver of the hidden moon. At the wood fort I peeled off forty guilders and stuffed them into the lining of the weather-worn pack, the one I had taken out to my father the night he went away. For him, I left that feeble offering.

12

Working on the water for months with Uncle Martin had tattered my hands, cracked my lips, and weathered my skin. My hands rubbing over my face caked up the salt grime in waxy little worms along my jaw. Most nights I slept in a spare bunk on board. In my sleep the sensation of floating, being levitated, always brought me back to Edwin. My dreams were spent chasing after a figure who was always ahead of me, until I woke to the noises of the boat rubbing against the dock, the lines groaning from being stretched with the tides, and my uncle snoring in his own bunk. I'd daydream of him garroting men with mooring lines, shoving heads into the moving propeller of his boat, and nailing minnows all over a body and dragging it behind the boat so large ocean birds would pick the corpse clean, the bones dropping loose and fluttering to the bottom of the sea. His country had not chosen sides, but Uncle Martin blamed the Germans for the loss of family and had made his choice.

When we didn't sleep on the *Lighthouse Lady*, we went home to visit my mother. Ludo and Hilda, who were both still working at the lightbulb factory, would join us as well. The five of us would spend our evenings in the living room with Fergus crawling between each of us looking for attention, his soft brown eyes reflecting the yellow light and a bare, honest pleading.

Ludo was terrified of us turning eighteen; we'd been told I would be joining the German army and he'd be assigned to a work crew. Each of us shipped to somewhere we had no say in. My mother couldn't handle talking about it and always wanted us to divert the subject. She had exhausted her voice pleading with us to run away. She wanted Martin to take us by ship, but he swore the whole North Sea was blockaded and that he had no way to pass through it.

"Give me time," he said. "I'll work something out for us. I swear." So we sat together and held our fears in our laps, letting the evenings wear down.

On a night when I walked Hilda home, we held hands. We stopped several times to kiss. I stopped to kiss her or let her kiss me. I kept stopping us like it were a new game. Before we got to her home, I hugged her, bent my mouth to touch the top of her head, and smelled her hair.

"I love you," I said.

She didn't say anything, but hugged me tighter. Then like before, she pushed her forehead into my chest and slid her hands into my pants. Wordlessly, and with a fierce, fast grip, she made me feel like a god breaking loose of my skin, and then all of sudden like a raw, new baby spilling out into the world, quivering and weak. She said nothing, reached up and kissed me, then ran into her house.

By the next morning there was a scab browning over the tip of my penis where she had rubbed me raw against the fabric of my pants. I looked at the scab and felt I should not have told her I loved her, yet was happy I did. I would say it again. I knew I would say it again. Next time I would ease my pants down too. Already all I could think of was the next time, and then the next.

When I wasn't on the boat with Uncle Martin, I passed the time at home doing the domestic chores to keep up the house. My mother cooked on our two burners as best she could, but there wasn't enough gas to use it for more than a half hour a day. At night we played card games. Uncle Martin did card tricks. He shuffled a deck taken from the soldiers, fanned out the cards, and then ran the edge of one card along the row of face-down cards so they rose up like a wave traveling back and forth beneath his fingers. Though we all used the same cards, they looked like something living in Uncle Martin's hands; they had a measure of grace plied from his touch. When it was dark, I went outside and did a lap around the house to make sure there were no unwelcome guests. Then we pulled our radio from the loose floorboard and turned on BBC to listen to the war news. The war so far had consisted of planes and ships bombing one another, but there was talk of the Allied invasion that made us all lean in closer, trying to swallow the words.

My mother finally wanted to talk about a plan before they came for me.

"What if he didn't have a trigger finger?" she said.

We stopped and looked at her.

"Well. I refuse to lose anyone else. That way, they couldn't send you to the eastern front to be fodder." She scrunched up her face and shut her eyes like she realized what she suggested. "Well, even if they didn't make you fight, they'd take you and work you into the ground. You might as well go into hiding. Go underground like your father." Her thumb made little circles against the inside of her fingers like she were kneading a tiny glob of dough.

It was the first time I'd heard her use the word *underground* regarding my father. I had been so consumed by my own struggle with his hiding that I hadn't thought of the ways my mother was trying to make peace with his absence. His absence angered me. More so because it dismantled the impossibly high regard I once held him in. The towering shadow from my youth. The giant in the hallway. At times I had pictured him cowering like a small animal—hushed in terror; a pile of orange rinds and artichoke leaves heaped in front of him; and even cloistered away in a monastery. To couple all of that with what my mother must have conjured him doing meant he was living so many other lives than one at home with me.

I didn't like those nights, sitting in the living room, getting a good look at what my family had become.

"I need your help tonight, Jacob," Uncle Martin said one evening in July at the house. He had on his rubber fishing boots, a heavy pullover sweater with a knitted collar and patch pockets, and a pop-tent cloth German hat. "Tonight is going to be a big night."

I knew the answer he expected and gave it.

"What time do you want me at the docks?" I asked, as if agreeing to such a thing had no weight to it. My hands were squeezed into each other. My nails left little pink crescents against the skin.

"Ten tonight," Martin said.

I went to my room to be away from my uncle then. Fergus came running in after me and slid across the floor into Edwin's bed, shifting the mattress. I went to put it back but instead lifted it off to see if Edwin had hidden anything the way I had under my mattress. There was nothing there, but it gave me the idea of looking through the rest of his side of the room, which I proceeded to do. And in a small box of colored pencils, I found a tiny spiral notebook full of etchings of disembodied breasts. All shapes and sizes, with different colored and shaped nipples, protruding from the page, seeming three dimensional. Page after page, he'd drawn them. I remembered Timothy from camp and how he'd described performing virginity tests, and how those words must have sunk like a little bomb into Edwin's mind. I flipped through the pages, and felt sad for my brother, who had all the same maddening bodily desires hidden away like I did. Though in a way, I was proud of him, as despite those impulses—which to me felt like a drain on any strength—he was still driven, determined to be every moment an artist.

In the same box as the catalog of breast etchings, I also found a miniature polished pine ottoman that matched the chest of drawers I'd stolen from Hilda's dollhouse. I held it up and tried to imagine all that we'd hidden from each other, then pushed that aching thought out of my head.

———

By the time I reached the dock that night there were several PT boats tied off. Traffic in the port had begun to increase.

"Do you think they're all here because of you?" I asked Uncle Martin.

He looked down at me and didn't say anything for a long moment. "I hope not."

"That guy Aldrich said the general and his platoon were coming here because of problems."

"I remember. I heard him."

There was a large, covered German truck parked by the water. A bald officer with a graying military mustache, wearing a long black trench coat and a stiff-brimmed gray and black hat, leaned against the truck's passenger side door.

"Martin," the officer said, "these two men will help you load. We leave at midnight."

"That will work fine," Martin said, knocking on the side door of the truck, so the two men would get out and help us. "This is my nephew, Jacob, who will be helping."

The two soldiers unlatched the back hatch of the truck, and we started unloading food and toiletry supplies into wheeled carts that they pushed to the side of the *Lighthouse Lady*. Once everything was piled up on the dock, the two soldiers handed it over to me, and I handed it down to Martin, who stacked it all belowdecks.

The two soldiers talked about all the good food that was in the boxes and how they wished they could take a box or two for themselves, but when we finished they went back to their truck, got in, and drove off.

Uncle Martin and I sat on the deck. We looked out at the German tents, which ran all the way up the harbor to the schoolhouse, which the officers had taken over as their headquarters and bunkhouse. During the day townspeople sauntered among the soldiers. They lined up outside the few shops to get whatever they could with their ration cards. It struck me then how much food and supplies we had loaded aboard, and how we could feed most of the town for a month if we passed everything out. My giant uncle in a Nazi uniform could play Robin Hood.

People in town distrusted Uncle Martin and called him a collaborator. They spat out his name because they saw him in the uniform, and that was all they needed to judge, even though he had been a Dutch

Marine. They couldn't have known how ashamed of Holland's surrender Martin was and how it burned him up so much that he wasn't done fighting. But the people in town had no idea what he was doing in secret. Being called a conformer meant nothing to him. He was above all of that. This was a gift his ruthlessness provided.

From the boat's bow I could see where the Germans had hung a poster by the pier about what would happen to locals who protected Jews or downed Royal Air Force in hiding. I'd seen smoking bombers dip out of the sky and watched for the gossamer fabric domes of parachutes dipping to the ground. All the children in town would race out to the fields to try to find the wreckage, but never found anything more than the burnt bodies in the charred fuselages of the downed planes on the outskirts of Delfzijl. The Germans would have seen the same planes landing and scooped up whomever they found floating down.

"A bad lot for them," Uncle Martin said about downed RAF men. "The Germans know that any German pilot floating to English soil is going to get a farmer's pitchfork up their ass, so they aren't too inclined to be nice to those RAF men."

"That explains the chocolate bars."

"I guess so," Martin said.

A few weeks before, low-flying planes dropped V-shaped chocolate bars over the town so that the Dutch people would take more kindly to any RAF men that crash. The chocolate bars clanked on rooftops and slid over the street, and people went crawling on the stones to snatch as many as they could. The wrappers said, *Compliments of the RAF.*

Most of the candy was scooped up and eaten by German soldiers, who were everywhere by then.

When we were rested, Uncle Martin had me untie the lines for us to take the boat to fuel up. On the way to the German-run fueling station, the bow of the boat pushed a pack of seagulls off their floating perch on the water, and the birds started hovering above the ship and squawking down at the decks the same way they would when we were out to sea fishing and tossing scraps overboard. While watching the birds, Uncle Martin handed me a large box of threepenny nails and a claw-handled hammer.

"Go to the steering hold and take out the box of potato masher grenades above the starboard bilges. Pry open all the boxes we loaded below and bury a grenade in as many as you can, then close the boxes back up."

"Oh god, Uncle Martin, I don't want to do any of that," I said.

"This is important."

"Please don't make me go out with you." My thumb ran over the sharp steel edge of the hammer's claw, and the fat pad of my thumb pressed between the gap. The seagulls were still calling all around the ship.

"I'll take care of you, I promise. But tonight I need your help. Now go do as I ask," he said.

"No."

"Go."

"I'll tell," I said.

Martin's open palm cracked the side of my head. My ear rang. It took everything not to let my eyes well over.

"Jacob. Do as I say."

I looked him straight in the eye and balled my fists, but he raised his voice and leaned into me and yelled, "Now," and I turned to do what he said.

In the holds I packed grenades into potato sacks, boxes of peppers, apples, toilet paper, and flour. I eased open the crates, scooped away what was inside and planted grenades like how my mother dropped tulip bulbs into the dirt, then tapped the nails back into place. The whole time I was ranting to myself.

Later, when the ship was fueled, the supply boxes had been stuffed with grenades, and the bald officer in the trench coat had returned, we cruised east out of the harbor, then north to the mouth where the Ems opens and spreads out like an alluvial fan into the North Sea. The bald officer rode up with Martin in the wind-shielded wheelhouse. I didn't want to be anywhere near the man, or even hear him talk. The officer checked his watch and then a map he pulled from his satchel every few minutes to compare to Martin's chart. At the dark mouth of the channel before the North Sea, where the water got choppier, Martin set the boat on a track to do large circles and turned out all his running lights. Fast-moving clouds swept over the star-wild sky. The officer stood ready by a large spotlight next to the steering column.

As we circled in the darkness, breaks in the cloud cover let the stars wink through. Whatever section of the moon was out was hidden. Drifts of diesel scent floated over the decks. The engine sputtered through the water as my legs got heavier and heavier, as if they'd become magnetized to the deck.

At 2:00 A.M. Martin faced the bow of the ship to the east, and the officer flipped the dual spotlight on and off in quick succession, flashing some code out into the dark. He did this for several minutes. My eyes followed the beam of light as it stretched outward, searching, then fading in the distance past the spot where the two beams of light converged. When the officer switched off the spotlight, the total darkness of some subterranean river settled over me, and there was my brother again in free float. Here came the rising wave of hurt. When the light switched back on, it made the mist look like a thick head wall of smoke moving in.

In the beam of light, the lustrous shadow of a U-boat's bow crested the surface. The sound of a large surge of water followed by a tremendous crash sent swells rippling over the calm surface.

"There," the officer said, "*Unterseeboot*," and pointed off the starboard side of the *Lighthouse Lady*.

Martin set the boat to circle alongside the U-boat. He came down the ladder from the steering column and waved me to follow him into the holds. Then he moved a Mauser submachine gun to the side panel of the ladder way. Next to that he put a large, black, steel box with an apple-sized glob of adhesive putty that looked like bread dough in each corner. He covered it with the jacket he'd been wearing, then put on a thicker black coat that he tucked a potato masher into the inner lining of.

"When we pull alongside, only tie one spring line in a slipknot from the center of the submarine to our cleat. We'll unload everything from there. They're going to stack it all at the bottom of the hatch column. When we have a few boxes left, this officer is going to go into their boat, and I want you to go to the helm and get ready to get us away from that sub as fast as possible." He rested a hand on my shoulder.

"I'm sorry I smacked you," he said, then climbed out of the hold.

Martin brought his boat parallel to the U-boat, a sleek, riveted whale. A close link chain assembly threaded through the hawsepipe and secured the anchor to the foredeck. There were four men in black oilskin jackets and wool hats on the top of the U-boat, and I tossed one of them the mooring line to tie the center of our boat up with from the middle of their ship. Once the lines were secure on their end I tied a slipknot to the cleat on our midship. The man on the U-boat handed over a meter-wide and five-meter-long wooden plank, which we secured to make a walkway between the two ships. The plank had been adhered to the outside bow and was slick and wet.

"You men can start unloading the supplies, while I go speak to the captain," the bald officer aboard said. He tossed his duffel bag over his shoulder and walked across the wood board. He handed his bag down into the hatch and then climbed down himself.

The men on the surface of the boat began loading the supplies. Someone reached out of the hatch and pulled the boxes inside, where they were stacked and then probably carried from hand to hand to the holds all throughout the ship. The resealed boxes went across. Some had bent nails pounded into the wood. One of the sailors on the U-boat went back into the hatch, leaving three above the surface. With only ten boxes left, Martin went below the hold and came up with a skinny lead anchor for a skiff. He handed it to one of the sailors.

"Put this right next to the hatch for now, would you?" The sailor laid the anchor next to the hatch and turned back to get the next box.

"I'll get the rest of these, Jacob, why don't you get up to the helm and keep us steady?"

Martin heaved a box over to the sailors standing on the plank. When I was on the helm, he went below the deck. He came back out with the black box cradled to his body with his left hand. He held his right underneath it for support.

"Let me carry this one across, it's heavy," he said, walking to the wood beam.

He took small, slow steps over the plank. His figure wavered against the dark night with each step, and for a moment I hoped that the plank would stretch far, far ahead of him, so whatever he planned to do would not happen near me.

The sailor on the beam helped Martin steady himself as he walked to the top of the U-boat. Martin crossed the plank, bent down, and pushed the black metal box onto the deck of the U-boat so the dough-shaped gobs smoothed down and adhered themselves to the deck. When he stood up, he pulled a Luger out of his jacket pocket, fired two shots into the chest of the man closest to him, and one shot each into the chest of the other two men, who both fell. The orange flash of the muzzle lingered across my field of vision as one man doubled backward and slid off the side of the boat like a wet rag. In what seemed like one fluid motion, in which I did not take a single breath, Martin stuck the muzzle of the gun down the hatch and started pulling the trigger, dropped the gun down the hole, pulled the potato masher grenade out of his jacket lining, twisted the top of it, threw it down the hole, and slammed the hatch shut. He twisted the hatch wheel closed and pushed the skiff anchor through the wheel so it would be jammed shut if someone tried to open it from the inside.

"Martin," I yelled, but it was too late.

One of the soldiers on the deck of the ship reached out with a blade that glinted for a moment before the man slashed it at the back of my uncle's ankle. Martin's leg gave way, and he kneeled next to the man who was about to gouge him again. I turned to get something to throw at the man or grab the machine gun, but when I looked back, Uncle Martin had lodged the hilt of his scrimshaw knife into the soldier's throat. Uncle Martin stood up and jumped off the side of the U-boat onto the stern of the *Lighthouse Lady* as the explosion of the potato masher pounded its way from out of the ship's innards and punched at the hatch door.

Uncle Martin stood up on the deck of the *Lady*. His left leg, cut through the boot, bent at the knee. He hobbled as he jumped to the spring line, which he pulled to release.

"Go, go, go!" he yelled up to me as the mooring line between the two boats fell loose.

A series of small explosions echoed at my back as the boat steered free. I looked back onto the stern deck to see if Uncle Martin was okay. He came out of the hold with the Mauser submachine gun, raised it to his shoulder, and fired at the black metal box he'd stuck to the U-boat. The fire red tails of the tracer bullets ripped into the side of the U-boat. His aim traced a burning line up to hit the mark. The box exploded, blasting the side of the U-boat open across the top and below the waterline. The percussion of more potato mashers echoed as the explosions burped out of the smoking hole that rolled and flooded. The hole pulled the honing tower down on its side before it started to sink.

A large surge of air bubbled up behind us where the U-boat sank.

"Steer a wide circle around it," Uncle Martin yelled up to me.

We circled around the sinking sub to make sure nothing or no one floated to the surface. Small potato masher explosions popped under the water and each let a little blast of bubbles breach the surface. Martin swept his spotlight with his left hand and in his right he held the Mauser. The gun's muzzle followed the sweeping light on our several loops around the area. For a while the U-boat's belly faced upward toward us beneath the surface. It had rolled upside down and shook as the last blasts pushed the rest of the air out. When we couldn't see it anymore and found nothing floating up to the surface in the wake of the white wash of air bubbles, I turned the boat back southwest, in the direction of Delfzijl. A small sliver torn from the far corner of the moon had come out. The sky lay dark and low as an osprey shadow circling beneath the clouds.

Uncle Martin climbed up and had me run the boat due west and then south to keep us at least five kilometers offshore the whole time. He set a course for the woods south of Delfzijl that we would reach by sunup. While I steered, he undid a metal panel under the wheel and pulled out a green radio. Years earlier before summer camp, I had seen him take this radio apart and put it back together. He hit a switch and static filled the wheelhouse.

"Turn this dial and listen for any calls of distress from that U-boat," he said.

All I heard was squelch. Static. A low hum breathing loose from silence.

Uncle Martin then took off his boot and we saw the deep groove of a wound at the top of his Achilles tendon. Once he stanched the blood flow with rags we could see the white ham fat-colored tendon and where the blade cut deep enough to slice part of it. He took off his belt, tied it around his thigh, and held a needle under several lit matches.

"Are you going to sew that back together?" I pointed to his tendon.

"I don't know how. Just the skin and hope it heals." It took him twenty sutures to close the wound. He lay on the wheelhouse deck, sweating and swearing to himself. He held up his hands to look at the blood on them.

"Jesus, Jacob. I cut that kid's throat open."

"Uncle Martin," I didn't know how to talk to him about what I felt. "This can't go on."

"What would you have me do? Disappear?" I looked down at him to see if he intended the sting of referencing my father. "Should I give myself over?"

When he got up, he hobbled down the ladder and went through the several boxes of supplies that had not been loaded onto the U-boat. He took out the rest of the grenades. One of the crates had a whole bushel of sour green apples inside. He filled the hem of his shirt with them and climbed up the wheel where we ate them for the rest of the night.

At first light, the mist coming off the water still looked like a thin layer of smoke. The smoke confused the horizon line between the water and air and creating an odd feeling of levitating. I felt that my life was being lived in that suspended mist, lost in the water smoke. My stomach started to turn from all the apples, but I kept eating, hoping that it would give me a visceral reason for feeling so beaten and cold, experiencing a dissipating hunger.

"I love the wind," Uncle Martin said, tilting his face up. The skin around his eyes was riven with hairline wrinkles. There was an inward curve along the ridge of his nose I only noticed in profile and a pinch of slack skin between his eyebrows.

The cool white flesh of the apples filled our mouths. Juice ran down our chins. We spit seeds into our palms, and lifted our flattened hands up and out the window to let the wind take them away.

When Uncle Martin dropped me off on shore near the woods, he handed me a small pillowcase full of apples and other food for my mother. Then his boat pulled away and headed north until it was out of sight. Walking up the beach to the trail in the woods that led to my house, the watermark wandered the sand ahead of me. I shut my eyes and walked, then stopped and vomited apple chunks, which mixed into the tide's foam and washed back over my feet. Still, something was left in my stomach. I stuck my finger down my throat and jammed it in over and over, trying to purge out whatever remained.

13

It was becoming common for the air raid siren north of town to go off all hours of the night. The loud, high wail rose in pitch as it washed over Delfzijl, sending people out of bed, through their homes, down stairs into their basements and cellars. People who lived in one-story brownstones ran across their streets to hide beneath their neighbors' homes.

After Uncle Martin and I docked the boat from a supply transfer, the sirens started. We had been bombed twice in the last several months, with each attempt knocking out the harbor, which then had to be rebuilt by the German soldiers.

"I'm afraid the RAF will think we're a major port now with all this traffic," Uncle Martin said.

We had already docked the *Lighthouse Lady*, and didn't have enough time to cast her off again. We ran from the port to the center of town and into the school's front doors. We went down into the basement, which had become a community air raid shelter despite the Germans setting up headquarters on the first floor. We were the last to descend the stairs. About ten families huddled in the dark. Some were wrapped in bedsheets. Their forms shifted back and forth or paced in the large open room. Despite the dark, many of the shapes were familiar. Mort Stroud was the father of one of my classmates. Mr. Johansson worked at the butcher shop. Then I saw Mrs. Von Schuler, my homeroom teacher. The word *Yeladim* rang out in my head and recalled the shame I felt from throwing rocks at rats years before. She sat in the corner with a small boy sleeping in her lap.

For a long time no one in the basement spoke. We took our place sitting along the walls. Eventually Mrs. Von Schuler reached out a hand and patted my knee.

"You're getting so tall. It's hard to believe." Her voice was the same as it always was, a sweet vocalization of affection.

I put my hands on top of hers. I'm not sure why. Because I felt she was scared. Because I wanted to apologize to her.

"Did you know your father used to bring me loaves of bread?"

I tried to make out her features in the dark.

"No."

"Yes. He'd just show up with them from time to time."

"I didn't know that."

"It was a nice thing for him to do."

As my eyes adjusted I could see how worried she was. How scared everyone was. If my father were there, he'd tell some story to help the children forget about being away from home. He could quiet their fears. He had been gone for so long, without giving us a word or sign. My mother kept doing her rounds visiting every household in town. She stopped asking if anyone had seen him. She'd knock on the door and simply look into their faces. Her trips became silent, penitent. Every part of me hoped my father was safe, but at certain moments I was furious with him. For leaving us, having crawled off on his belly like a coward. Though in that basement, more than anything, I wanted to hear one of his stories. As we sat in the dark there were no voices to soothe our fear.

Four waves of bombers flew over Delfzijl that night, but none dropped ordinance on the village itself. We huddled together in our sleep vigil. "Maybe they'll drop chocolate again," the little boy in Mrs. Von Schuler's lap whispered to her.

In the morning, Uncle Martin and I were the first to walk up the stairs into the slant of light coming through the school's windows. Puffs of black smoke rose from the north. The sun caught and outlined it with yellow and glowing gray that rose into the air like a column of illuminated steam. From what we could tell, the bombers didn't make a run over the city or port, but as we walked ten minutes north, we realized they had lobbed a volley along the shore, knocking out the air raid siren and the antiaircraft guns.

"They're smart, they know where they've taken fire from and made sure to clear the path for their next run-through," Martin said, as we looked at a pit of earth where a heavy flack gun bunker had been.

"You mean the British, right?" I asked.

"Yes."

"Are they bombing us because of all the new soldiers here?"

"God, I hope not," Uncle Martin said.

Walking farther north of town, we saw the heap of twisted metal and splintered and burnt wooden posts that had been the siren. "At night from now on, we'll either have to be on the boat out in the water or at your mom's house. That's far enough from town to be safe."

"What about the bomb that almost cut our backyard in half?"

"I can't explain that one," he said.

We walked back into town. When we got to the main square, a

group of people huddled together in a large circle. We pushed through them and saw two bodies on the ground. Both lay face-down with wet red holes in the backs of their heads. A man and a woman, side by side, shoulder to shoulder. We moved in closer. It was Gerard Van Den Bosch and his wife, Annie, the factory's accountants. Annie's dark blood-smeared hair was matted forward like a waterlogged blanket covering her face.

Everyone in the circle of people was hungry and scared. Hilda and Ludo stood across from us. Hilda looked down at the bodies. Ludo's face was white, and he kept rubbing his palms together like he did when he was nervous. Ludo didn't take his eyes off the bodies until he whispered something to Hilda and exited the circle. He walked about twenty meters and then started running in the direction of his home.

"What happened?" Uncle Martin asked the man standing next to us.

"Wouldn't you know?" the man said, eyeing Martin's German jacket.

"Tell me," Martin said, a sharpness entering his voice.

"Soldiers dragged them out here and shot them."

"What for?"

"A few soldiers went to hide in their basement during the raid and discovered Maud Stein hiding down there. They were hiding her."

Maud was Jewish. She lived by herself in the apartment building downtown. She'd disappeared years before without a trace. "They killed them for that?" Uncle Martin said. He didn't ask what the soldiers did with Maud.

At camp the counselors had said they would need one giant, violent push to clean and unify Europe. As a boy I had never thought to ask what that would look like, where the ugliness would actually fall.

That night, Ludo showed up at my house. He knocked on the door and stood back off the stoop. His body weight shifted back and forth on his heels.

"Ludo, come in."

"Can we talk outside?" he asked.

We walked from the house back into the woods to the tree fort where, night after night throughout the past winter, I'd go trying to catch a glimpse of my father, always avoiding the pseudo grave of my brother. Ludo moved quickly, his spindly arm raised up in front of him, pushing away the low branches without paying attention to how they snapped back behind him. When we got to the fort, Ludo stopped and faced me.

"I need your help with something," he said. "But I have to know you'll keep this quiet. You have to promise me. Whatever you think about all this insanity in town and this war, you have to promise to keep this quiet. Can you do that?"

"Okay, what's going on?"

"Today, those soldiers killed the Van Den Bosches for hiding a Jew."

"Is your family hiding someone?"

"You have to promise me you won't tell anyone, Jacob," Ludo said. "That could be my family dead on the ground."

"Who are you hiding?" I wanted it to be my father. I wanted it to be connected to his disappearance.

"My father found a British airman who'd been shot down last week. His leg was broken, and he would have been captured."

I rubbed my hands over my eyes. "Why didn't you tell me before? Why now?"

"I don't want what happened to the Van Den Bosches to happen to my parents. I'm terrified, and now they are too. They won't send him away though. How could they?"

"What a mess. Where is he?"

"He's in our house."

"Where?"

"We have a hidden cubby off the attic. Can you—"

"Can I what?"

"Martin knows people." Ludo said. "People suspect he's part of an underground escape system. But no one will approach him about it because they're afraid of him. Can you and your uncle get him out on your boat?"

"Don't you think we would have gotten ourselves out? We're all trapped here."

We stood staring at each other in the early dark of the evening. The trees around us that had always been so familiar seemed to create a barbed meshing that walled us in.

"I don't know what else to do," Ludo said.

"Ludo, I don't know how to help you."

"Promise not to tell anyone. Promise, not even your uncle if you don't think he can get him out of here."

"I thought you wanted me to ask my uncle?"

"I did, but if you know he can't do it, I'd rather he doesn't know. After all, he works with the Germans."

That phrase sank into my heart. I also worked with the Germans for all Ludo knew. That was why he hadn't told me anything about the downed airman until now. Ludo walked back through the woods toward his home. I was hurt by his distrust of me or my uncle. All my plans, no, they were fantasies, but all my fantasies of getting away had included him. He was my best friend, and it felt like this conversation wedged suspicion between us.

I tried to picture life in Ludo's attic for the pilot, which must have felt claustrophobic and cramped compared to the giant sky he cut through in his plane. The darkness of the school's basement filled my mind again, the palpable worry over how and when death would come for each of the huddled townspeople. I walked to the overturned stone with my brother's name carved into it and rested my palms flat trying in some way to communicate with those missing. In the woods that night, it seemed all of the light in my country was now going dark or being blocked by some antiaircraft cover. Chaos had shattered my own family and now worked its way along the seams of the only place I'd ever known.

Two nights later, after finishing work on the docks, I went to my father's factory and waited for my mother to walk home with her. They had covered the entire building with a giant mesh tarp that was supposed to hide it from bombers.

"Your father's factory is having a little camping trip," my mother said when she exited. She was hunched over and exhausted. She wore a smock over her clothes so the fabric of her dress wouldn't get rubbed thin from leaning against the metal conveyor line all day long.

We walked out of the village. On the road out of town were several orange splatters on the gravel. They were spaced far apart and looked like rain drops. One smudged into the dirt when my shoe slid over it. My hand looped under my mother's elbow and she relaxed under my touch. Her stern face slackened, and she looked like she could fall asleep while walking. I wished she would. She had not been sleeping well for months, and though she had gotten into a routine, she had been up every night for the last few weeks, worried about my eighteenth birthday and if or when and where the Germans might take me. She kept trying to find a way to hide all of my records, to claim I was younger, in hopes that some Allied force would liberate Holland within the next few years.

Several hundred yards from home, something moved off to the side of the road ahead of us. It looked like a waterlogged and deflated barrel. Then it moved again. It was a brown blanket huddled over someone's back and head. The person leaned their shoulders against a tree. My mother saw it too. Part of us both must have wanted for it to be my father waiting for us. We both wanted every shadow to be him or Edwin returning.

"Go. Go look," my mother said. The gravel crunched under my feet and rolled away after each footfall. The person under the blanket was no bigger than a teenage boy. Maybe it was Edwin, who had been preserved under the water, I thought. A sick thought. A desperate thought, that he had not grown, and had just now found his way back home.

"Hello," I said. The person balled up and pressed farther into the tree and whimpered. Their knees pushed into the dead leaves that covered the ground in wet clumps. The blanket was rust brown and covered in bright, orange drops that splattered across it. Then I saw the split lip and naked thigh.

I kneeled down. "Are you okay?"

The head under the blanket lifted. There were those supple green eyes.

"Oh. No. No."

Strands of red hair were glued to her face by orange paint and blood. "Hilda. No. No. Not you."

Beneath the blanket, Hilda was naked and trembling.

My mother ran up to us and helped Hilda stand, and I caught a glimpse of her pale left breast and soft pink nipple. Her bare spine was beautiful. But this was so far from how I imagined her when we had kissed and I imagined my hand inside her dress. She had been beaten, and her eyes would have been swollen shut if they hadn't burst open and bled over her temples. Her head was shaved and covered with orange paint that smeared down her neck and on her hands where she tried to rub it off. The fine red hairs over her ears that cupped her face in parentheses were the only hair she had left on her head. The rest had been shorn off, and there was a cropping of red, bloody dots on her skull.

Hilda leaned into my mother's arms and started weeping.

It was foolish of me, but I had always thought of her as virginal and pure and this new reality filled me with confusion, anger, and shame. I helped hold her up despite an immediate desire to banish her from my life. All memory of Hilda and Hilda's touch—I wanted to whitewash it away.

"We'll take you inside, dear," my mother said.

"Take me home," Hilda gurgled out of her swollen lips.

We helped lead her the rest of the way home, crumpled between us as we walked down the road we had followed so many times as children.

The blanket barely covered her body. So many nights I had dreamed of her naked body, each contour and mystery, and here it was, battered, bathed in orange, and I knew what that meant. She had been with a German man. At least one, and often enough to have been found out by the townspeople. As we walked, I grew equally upset at the Germans who had touched her and the Dutch who had punished her for letting them. I felt the orange paint dry on my fingers. Though there was much I didn't understand, about the townspeople, about the Germans or Hilda's own desires, I knew none of us would come away unchanged.

14

December snow dragged itself over Holland like a heavy, wet sheet, and once its deep chill set in, on the boat Martin and I had to spend our time in the covered wheelhouse or below deck as much as possible. When we were not transferring troops or supplies, we tried to fish, though it was often too cold to be on the open decks for long enough to roll out more than one net. It also made it harder for Uncle Martin to show sandbars to the soldiers he ferried, which was good, because it meant I could avoid participating in his covert plans. I was afraid of being caught and killed, and I said as much to him, but I hadn't pushed the issue after my mother and I found Hilda beaten on the side of the road. Part of me didn't care who lived or died beyond my own family anymore.

When we were out fishing, we caught onto a school of herring. The fish flittered several feet under the surface. They'd drift apart and their sides reflected the running lights like dozens of sinking coins. Then some movement of the boat or something beneath brought them back together into a tight teardrop-shaped shadow. They drifted apart again before tightening back into one mass moving in time like a giant heart-

THE BOAT RUNNER — 207

beat. We took turns pulling the sprawled net out of the water and spent a day and a half getting one hold container full. Martin still limped from his leg wound. His gap-tooth whistled as he gave me orders. On the decks the cold wind burned my face. I hauled in the nets fearful of dragging up the bones of the dead drifting apart beneath us. When the one hold was full we headed back to Delfzijl, where we were scheduled to make a troop transport. The transport would be a one-way group of soldiers who were supposed to be dropped off at the mouth of the North Sea to work their way inland. If the opportunity arose, they wouldn't leave the water alive.

It was early morning when we began working our way back to shore. Martin was belowdecks getting ready for our next transfer. The sun was all the way up and everything looked empty and new in the clear, cold air. The cluster of the town's buildings shone in the fullness of the day. A glint of light flittered in the sky beyond the town. I focused on it and then saw another, then a third. When it got closer I realized it was a formation of airplanes, four, five, soon over a dozen flying low and toward Delfzijl.

"Martin," I yelled down into the holds, "Martin."

Martin limped up the ladder into the wheelhouse and I pointed.

"The air raid siren is still out," he said, a subtle whistle where his tooth had been.

"They wouldn't come during the day. Would they?" I asked.

"They took out all the guns. They can do whatever they want," he said, reaching for his radio. He switched on the console and tried hailing the harbor. "*Lighthouse Lady* to Delfzijl Pier, *Lighthouse Lady* to Delfzijl Pier."

Then he kicked and pulled back the dented panel with his hidden green radio. He jerked the radio out, slammed it on the desk, and began yelling into it in English. "Planes over Delfzijl. Planes over Delfzijl, pull back. Planes over Delfzijl." He adjusted the nobs and kept yelling in English.

The formation of bombers dropped lower out of the clouds so we could see the size of them, broad-winged, deep-bellied RAF Manchester heavy bombers.

"No. No. Please," Uncle Martin screamed into the microphone.

The first plane in the formation dropped flares over the town to mark the targets. The flares corkscrewed downward in burning-iron-orange light. The flares were followed by the horrible whistling sound of 2000-pounder bombs. Each of the planes sprinkled the black dots of bombs after the flares, and they fell in the sunlight, each a miniature golden teardrop descending on the town. In seconds the planes roared over the top of the *Lighthouse Lady*, and the town of Delfzijl was engulfed in a growing orange and black cloud that breathed upward swallowing all the brick, wood, and air in the blue sky above. The crystalline morning cracked open with high whistles that erupted in a pounding that echoed across the water with each ball of fire thrown.

"No. No. No," I screamed. I felt a digging pain in a secret part of myself. Strings of electricity cutting under my ribs. The same sensation as being shocked by my father's bulb. Now it felt like I was licking the socket, taking in all the shock and tremble.

The roar of the low-flying bombers swept through the sky above. They started to bank off of our stern and head up along the Ems to the North Sea, where they gained elevation again, light, empty, and on the return trip to England.

We steered the boat to the harbor and put the engine up to full throttle. The freezing wind cut into my face. The taste of burning smoke on the air drifted in from a kilometer out. Then came a subtle warmth from the shore pulsating over the bow. In the wheelhouse, Martin took two long strips of cloth and dunked them in a potable water bucket. He tied one around his face to cover his nose and mouth and tossed the other to me. We breathed through the wet cloth as we slowed down and steered the boat into the harbor. Gray drifts billowed down the town's main street and blanketed us. From what we could see, the harbor was leveled. Masts of sunken sailboats peeked above the burning, oil-slicked surface. The bombers leveled everything in a wide strip, from the far side of town up to and through the harbor.

Martin swung the boat toward shore. None of it seemed real. The air around us turned gray like we'd been sucked up into a thunderhead. I stood leaning over the bow to help him steer clear of floating debris. The skiffs that had been tied to the break wall had sunk. A robin's egg blue rowboat floated loose, the inside of the boat was on fire, two benches and parts of the inner hull were burning, a little cup of flame drifting out to sea.

"We'll steer north to the old fishing pier and tie up there," Martin said.

North of town, the wood pylons from an old pier still jutted out from the shore at odd, sloping angles. It would be the closest place outside of the ruined harbor to tie the boat up. We turned the boat north and had to cruise through the dense, black cloud of smoke that drifted onto the water.

"Go. I'll be right behind you," Martin yelled as he prepared a spring line.

Onshore the giant drift of black smoke rose up into the air and darkened the whole sky. I ran to my father's factory through several blocks of untouched homes and buildings closer to the village, where gasoline burning from the bombs choked my lungs through the damp rag over my mouth and nose.

At the main square of town there were dirt craters where the Germans had set up their camp. Beyond that was the leveled pile of brick that had been the school. What was left of the church was on fire up on the hill. Shell-shocked soldiers wandered around town with guns held out in front of them like they could fight off the smoke and fire. One of them had blood running out of his ears. Another's face was burnt and his skin looked like raw chicken. Ash fell over the street. Several more soldiers ran past me with their hands covering their faces, and I feared they'd taken in some poisonous gas.

I stopped running and tumbled toward what was left of the factory. The office part of the building was a pile of rubble. The factory's tall steel-sheet- and wood-sided walls stretched the length of half a football field but had nothing of their previous form standing upright. Pieces of steel jutted out from the ground in concrete piles. There was a large chemical fire toward the back corner where the gases were stored. A sour smell that drifted from the chemical vat stung my eyes and left a sulfuric tang at the back of my throat. The flame lapped up at the sky and shimmered in iridescent green and red undulations. The heat had twisted the assembly lines into extraordinary shapes. Copper base mounts of unfinished lightbulbs were spread over the ground.

I climbed onto a heap of brick and froze at the lip of the caldera. My mother. Hilda. Ludo. Ludo's mother. All those people.

Martin staggered up beside me, bent down to massage his wounded ankle, and took in the ruined factory. He ran to the flattened assembly lines. There were bomb-lopped hands, legs, and whole torsos sticking out of the rubble piles. I pulled a hand from the pile and saw the scar crisscrossed deep into the meat of the forearm muscle. Edward Fass, who had shown me how to work on the assembly line all those years ago. I dropped his dead arm and went looking further among the debris, going from body to body, each of which looked like a limp and ashen version of someone I'd once known, digging with my hands into the stone that was hot to the touch despite the frozen air. Every few minutes I fell to my hands and knees and hacked up some chemical gas from deep in my lungs. When I stood back up, I tried to picture the layout of the factory, where Hilda, Ludo and his mother, and my mother would have stood, but couldn't make sense of what was scattered in ash around me.

The roof had collapsed. Where the ribbon machines had been, a set of legs stuck out. Whoever it was had their pants burned off, and the rubber soles of their brown shoes were sticky from having melted to the floor. I grabbed the legs at the shins and pulled, but the skin tore loose and bunched down at the ankle like a soggy sock. All I could do to keep from screaming and collapsing right there was to wipe my hands off on the front of my shirt and try to disengage from all memory of touch.

Martin breathed in and exhaled little puffs of fumes as he crawled through the rubble like an ash-covered spirit collecting last breaths. He scurried from body to body, ignoring the yelps of the living that he found like he'd fallen out of one of Blake's poems, reaching down with hungry fingers for human souls.

A wide swath of human skin spread flat against a crumbled cinder block, flash-heated and sealed, as if the whole building had been a living thing.

"No," Martin yelled, then scaled a mound of crumbled cinder block in front of him and started digging at the rubble. When I scaled the mound of brick, I saw him pull my mother into his lap.

Her body hung in his arms. What he held was shattered, bloodied, splintered with shards of steel from the assembly line she must have been standing at. Her cheek was in the light, dirt smudged and bruised along the jawline. Her midsection from her hip bone to her rib cage had been filleted open. A balled knot of skinless snakes poked out of the gaping wound. The kinky knot of intestine was red, purple, and coated in ash. I looked at the white bone and otherness of her torn skin. Blood had pumped out and flooded her clothing. Her teeth were cracked across the top, and the exposed roots nudged out in gummy pink spires; a forehead lump over her right eye split open her small frame, as pale and lifeless as the brick she lay on.

I leaned my ear to her lips. Breath wasn't good enough. I wanted her voice. An I love you, or just the word love, a word I could feed on forever. But there was nothing.

My ash-covered uncle staggered back with a mad scowl twisted across his face. The tint of his eyes lined up the world around him and made me think he was going to explode. All that he had been holding back couldn't be contained any longer.

I looked up to the sky expecting more of the bombers. I wished I had been there when the bombs fell, to have opened my mouth and swallowed their ordinance. Then spit it all back at them. I hated them for their ability to fly, for what they had done. I wanted to match my uncle's rage with my own, but who was there left to hate? The only choice was to hate everyone. Martin undid his jacket and covered my mother with it. Then he scooped her body off the ground.

Hilda with her fading bruises and half-inch-long hair. Ludo with his half-limp arm. Ludo's mother with her nine lost pregnancies. The men and women whom I'd worked with and my father had employed for almost two decades. Their lives. Their stories. I didn't want to look and find them. I didn't want to find scraps of their bodies, the certainty of their death. If I didn't look, there was a chance they had survived.

"We'll take her home," Uncle Martin said. He walked past me in the wreckage and started toward the house.

I followed him in a numb haze until we got to the back of the Protestant church where the body of a German officer lay face-down in the dirt. When no one watched, I walked up to him, rolled him over, and pretended to check his pulse in case any other soldiers were near. Then I unclasped the front of his heavy jacket. The officers carried Lugers on their belts, and when the dead man's jacket opened, I pulled out the Luger and shoved it into my pocket. The only person around me was my uncle, carrying my half-opened mother home. Her head dangled loose from his arm.

The handle of the Luger was smooth and cool. My fingertips ran over the stock as I turned away from my uncle and ran down the bombed road west of town.

It looked like the world had ended. Several blocks of town were leveled. At a familiar corner outside the main square, none of the houses had been touched. I stood in front of the third house on the right, the three-story brownstone where Ludo had lived his entire life. I looked for some other unseen window in the attic, scanned the house for a moment, then walked up to the door and pushed it open.

"Who's here?" I yelled.

Ludo's family and the rest of the town either would have been in or were now digging away at the rubble of the factory or the town center's office buildings. There was no knowing who was and wasn't alive. When no one answered, I started up the stairs with the Luger held out. I started up the stairs oozing a dark rage. The attic door opened up to a large storage space. Boxes lined the walls.

I scanned the room and yelled, "Come out," in English. "I know you're here." I listened for any movements. There was one small window that looked out into the front of the street and cast a square of light onto the floor. The wood beneath me creaked the way old houses do with big wind gusts. I moved several boxes and then came to a bookshelf that looked built into the corner. I swept the books on top of it to the floor and pulled the shelf away from the wall. It swung on a hinge, and I stepped back to see the small cavity in the wall.

The smell from a shit and piss bucket by the opening made me gag. Through the dark hole, a pair of dark eyes blinked shut, and an overpowering desire to unload the gun into the dark space between them flushed through me.

The man's body bent forward over his straightened legs. His head rested on his kneecaps, and he looked like a giant larva embedded into the wall.

"Get out here. Get out here now." I motioned with the gun for him to come out. His shoulder rubbed against the horsehair insulation that bulged between exposed wall studs.

He rolled to his side and stretched out his body like everything had gone numb from squirreling himself away. He looked up at me and said, "Prisoner of war," then looked at me for a long moment. *"Speekt u Engles? Churchill. Queen Wilhelmina. Kamerad,"* he said, making it clear he spoke no Dutch.

When he was out of the hole, he pulled himself up along the edge of the chest of drawers. His left leg was splinted by a handmade wooden brace with a smooth hone done by an expert carpenter. He wore a Royal Air Force jumpsuit with pockets on both pant legs and over his chest. On the chest pocket was the word *Yarborough*.

"What kind of plane were you in when you went down?" I asked in the best English I could. He kept looking at me. The expression on his face slackened. "Answer me."

He studied me and my clothes. The ash darkening my skin. "I've been here for a long time."

"What kind of plane?"

"Wait."

"Was it a Manchester heavy bomber? The same kind that just went over?"

When he stood straight, I wanted to shoot him for being part of those who had destroyed my town and killed my mother. A vision of the innards of his head splattered across the back wall filled my mind. I wanted to shoot someone. The bent inside of my finger rubbed against the trigger.

"Walk over here."

"Okay. Easy," he said. He had a thick British accent. His black hair and beard were unkempt and greasy.

"I can pay you, I have a barter kit." The pilot took out a thin, black case from his leg pocket. He opened it, and inside there were three gold coins and three gold rings. "Look, I can pay you. Please don't shoot. Please. I need help."

"Help with what? To get back to England? Get a new plane? Drop more bombs? Kill more of my family and friends?" I held the gun so close to the man's face the barrel touched his nose. "Put that on the floor and take off your clothes. The brace too."

The pilot didn't move.

"Now," I said like a spitting lunatic, stepping into him, scraping the muzzle of the gun from his nose to his forehead.

He stripped off his wooden brace, then unzipped his jumpsuit and peeled it off.

"And leave your boots."

Once the RAF pilot was only in his underwear, I could see that his skin was covered in sores from his calves up to and over his shoulders. The rounded knobs of his rib cage grotesquely protruded, and the dark blue, swollen left knee was the size of a grapefruit. He kept hopping up and down to keep his balance and not put pressure on his wounded leg. His left ankle had dark yellow bruises from what looked like the knee draining down. I went to the entrance of the cubbyhole and picked up the jumpsuit and the barter kit.

"Downstairs," I said.

He hobbled when he walked, leaning against the banister and jumping to get down the stairs. Pictures of Ludo's family lined the stairwell. I hadn't paid any attention to them on my way up, but coming down the black and white prints hurt to look at. There was no knowing if any of them was still alive.

The photographs made me want to boot the pilot in the back to tumble him down the stairs, to inflict pain on him.

On the front porch, the man began to shiver. The sun hit his open sores and they shone like dew. He looked so lean and needy with the cold street and row of dull brownstones behind him. The scrape from the gun's muzzle was pink against his white forehead skin.

"Go," I said. "Run. Run like hell."

The pilot looked at me, then out into the cold street, a look of total confusion on his face. I thought again of kicking the pilot hard between the shoulder blades so he'd fly down the porch steps, but I didn't do that. I'm glad, at least, I didn't do that.

He may have thought I was going to shoot him in the back, but he turned and worked his way down the steps, hopping with his swollen leg held straight out in front of him. He hobbled across the street and shimmied up the road. His body almost buckled every time he put weight on his swollen leg. By the time he ducked behind some other house, his skin was already turning blue. He slunk off into the bombed and occupied town with I thought about the same chance my father was given.

I walked home with the officer's gun and the pilot's suit and black box under my arm in a bundle. In the pocket of the suit were his papers. *Herbert Yarborough. RAF.* It was easy to see myself in his clothes, high in the clouds, drifting far above any human concerns.

At home, Fergus barked into the bathroom, where my uncle knelt on the tile floor between my mother and the claw-footed bathtub, washing the ash and dust and blood off of my mother with a wet towel. A second towel wrapped around her midsection kept her intestines from spilling out.

"What are we going to do with her?" There was a quick flash of desperation in my uncle's voice—something I didn't know could exist. "The ground is too frozen to dig a hole."

"Stop barking," Uncle Martin yelled at Fergus. A tragic tremolo floated at the end of his words. "Stop barking. Go dig a hole with all that energy. Help us out and dig a hole."

Fergus ran to me, nudged my hand with his cold nose, and then went back to bark at my mother.

The shape of her body looked plastered to the floor, mummified with rust-colored puddles of her watered-down blood on the tile. Fergus whimpered at the doorway but wouldn't go any farther into the room. I put my hand on the dog's head and let my fingers scratch the velvet tips of his ears. Then I stepped into the bathroom, kneeled into the puddle, and felt the blood-water soak into the cloth and cool my skin. I put my hand on her chest and felt compelled to start pushing down, with all my strength, to make her heart beat again. But, once something was dead, it was dead forever. I knew this. The towels were still wet to the touch. I peeled the topmost one back to make sure it was really her. That this was not some awful mistake. When I looked down into her battered face, I knew there was nothing left for me, so I kissed her forehead, pulled out her left hand, kissed her on each fingertip, and covered her once more.

"What are we going to do?" Martin asked.

He ran a fresh wet cloth over her face. His own face was coated in grime. I stood up and walked out of the room. Out the window was the huge pit, which was now a sunken little ice pond, a jewel of frozen water.

"Where should we bury her?" echoed out of the bathroom when I went into the living room, the room she used to dance in, and curled up on the couch. I picked up a pillow. A hexagon patchwork with a thick blue chord sewn along the edge and port wine-colored tassels. Homemade. I held it. Touched by the care and delicacy of her work. I hugged the pillow and lay like that, listening to my uncle ranting and cleaning her off in the bathroom and Fergus's barking choir until everything in me succumbed to exhaustion. The last vapors of the massive rush that had kept me going drained away. This was the day my mother died. There would never be another day like it. Still, I could not yet mourn, not yet cry, and had spent a quick and horrible burst of anger on Herbert Yarborough, and could do nothing else but fold inside myself and fall asleep.

I woke to my uncle standing over me. There was a hot, sweet smell on his breath, peat moss scotch, engine fumes, and burnt hair. Streaks of water cut channels down his filthy face. He had no reason to wash.

"Get your things," he said. He walked into the kitchen where the pantry door popped open.

I lay back down and tried not to wade into the river of faces of loved ones who were now gone. I shut my eyes and tried to be Herbert Yarborough, loose in the sky cut by the white triangular whirl of propellers.

"Where are we going?" I called out.

"Get your things and I'll show you."

I packed my backpack with my identification papers, warm clothes, the German officer's Luger, and Herbert Yarborough's barter kit, jumpsuit, and papers. Then I went to the bathroom door. My mother was no longer there.

"Where is she?"

"Come on."

I followed my uncle outside, where he headed through the woods. I could picture another chiseled rock laid out next to the headstone Ludo carved. But Uncle Martin walked past the upturned headstone toward the dock by the water.

"What's happening?"

"We're going to give your mother a burial at sea, Jacob."

The idea of dumping my mother off the side of the *Lighthouse Lady* made me stop. The image of a heathen ceremony came to me then, as dumping her in the water was no different to me than if we torched her in a funeral pyre, or draped her from the limbs of a tree and offered her up to carrion birds.

The boat was tied to the old pier through the woods. He untied the line as we stepped aboard.

On the deck of the wheelhouse lay my mother. There was a clean sheet over her body but I could see he had cleaned and dressed her. He started the engines and maneuvered us into the heart of the Ems.

"What's happening?"

"They're sending a large group of soldiers over to check the wreckage. They called us to get them. We're going to get all of them this time. We'll bury your mother and then we'll cause some real damage. Something real," he said. "Real." His eyes were red and spiteful—crazy spiteful, like he had no intention of hiding his true hatred tonight.

My mind flashed forward to what my uncle would have me do if I continued with him. He would smile and nod throughout the whole war to disarm the Germans, and then massacre them when they let their guard down. He would go on bigger and bigger missions, and take bigger risks with the hope that some Allied force would again step foot in Holland and defeat the Germans.

At the time I didn't believe that would ever happen. I had seen the child army practicing at the camps and remembered the two thousand boys running to the beach and playing in the water. There were so many boys. There had been groups like that all over Germany. All trained to answer a unifying call. They were too plentiful and too well organized to lose the war. Uncle Martin would rage against this undying force and be killed, and there was nothing I could do. I knew all this. To me, the outcome was inevitable. Fire and ash and death would continue until the war was over. At the time, it seemed to me that to end it all as soon as possible was the only way to alleviate the suffering.

I kneeled next to my supine mother, lifted the hem of her blue, flower-print dress, pressed the collar to my nose, and smelled it. Breathed it in. Everything in my body pounded like I was touching my own heart. I thought of my father holding the empty burlap sack in the water thinking it was Edwin, and only now felt I could relate to that kind of emptiness. Tears burst out of me. I tried to catch them in my fists but they spurt through my fingers. The thought of my mother lost to the cold water was too much.

"I can't do this."

"The ground is too frozen."

"No. Go out with you, again. I want this all to stop."

"We're already on our way."

I looked over the side of the ship. We were a hundred meters from the shore. "I need you to take me back."

"No going back now," he said.

"Uncle Martin. I can't do this."

He did not say anything; either he was not listening or he did not care.

"Why do we have to do this?" I said. A burning lump lodged in my throat. "It was the RAF who did this. They destroyed everything."

Martin looked back at me. So many different expressions crossed his face I thought it would split open. Wet light filled his eyes. He had caused enough trouble in town that the Germans had set up a whole battalion here, and it was probably that massing that caught the RAF's attention. He must have felt that burning responsibility, only increasing his rage. Some devil sat up inside me and, again, I saw what lay ahead of us. More men gunned down and boats sunk. More atrocities. He would continue to fracture the world into more ruined shards. I was certain then that my uncle was wired to explode, and I wanted no part picking up the leftover pieces.

"I need you to take me back."

He kept steering the boat. My mother's body, everything familiar to me, lay between us.

"Martin. I need you to take me back."

"Sorry, Jacob."

I didn't know what to do. I felt that the *Lighthouse Lady* was pushing toward our deaths.

Make it out of this nightmare is what my mother had told me. *Make it out of this nightmare.*

I crawled on my hands and knees to my backpack, opened the drawstring on top, and reached inside until I felt the handle of the Luger.

"Uncle Martin," I said and raised the barrel toward his back. "Uncle Martin."

When he glanced back he did a double take and his eyes leveled on mine. I held his gaze. Something went out of him then. A ghost. He turned back to the water and his shoulders sank over the wheel.

"Okay," he whispered. "Okay, Jacob."

He spun the wheel so that the boat started a slow arc back to the shore. I was crying. Still aiming at his back. If I fired, the bullet would have traveled over the body of my mother to find my last blood relative. I had been trained in many languages but had no word for such a feeling.

When we were close to the dock, I grabbed my backpack and stepped out of the wheelhouse.

"I'm sorry," I sobbed, as much to my mother as my uncle. There was no need to toss a line to the dock. I jumped off and the *Lighthouse Lady* finished its circle and headed back out to the Ems.

I stumbled through the woods back to my house.

There, Fergus wandered from room to room barking, then sat in front of the bathroom and started whimpering.

"Come on, boy. Come on, Fergus," I called, but that only raised his volume to a howl. When I pulled him away by the scruff of the neck, he yanked free and started another lap of the house, barking into each room.

"Fergus. Fergus. Please come. Fergus. Come." I kept calling but the dog did not stop and was half-crazed by fear or sadness and didn't listen to me.

I was still bawling with big chest-heaving sighs as I emptied the giant bin of dog food on the floor where we had kept Fergus's bowl. Then I propped the back door open for him.

"Come on, boy. Please." I tried one last time. "Please," but he didn't come.

In the woods, at the fort, I left a note for my father between two slats of moldering planks, then walked to the rock Ludo had carved as a tombstone for Edwin. I heaped snow, leaves, and dirt on top of it until it was covered. Even if Ludo and his family were still alive, I'd never be able to look them in the eye after what I'd done to the pilot, even though the man's presence could have gotten them killed.

I left the woods and walked past my house. Inside Fergus kept barking. This was my final look at my home. It was a beautiful house—almost opulent. My mother had once draped all the windows in great sheets of cloth that she had cut and sewn, making billowing curtains she could cast open to let in the light. It seemed, now, that there was no more light to let in.

I walked to town, past the spot where Hilda had lain huddled and beaten, past the flattened church where the priest's, storyteller's, and now organist's voices were silent. In the harbormaster's office the Germans were already setting up a new office. They had boats anchored offshore and were ferrying in men and supplies on motorized skiffs. I walked around the harbor until I found one of the men in charge. Uncle Martin had dealt with the man on almost all of his ferry trips, and the man had seen me with Martin aboard the *Lighthouse Lady*.

I'm not sure if I was thinking clearly in that moment, but there were certain facts, truths I was holding on to. The Dutch had drowned my brother and the Allies had killed my mother, and on the Allies' behalf my father had sabotaged his safety and was forced into hiding. Hilda didn't really care for me and Ludo didn't trust me. My uncle would not belong to this world much longer with what he was doing. He would probably die soon—or continue—killing, killing some more. It was a conscious choice. So, so naïve, but conscious.

When I was in front of the German officer, the man looked at me. "Are you okay, son?" he asked.

"The Allies just killed my mother," I said, not having any of the right words for what I felt.

The officer didn't say anything.

It surprised me it was my voice, in my mouth, speaking again. "I'll be eighteen soon," I said, "but I'm ready now."

THROWING AWAY THE OAR

15

I was taken to Kiel by train with written orders from the officer in Delfzijl explaining that I knew boats, was water-smart, and would be valuable to the Kriegsmarine, the German navy. The train heading across Germany stopped every ten or twenty kilometers and had to ease over the repaired sections of railroad that had been bombed, or pass through some check station, where cars were added or taken off. Each station was full of soldiers, thousands of them. The world was flooded with soldiers.

There were several officers on the train who were responsible for me and the other new recruits. The train ride took us through dense forest areas, a defense line with cement pillboxes for machine-gun nests, small towns that bore the scars of bombs cut through their cores, and rows of factories that had been covered by mesh tents and blacked-out windows. The whole country worked toward the war effort and on the train ride, I looked out at the German countryside and wondered why they needed more territory. Wasn't this sprawling place enough?

In Kiel the officers on the train led me to a set of buses in the parking lot with more young men. It was all eerily similar to the movement of boys at the youth camp.

The buses took us to the naval training base north of the city. The base had a large open field, rows of barracks and office buildings, and a port with ships and several U-boats docked inside the break wall. The U-boats were identical to the one Uncle Martin had sunk. The one I helped sink. When the buses unloaded, all the new recruits lined up on the open field. Soldiers organized us in rows and we dropped our bags at our feet and stood straight with our arms at our sides. Like being at the shore during camp years before, I wondered what brought all these boys here, what faith or failure had delivered them.

An officer wearing a long leather jacket that smelled of pipe tobacco marched up and down the lines inspecting everyone. Though he was well into his sixties, he still had the firm build of a laborer. His thinning silver hair was cut close and combed slick to his head. Tong marks dented his skull, each a shadowed crease above his ears where the forceps yanked him into the world. Medallions hung off his pressed uniform, which looked like it restrained him from swinging an axe, or tossing concrete blocks from pile to pile and other motions befitting his build. In the full daylight, his smoky blue eyes pinched at the corners and sharpened his direct gaze. His presence unnerved me from the start, and perhaps that was how he commanded such attention.

"I am Lieutenant-Major Erich Oldif, commander of Kiel Training Station, and you are Crew X-41B." His Adam's apple jumped up and down in his throat as he spoke. "You will be trained in body, mind, and spirit in order to make your proper contributions to your Fatherland. Your time has come, so be proud of who you are and where you're from." As he spoke, a soft purple vein wobbled on his forehead and wormed into his right dent.

Major Oldif's officers called out our names and led us to a supplies building, where we were issued uniforms and identification books, then shown to our bunks. The bunks were long tent houses with wood-burning stoves at each end. The forty bunks each had a wooden chest at the foot of it.

The blue service suit we were given contained a jacket, a pair of trousers, a white and blue shirt, a shirt collar with three stripes, a silk neckerchief, gray gloves, lace-up black boots, and a cap. The men around me put on the neckerchief, as well as golden badges, which signified rank and went on the left shoulder. The uniform was similar to that of the men in the U-boat Uncle Martin and I had destroyed. I could see those men again, their shadow forms waiting in the dark; I knew what they never saw coming.

For our first three weeks in Kiel, we recruits were put through basic military training, calisthenics, small arms and rifle work, first aid, and land strategies. It all seemed so familiar. In that short intense time of training, there was no time to dwell on crushing loss after loss, which is what I needed.

The major showed up throughout the day and shouted at the training officers and my group. The dents in his head flushed with the reddish purple flow of blood. We were awakened at five in the morning, marched and run around all day, and fed twice. My weight whittled until I became a thin rope of muscle, hard hands, and mean, knobby elbows. Despite my outer toughness and the growing inner swamp of anger fueling me, I was terrified of the major. When he decided to ride us harder, or call me specifically a "puny bitch of a man" or "Dutch dog," I tried to hold his gaze but I always found myself blinking uncontrollably.

"You stank-filled gut snake. Hold your weapon higher. Tuck in your shirt. Kick your heel up higher when you march. Fall in line—move." The odor of tobacco drifted from his clothes.

"Did you know that the Dutch language is a disease of the throat? All those phlegmy words," the major said so everyone around could hear.

"Do you hear me?"

"Yes, Major."

"I can't hear you."

"*Yes. Major,*" I screamed.

His bladed face was as lined as an autumn leaf. Loose skin around his jowls gave him a second chin that hung down like a shriveled turkey neck.

The major smoked long cigarettes and flicked the stumps, which arched like smoking orange bugs, into the snow. Burnt butts littered the training grounds, and there was a special detail to make rounds and clean them up. At the back part of the grounds, there were bullet-riddled barrels used for target practice. The major walked behind us as we fired. If he felt he needed to, he'd bend down next to us and instruct us how to hold the stock of the rifle taut against our shoulders to steady the shot, or how to spray the muzzle of a machine gun back and forth to level a target.

———

During my fourth week of training, I walked into my barracks at the end of the day and saw a tall soldier sitting on my bunk.

"Excuse me," I said.

"Oh," the man said. Then he looked at me for a long moment. He had a gap in his wide front teeth, and wore an ensign's uniform like me but with more stripes on his shoulders. "I heard Major Oldif barking at some 'Dutch dog' on the parade grounds today, and I thought you looked familiar. I looked up the names of the recruits and saw my old charioteer's name there."

"Pauwel," I said. His words somehow transformed the unknown features of his face into my old friend with those dark, exotic eyes, and square teeth. He was lean, and had no traces of the baby fat that hung off him several years before. He had grown over a quarter meter and stood with a confidence that seemed like a new coat on him.

"What, you don't remember standing on my back?"

"I'm sorry, I didn't expect to know anyone here."

"Well, neither did I, but here we are. Good to see you, Jacob. How's your brother?"

I sat on the bunk next to Pauwel. I let my arms rest on my knees and my head drop between my legs. Seeing someone I knew before I lost my family and then thinking of Edwin was too much. Winged sorrow sliced through my chest. "He went missing a few years ago."

"Wait, what?" He went silent for a moment. "I'm sorry," he said.

"Ludo?" he asked.

I shook my head and shrugged my shoulders.

Already, I could tell that my memory would no longer be a solid picture but a mosaic. Edwin biking down Junfanger Street. The sun ablaze in Hilda's hair as she walked the strand at Einflound Beach. Ludo lobbing a lightbulb through the trees. The long strides of my father across the cobbles of market square. My mother's soft palms bedding down the pixies in her tulip bed. My uncle pulling up nets from the Mulway shoals. The memories of each of them came easily, but when I let up, each image was an origami bird lifted up to a strong wind.

After that first month, my training shifted from mostly physical to classroom work. Between lectures, Pauwel joined me for meals in the dining hall if he was not out on a training trip or sea trials. The dining hall was a long wooden building covered in the red and black Nazi flags. A mess line separated the kitchen from the rows of tables and folding chairs. It smelled like boiled cabbage and mud dragged in from an army of boots. When the room was full of ensigns, wearing the same clothes and all eating the same food, there was a current of a common goal that moved everyone, our training was brought about with an unquestioned intensity. Several nights during those first few weeks, we assembled in the dining hall for speeches and patriotic singing. Afterward we sang the songs we wanted, and the men started up with their own chorus of the "Lili Marlene" song, which had been playing on the Radio Belgrade station in the bunkhouses. We all sang together:

> Underneath the lantern, by the barrack gate,
> Darling I remember the way you used to wait.
> 'Twas there that you whispered tenderly,
> That you loved me, you'd always be,
> My Lili of the lamplight, my own Lili Marlene.

There was a three-day artillery school, and a twenty-hour course in submarine subjects covering the fundamentals of positive and negative floatation, how to blow and fill the ballast tanks, use of the horizontal rudder, bow fins, diesel engines, and storage batteries. We followed this with training patrols on small minesweepers and U-boats. Tactical instruction on torpedo firing was followed by antisubmarine-warfare lectures and a day spent in a deep-sided, aboveground pool training in the use of escape apparatus to get out of sinking submarines. This expertise explained why Uncle Martin circled the sunken U-boat with a spotlight and a gun in his hands. In the pool we practiced with valves and equalizing pressures, and then moved on to sea survival: how to keep afloat if adrift, and then deal with hypothermia.

I was good at remembering everything and thought, This could be what I become, what I am meant to be—a soldier, a sailor.

After the basics of seafaring, Major Oldif picked me along with several other ensigns to do another round of training. "Our success depends on stealth," he kept saying. And, "The U-boat is the most successful conveyor of torpedoes." The main point of the second round was to learn underwater maneuvering. First, we learned the principles on a submerged steering trainer, which led us to go out in real boats. For a while it felt like days swirled into each other, and I'd been smothered by a giant bomb of information. I liked how busy they kept me, as whenever there was downtime, my mind would get caught on the same loop of broken memories. There were days I wouldn't think of anyone by sheer act of will, but then I'd touch the loose cloth of a curtain or smell the hint of crushed garlic in the air, and it was as if I was standing in the living room of my childhood home, and then I'd have to experience everyone I loved disappearing once more.

The few hours at night I did sleep were spent dodging those images or crawling from my bunk and walking around the base. There were mandatory blackouts at night. Everything was dark. I wished the war would be over and there could be lights burning again, as many as could be made. Lights meant for reading and prayers and families, and the last moments of night before sleep. My father, a good man, could come back to his factory and continue to light Europe and spin thousands of stories under that light.

One night, on a walk with Pauwel, we moved among the shadowy figures of guards on their rounds, the menacing fingers of searchlights snapped on and sliced up the great inky blackness of the sky. We watched as a bomber was caught in a cone of light and flack fire opened up all around it. The tail burst apart and the nose of the plane dipped, and its fiery, orange descent streaked across the air. I thought of Herbert Yarborough, screaming through a spinning terror of a free fall. Three parachutes blossomed white beneath the flame, but they disappeared in the darkness soon after deploying.

"What unlucky bastards," Pauwel said.

We kept walking around the compound and a feral little dog came running up to us. When I bent down to pet it, Pauwel stepped back and said, "Don't touch that. It's filthy."

"You don't like dogs?" I asked, petting the little brindle mutt on its matted fur. I missed Fergus very much.

"I hate dogs," Pauwel said.

"Why, look at this guy, he's friendly." The dog had flipped on its back and clawed the air to get me to pet its stomach.

"I never told you my dog story?" Pauwel asked.

"No."

"When I was a boy, before we went to camp together, my father had this hunting dog he loved, a big rough springer mix. He wanted to have this dog forever, so he got a female for them to have puppies. When the dog gave birth, she kept sitting on the puppies like a chicken and suffocating them. We tried to keep her away from them, and had to stand guard while the puppies nursed. When it was my turn to watch in the garage, I lay down next to the little nest we made them and put my head on a big sack of fresh sawdust and fell asleep. When I woke, the mom was sitting on the last of the pups. A little paw stuck out from under her. The four other pups were all motionless on the ground. I stayed there for a long time before someone came and checked on me. They found me staring at that dog sitting on its dead pup beside the other dead ones.

"'Did you just keep watch?' my father had asked, looking at me like I was ill in the head. I'll carry that look like a disease the rest of my life. It's a shame I'll always feel."

I didn't say anything to Pauwel then, but his story left a deep impression on me. Not the story of the dogs, exactly, but how he could speak openly about something that made him feel low and weak. His story was a gift to me, a model for release I knew I'd someday need to follow.

During training Major Oldif kept telling my troop that they had special missions for us. We kept practicing steering a straight course under known conditions and with difficulties, overcoming trim-distribution problems, which eventually led to diving maneuvers. Once we had demonstrated the basics of those operations, we took a basic course in hands-on underwater maneuvering.

At dinner, Pauwel and I shared what we learned and ate mush and potatoes. Pauwel had been on the same track, but with the prior recruit class. He was also told there was some special mission awaiting them.

In the morning, general boat knowledge training began with technical motor and engine skills. We started with training diagrams, and charts, then by lunch moved on to cutaway models, and by dinner we worked in a factory on full engines, which we were tasked with diagnosing and repairing. At the far end of the factory, laborers were working with sheet metal at drill presses, engine lathes, milling machines, and grinding wheels.

The next day we studied navigational charts, currents, and then tide charts for the North Sea and the Atlantic Ocean. Each map was similar to Uncle Martin's except larger, and less creased.

"We will make several runs in these ships, then you will all be transferred to a naval base in La Rochelle, France."

We had a few-hour course in ship identification, simple navigation, and the absolute basics in training for meteorology, astronomical navigation, and flag and light signaling. The information was thrown repeatedly at us as we were needed; every last body was needed for something.

"My head is going to explode," Pauwel told me. He didn't often talk about details from home life, nor did we talk about our early camp days. We discussed what we had learned and tried to help each other through all the information. We rehashed the language we had been fed in the classes, speaking of enemy warships and merchant marine vessels by acronym names and based on tonnage. The language was cold. It was all the operational terms that dealt with machinery, and that is how we thought of it, as we went through a flip chart to identify the kinds of ships at sea and the flags they flew. It was all only metal— all machinery—nothing animate.

On the morning of February 24, Pauwel's and my entire cadet classes transferred by bus farther north of Kiel, to a small port camp along the water.

Us ensigns marched off the buses into the port compound. The tents had mesh over them, and anything that could let out light was blacked out or had a cover over it so it could go dark in case of air raids. We marched into a small meeting tent, where we waited for further instructions. We sat in silence for several moments until Major Oldif came and stood in front of us.

"It is because of your extra efforts and abilities that you have been selected for this assignment. We are about to launch a new weapon that you will each be in charge of. You are bestowed with the opportunity to turn the tide of the war at sea." He held up his pointer finger and tapped it into the dent at his temple. Then he nodded to several soldiers who had come into the tent with him. Each soldier had a box and started handing out folders from the box to everyone sitting down. Inside my folder was a diagram of a miniature submarine.

"What you have in front of you is the layout of our new model of midget submarine, the 'Negro.' They are one-person vessels capable of delivering one torpedo strike, and you will be our first wave of captains."

Major Oldif went through the folder with us. Then he walked us all across the compound to a warehouse. Inside there were several Negro subs propped up on large cast-iron sawhorses. For the rest of the day, engineers described the subs, their purpose, and their capabilities.

The following morning we met at the pier where groups of five were assigned to work with one of the subs, which was already in the water. The Negro sub was nicknamed "Human Torpedo," and was nine meters long, displaced five tons of water, and had both an electric motor and a gas engine that gave it a top speed of twelve knots. The entire thing was the same shape and size of the torpedo latched underneath it. The only visible difference between the two was the glass dome of the cockpit. In the cockpit of the sub, the waterline was at my shoulders, and the glass cover over my head was tinted black to decrease the reflection.

"Grab that seat with your asshole," one of the engineers told me, "and focus on these controls and gauges here."

Space onboard was limited to the basic equipment: a tiny cockpit, the life support systems, fuel, the propulsion system and the equipment needed to run it. When it was my turn to take the Negro out for my first pilot run in the harbor, it was uncomfortable being in such a confined space. My legs were too long. They were growing into my father's legs. The iron walls adjusting to the pressure of the water let out soft groans that rose up through my bones. My knees barely slipped under the steering column, but there was enough room behind the seat for extra gear. The tube felt like a coffin that was ready to be pounded into the ground or to sink to the sea floor, holding me there until nothing of who I was remained. By the end of the first full run of test trips, many of the crew got sick from the waves and vomited in the bilges. The hatches couldn't be conveniently opened while under way at sea so they had to steer with their own foul odor doubling their nausea. On the third day, one of the Negro subs floated out of the harbor and by the time it was towed back to shore the ensign inside was dead. It wasn't until later that night that the engineers figured out carbon monoxide poisoning had caused the drowsiness and nausea and the death of the lone sailor.

"I hate those things," Pauwel whispered across the dinner table to me. "I'm claustrophobic in them, and the visibility is shit. I feel like a lab rat."

At the end of the first week of training with the midget subs, our forty-nine-member crew was put on a low-fiber diet and issued food tablets for twenty-four hours and then energy tablets for the duration of our time before shipping out, to prevent us from needing to use the bathroom on our deployments.

"Due to lack of toilet facilities, a regular diet would cause you extreme discomfort," Major Oldif told us.

As the major gave us our first orders, Pauwel leaned over to me with the diet pills in his hand and whispered, "Do you feel like a rat now?"

16

In the mini-submarine at night, skirting along the black edge of the world, the thinnest cloud covering created a perfect inky darkness that rolled in and away with the waves. I forgot about my old life. Being in the submarine, it was as if I had no past. My life simply started as a sailor, and that sufficed. In the open water during training exercises, I thought about throttle levers and current strengths, and never about what life was like before coming to Kiel. Being on the water was an empty slate.

When my fuel levels and time chart told me it was time to return to the base at Kiel, I turned the Negro back to shore. At the base, the Negros sat moored side by side along the pier, like giant cast-iron water slugs.

Major Oldif's fierce eyes moved from the boats to me walking down the pier. His pupils seemed to grow and his brow furrowed. He put his head down and read something on his clipboard and walked toward me, moving to the dock as if feeling his way with a pair of antennae.

"Ensign Koopman," he said, "your training run went well?"

"Yes, sir."

"Good. You keep this up and you may be a credit to the Dutch."

"Thank you, sir."

Another Negro was docking, and after the sailors roped it off, I saw it was Pauwel's sub.

"It's hotter than a snake's asshole in here," Pauwel said from the seat of his boat. He was coated in sweat and his face was drained of color, but he bit off a short smile and pushed the glass dome open higher so he could get out.

"Good god, I hate that thing," he said to me as we walked down the pier. "Those are going to be the end of us."

After our training exercises, which consisted of taking our subs out for a cruise of the harbor where we stayed on the surface, and then another that included a brief submersion, the Negros were loaded onto a battleship by a flat crane mounted on a hopper barge. Major Oldif had given us our orders.

"Our entire unit will load the ship on March fourteenth. We will sail for two days beyond the German naval blockade to the open Atlantic. There you will be released to hunt for live targets."

During that two-day cruise I saw what Uncle Martin had been talking about with the heavy traffic of German naval ships arching across the ocean, sealing in most of northern Europe.

We were allowed out on deck at night while the ship was sailing with all its running lights off. No one was allowed to smoke on the decks at night. Almost every hour planes could be heard crossing overhead. Both British B-17 and Grumman P-65's, and German Ju 88s and Dornier Do 177s lobbed bombs at one another. Then came the lone whine of long-range Messerschmitt reconnaissance planes thrumming through the dark sky. On March 16, when the battleship we were on was due south of Iceland, we were given our orders by

Major Oldif. Each Negro pilot was to push off from the ship in his assigned direction and engage any Allied vessel, either navy or merchant. The battleship would do a wide circle, dropping off Negro subs at a prearranged dot on the ocean map close to shipping lanes. Each sub would sail from its drop-off point and return to that spot twenty hours later, where the battleship would collect it on its second circle.

"Timing and precision will be the measure of success for this mission," Major Oldif said. "This mission is part of a large-scale Atlantic attack force beginning tonight. Do your country and your Führer proud."

With that we were ushered to the holding bay. Pauwel drummed at his hips with his open hands, hammering out some wild beat. When he shook my hand, his eyes were wide with fear of the unknown and he said, "I hope to see you again."

Seven subs launched from the cargo bay door of the battleship before Pauwel went. Ten more subs deployed before it was my turn.

"Ready, Dutchman?" Major Oldif asked.

"Yes, sir," I said. The sailors around my sub closed the glass cockpit case, clicked it shut, and looked down at me through the little half-bubble. One of the sailors held up his hand to me with his fingers splayed. Then he tucked in his thumb, then his pointer finger, and then the next until his pinkie wrapped into his fist, and with that they pushed my Negro down a sliding ramp out the cargo hold into the sea.

The nose submerged and then scooped upward to right itself. The small chop of the waves rolled the Negro from side to side, until I hit the ignition and the hum of the motor growled to life. The engine rattled the whole sub and the torpedo connected beneath. A wave from the wake of the battleship rolled over the glass and the white foam rolled off.

Panic ran through me as the ship sailed away, leaving me in my tube in the middle of the vast ocean. That night a blue haze slid from the sky. I steered my boat on its designated course and then focused on the sliver of moon to calm my nerves. I breathed in the moonlight. My father had told me and my brother to "breathe in the moonlight" when we were younger and lay scared of the dark in our beds. *"Breathe the moonlight into your lungs, let it beat through your veins, fill your heart like a lightbulb, then exhale it and send it all the way back. That's how you become one with the night and stop being afraid of it."*

But there in the sub, breathing deep in the hold, I only tasted burning diesel and the heartburn bile that the food supplement pills had left. The silver light on the endless dark water scared the living hell out of me. It was the first real emotion I'd felt since leaving my mother on the wheelhouse deck of the *Lighthouse Lady*. I'd sealed up that part, the feeling part. Now, whatever cord that had run so taut between my mind and my heart tore loose. There in the hold, I focused on the chart to quell my rising fear.

My chart had me follow a northwest track to the southern end of Iceland for several hours. In the mini-sub, my thighs itched, my legs were sore from the vibrations, and being crammed in upright made each link of my spine feel welded together. After several hours, everything in me ached to be out of that machine and a newly formed claustrophobia seized me. Where the clouds broke, a wide swath of stars above poured through. Where the cloud cover was dense and hid everything, I felt like the last living person on earth.

I cruised on course for five hours without seeing anything. Then, in the distance, something shifted in the dark. Through my lenses, the small halos of light beneath the running light covers of a large ship slipped past. The ship had a conning tower and large guns mounted on the fore and aft decks. The flags were dark but the white paint trim along the bow told me it was an Allied troop transport vessel. A British light cruiser of the Aurora class. It was sleek and graceful, low to the water and slow as it cut through the swell. I marked my exact position on the chart and deviated my course forty-two degrees to face ahead of it. The ship didn't have spotlights on so I stayed on the surface to close the gap faster. Within ten minutes I was five hundred meters away and could make out the transom, stern, antenna mast, funnel, and the ship's boats.

I wish to god I had another story to tell—but I have only this one.

I fired.

I led my shot ahead of the ship to hit aft of the centerline at its fuel tanks. The torpedo disengaged from the hull, its propeller roiled up the water as it dug forward and made a tunnel of white bubbles for about fifty meters before it disappeared. For a moment, just as the weapon released, I felt an overwhelming mixture of exhilaration and power.

Fifty-six seconds later by my watch, a volcanic blast of water leapt up from the ocean. The ship flinched like a wounded creature. An explosion from the ribbed framework of the ship and the long waterline of the vessel bent off the surface and slammed back down. The concussion of the blast rippled through the water and wobbled the jelly between my bones. The echo rocked my sub in waves.

The hit broke the ship's back, and it heeled to starboard. A large fire billowed out of the hull even as the hole the torpedo created flooded with seawater. The shot hit right at the watertight doors separating the middle and aft sections at the fuel tanks.

Watchmen shot white incendiary flares off the sides, which flew up and glowed on the placid water. The reflection pierced the darkness and I breathed in the light. For a moment I was calm inside the hull of the Negro. But the glass top of my fuselage reflected the flash and the ping of a watchman's gunfire pierced the bow of the Negro.

My boat was shot at once more before the whole aft of the British ship exploded into flame, and the top decks became brilliantly illuminated by a deep orange glow. Fire rose up into the air in a giant column. The starboard-leaning burning section of the aft tilted toward the waterline at an impossible angle. The middle and bow of the ship cruised forward, both sections intact but no longer connected. In the eerie light of the flares and orange glow of the flame, the ship's conning tower leaned down to the sea, which pushed its bow into the sky. Water around the tower bubbled up, drinking the ship down, gulping up its side until it vanished, pushed under by the upright and sinking bow. There was a large white churning of water after the bow sank.

The aft of the ship was still a billowing tower of black smoke and flame and in the distance, the crew who made it up to the deck leapt off the sides into the burning water below them. One of the jumpers was on fire. His arms and legs kicked at the air to shake the flames loose as he plummeted toward the waterline.

The shadows of burning men jumping from what I had convinced myself was only machinery, tonnage, and supplies seared hot and terrible into my mind.

When the aft tilted forward into the sea, the last of the white flares dropped to the water. Deck by deck the flaming ship's aft half-sank, leaving the wide gas spill burning on the surface.

My mind took in every detail like a camera taking hundreds of shots per second, all of which settled at the stem of my head, deep in my snake brain. I imagined being onboard, iron sheets squealing as they unhinged. Rivets wrenched loose. Overheads in the passageways sucked down by the blast of heat, and the mêlée of movement of all the sailors running into the smoke filling the holds with clotted air. Charred armament. The sibilant wheeze of air pumping from the bilges. The gunmetal gray world buckling in around them. All those men billeted there. The bunk room now a bellows. Warping. The dizzying truth of what was to come. The vitals of the ship gutted by fire. Paint boiling off the bulkheads.

These flecks of images sliced beneath my skin. There was no returning to who I was before. There was no being someone who did not take that shot again. I was now something different. Those images would never be dislodged.

I steered the Negro to pass through the wake of the troop carrier to avoid any of the wreckage. That's when a yellow dog swam by me. It barked, and barked, and barked, and the sound of it filled the capsule of my submarine. The dog swam away from the burning surface of this ship, farther from any direction where there could possibly be land. It swam and barked, moving deeper into the ocean. This was something I had not prepared for. The cold language of class, of ship, and of tonnage made it all sound like a game, and removed any talk of people and their lives. I'd been trained to sink floating sections of warehouses and had done so. But the sound of the dog barking, barking like Fergus, barking until the cold pulled it under, coupled in my brain with the images of the burning man jumping into the sea.

A garbled swishing rose in my stomach, then a familiar stabbing pain. Wet heaving noises croaked up from between my ribs. Yellow bile splattered against my lap and ran off in runnels of spew down my thighs. After recovering, I turned the Negro around and set my course for the German battleship's rendezvous point. I used my neckerchief to clean vomit from my lap, and where it soaked into my jumpsuit down my leg. All the thoughts in my head dissolved into something dark and grainy, and my bowels felt like they were on the verge of collapse.

I lit a cork with a match to mask the smell of the sour bilge.

Heading back to the meeting point with the German battleship, I retraced my exact movements so as not to make the slightest calculation error that might send me off course into the middle of the ocean. It took me six hours to get back, working against the current. By then it was well past sunup, when the sky opened and I hoped that any plane that saw me would mistake me for an algae patch, driftwood, a naiad, the back of a rippling wave. At 0800 hours, I was at the correct meeting point at the meeting time, but the battleship still had not appeared. By 0900 hours my sub was almost out of fuel. I cut the engines and let myself drift, then restarted and worked my way back to the meeting point. With each passing minute came the terror of being in the wrong spot. I checked and rechecked my calculations. As I waited, a profound regret for sinking the ship built up in me, and I realized that it would have been a worthy punishment to be abandoned for such a sin.

Now, I think, perhaps I *was* cast off.

Then at 1000 hours, with aprons of bright white clouds bordering the sky, the battleship steamed over the horizon toward me with the white waterline pulsing where the bow turned up the swells. It was broad daylight now, a poor time for any motion in these waters, but the ship gave me such a lift of hope. I'd managed to stay alive. A man on the bow used signal flags to communicate with me, but I did not understand what he was trying to say.

When the ship was alongside, they lowered a sailor on a cargo line by crane. When the sailor stood on the bow of my submarine, he raised his hand and saluted me. His body looked like a statue riding on the swells. Then he tied a line off to the bow that the crane pulled into the open cargo bay door, where it was hooked up to more lines and winched aboard. In the cargo bay there were only three other Negro subs. I'd been the nineteenth to launch, so there should have been eighteen boats. The three Negros in the hold had their torpedoes still adhered to the bottom. Crew members unlatched my cockpit cover and pushed it up.

"Ensign Koopman," Major Oldif said. "Where is your torpedo?"

"I fired it, sir."

"Did you make contact?"

"Yes, sir."

"With what?"

"A Class 8 armed troop carrier, sir."

"Yes. Yes. Yes. You're the one then. We had radio transmission from the ship that went down. That was you. God damn it, good job, Dutchman." Major Oldif reached into the sub and squeezed my shoulder and gave it a shake. I wanted to hug him for touching me, for bringing me away from the endless drift. Then he looked at me and noticed the vomit on my clothes. He pulled his hand off my shoulder and wiped it on the leg of his trousers. "Sailors, get this man out of here. He's a goddamn hero, help him up and take him to the medics." They lifted me out of the submarine. A heavy-caliber bullet had punctured the forward planking. My legs were so stiff they locked up on me and the men had to drag me to the medic.

"Why are there only three boats?"

"We'll find more," the sailor said.

In the medic's office, Pauwel was lying on a cot and mumbling to himself, thrashing around under a sheet.

"What's wrong with him?"

"CO poisoning," the medic said.

Pauwel turned toward me and squinted. "Thank god it's you. Thank god."

The medic helped me out of my jumpsuit. On the cot he started checking all my vital signs. He squeezed the black egg of the blood pressure cuff, which inhaled tighter around my arm. There were two other ensigns in the bunks next to Pauwel. One had his hands in a prayer tepee covering his face and the other was asleep on his side with a blanket over his head. After the medic checked me, he told me to go get something to eat and get back to my bunk.

"Pauwel. Are you okay?"

"I will be."

"What happened?"

"There'll be time for all that," the medic said. "Go get something to eat."

Pauwel nodded his head and waved me away. "I'm fine."

I was starving, and I got myself a meal. I took a slice of sausage for Pauwel and brought it to the outer deck of the vessel to watch the rest of the Negros getting picked up. The sun was full and rising to the middle of the sky. The open water all around the ship was calm in that dull blue-glossed-brown color. In the distance was a glint of steel, the next Negro to be retrieved. When we got closer what I thought was the glass cockpit of the fuselage I saw to be the long cylinder of the torpedo. The Negro was upside down. When the crane hooked the boat up, I peered over the deck to see them hook enough lines to flip the boat right-side-up. When they did the slumped head of the pilot slapped against the glass. When the upturned Negro was pulled in, the ship picked up its speed to meet the next vessel, which was not there. We slowed for a moment and then moved along to the next.

"All day, like this," a watchman standing by the 16mm guns said. "All day these subs aren't there." The man wore a leather jacket and a fur hat with long ear flaps cinched tight by a thin cord tied in a bow under his chin. His fur collar was pulled up high over his neck.

The rest of the afternoon the ship picked up seven more Negros. Two had dead pilots from CO poisoning. One of the Negro pilots poured yellow dye into the sea to make himself more visible. It was only to be used if we had drifted off too far, out of reach of the support vessel. The pilot must have been frightened out there waiting for the missing ship. He must have deployed the yellow dye, which in turn hailed an Allied plane out of the sky that strafed it with machine-gun fire. A stripe of fighter plane bullets ran up the length of it and had shattered the pilot's lap, chest, and head. The next stop had a loosening slick of yellow without a sign of a sub. That made eleven survivors from the forty-nine that had set out. When the battleship spent the rest of the day doing another circle to check for lost boats, I went back to the medic's office to sit with Pauwel.

He opened his eyes and looked at me. "If I'm dead, you're one ugly angel."

In the medic's office the pilots discussed what happened to the rest of our rank. Some pilots were lucky, they decided, as they probably fell asleep through strain or lack of oxygen under their tiny glass domes. The vessels had been tested for making headway against the current so that the sub could go out on the ebb tide and return home on the flood, but in the open waters, some of the boats would have made no progress and, sooner or later, would be lost. All of us in the medic's office who had returned had not submerged our ships. We figured some that had submerged never came up. Others may have fired their torpedoes but the clasps failed and they were carried along on the backs of their own bombs. We each sat in our own bunks and talked of the ways the lost men did not come back.

"I thought they figured out the CO problems."

"Apparently not."

"What about the ones that are left out there?"

"They're smart. They'll send a recon plane out for them."

"Yeah, but the recon plane will probably make sure they sink so that no one else gets their hands on them." This made everyone quiet for a while.

Then one of the pilots confessed. "I didn't go anywhere. I circled the same spot over and over." He gave us a nervous smile and kept rubbing the palm of his hand over his chin so his fingers squeezed into his cheek. Then he shook it off as if it were a joke.

"Didn't they want to know what happened?" I asked.

"I told them it was a technical fault and that I had to turn back early."

None of us questioned why he had done this as on the battleship's third loop around, no more Negros were found.

On the final evening of the two-day trip back to Kiel, Major Oldif sent a sailor to bring me to the bridge. In the conning tower, the major paced back and forth, and looked out at the water. Low growls of static trundled from the radio console. A machine beeped every twenty seconds. Soft. Steady. I counted to twenty. To twenty. To twenty, until Major Oldif turned and waved me forward.

"Ah, Ensign Koopman. Good, good, come in. Are you feeling okay?"

"Yes, sir."

"Good, that's good. I want to congratulate you, son. You made this mission a great success. That ship you sunk was a big victory for us.

Do you know how much manpower and effort it would be to deal with those soldiers and supplies once they landed in Europe? Every ship we take down is the equivalent of a land battle won. And you won a big one for us, ensign."

"But the lost subs, sir."

"Yes, a shame, but you're not seeing the big picture. We tested the Negros and they work. They will work better running along the shores. When the Allies mount an invasion force, we now know we have these weapons to use against them. Now, maybe we can get you some publicity for your success, and we can use that to round up some more fine Dutch to come captain for us."

"Yes, sir," I said, feeling sick all over again, knowing this meant the pilots who spent the night circling the same spot of ocean would have to go out again. This would become a tactic now. The major made to squeeze my shoulder, but maybe the memory of seeing me covered in vomit made him stop short.

17

The morning after the battleship returned and disembarked at the training center in Kiel, Major Oldif ordered me to report to his office in my full dress uniform. A film of dust coated the lamp on his desk but there was an oyster blue porcelain vase with three red tulips that looked fresh and new. A man with a camera had draped a dark sheet against the major's office wall.

"Stand here, please, ensign," Major Oldif said, pointing to the front of the sheet. "Take one of just him first."

The photographer, who had a thick, scissor-trimmed beard, moved in closer to me and told me to stand straight and look at the camera, then he took a picture. The shutter clicked. Then clicked again. Each time the camera flashed, I hoped it would bleach out my skin, blot out part of me so the images would eventually show some unidentifiable, nondescript figure. "Good, now take one of us." Major Oldif stepped next to me, and we shook hands for the next picture.

"Son, I've arranged for you to receive the Knight's Cross for your work on our mission. It's the highest honor you can receive. We're going to make a great example out of you, ensign. A Dutch boy does good for the German navy. We'll put it in the papers to sign up more of your countrymen."

"The papers, sir?"

"You're a hero. We're going to treat you like one." Major Oldif patted me on the back and led me out of his office. "You keep up your good work."

I had been up all night thinking of the yellow dog in the water. Hearing it barking. Barking. Barking.

"Yes, sir," I said.

I held back from revealing any of my hesitation. This was something I was becoming an expert at. Still deep down, I doubted everything. And my voice, *that* voice, my real voice that had not breached the walls of meekness, fear, rancor, and subordination I had boxed myself in with, was still incapable of saying what I really felt then. Weak. Insignificant. It was hard to put into words that smallness, but it made me hate myself.

I had another checkup with the medic that morning and then a mission debriefing after that. At the briefing, Pauwel and I and the other remaining crew members joined in a meeting with a new wave of recruits. Major Oldif stood in front of us and told them all about our previous mission with the Negros. He said it was a great success and what we learned had already begun being implemented by the engineers into upgrades. Then he had me stand, and he told everyone that I was to be awarded the Knight's Cross. Everyone in the tent clapped for me. Even Pauwel, who still looked pale despite being back on land.

The next day my picture was on the front page of the German newspaper *Der Strosstrupp*. Major Oldif was quoted praising me, the young Dutchman, as a "credit to his country, whose lead more men should follow and join the German fighting forces." It talked about the award ceremony to be held for me and mentioned how I couldn't wait to go back out and fight. It mentioned that from March 16 through the 20th, German naval forces sank twenty-seven Allied ships. "Ensign Koopman was part of our great success," Major Oldif said at the end of the article.

After we returned, Pauwel moved into my bunkhouse. He hadn't been able to sleep one night since our mission. I woke in the middle of the night to find him sitting up in his cot, his hands kneading his hair back, tapping some beat on his scalp. Each night Pauwel had been like this, and the deep bags under his eyes were getting darker by the day.

Then, because he was the longest tenured among us, Pauwel got pulled from the midget-sub training group and placed on a U-boat crew that was outbound for a seven-day trip.

"I hope I see you again," he said before loading onto the U-boat.

The ceremony was set for me to receive my award. Everyone at the base was invited into the tent. There were full steins poured from wood casks of wheat and dunkel beer. Rations of brandy. The cooks made pretzels we dipped in spicy mustard, and we had schnitzel, some of the first meat we'd eaten in a month. I wore my dress blue uniform and was called to the front of the room to stand next to Major Oldif for the ceremony. The major gave a speech about how fine a Dutchman I was and a fine example to other Dutchmen considering joining.

Who would take my lead? If Ludo was alive, as I often imagined him stumbling from the ash of the factory, would he join the Third Reich's navy because I'd shown him the path? The image of myself being a Dutch hero once the Germans won the war ran through my mind. It wasn't hard to do with the whole troop of men there to cheer me on. It was the second time in my life I was lauded by a group of Germans. My daydream lifted and dipped on the major's words. Then I looked out over the crowd of soldiers.

In the back of the room there was a man much taller than everyone else. I squinted to get a better look. He had a German naval hat with the brim low over his forehead and a German jacket with the collar popped up enough that it would have hidden the fine line of tattoo ink I knew rose over his shoulder and up his neck.

Uncle Martin looked right at me, inside of me, at the blood flowing in my veins. Tears started forming in my eyes.

"And so with no further ado, I present our highest honor and these papers of valor signed by the Führer himself, to one of our own, Ensign Jacob Koopman." Major Oldif clicked his heels together and saluted me. Then he fastened the Knight's Cross on my chest. It was a large iron cross-shaped brooch with a tree molded into the middle.

"I know. I know," Major Oldif said and patted my shoulder when he realized I was crying. Then he stepped back and raised his palm up flat to me again.

I looked down at the broad cross, hanging from a thick black and red cut of ribbon. It had small shards of diamonds studding the outer edge of it, which reflected the tent's overhead lights.

"Face them now, ensign," Major Oldif said.

Everyone else in the tent stood with their arms raised straight out and over their heads, except for Uncle Martin, whose finger pointed right at me. More fear shot through my body. What decision had I really made? Had he come to kill me? If I pointed to the back of the room and cried out that there was a traitor in our midst, could I save myself—from getting killed, from looking into my past and seeing what had been taken from me since the war began.

The medal lay flat upon my chest, opposite my heart, and hung there like a cold omen. A photographer snapped another picture. If I could have made my own headline at that moment, I would have changed the names, changed the story, changed everything.

Major Oldif led me to several photographers, who took more photos of us shaking hands. Then the major walked me through the tent, introducing me to other officers and telling them my story of downing the troop ship. All that time my uncle circled the tent, probably dropping explosives under each empty seat. Major Oldif handed me a tin cup of dark roasted coffee with whiskey in it, which warmed me on the way down but burned once it hit my stomach.

When there was a break from shaking people's hands, Major Oldif leaned into me. "You have earned the right to test our new midget submarine. It is called the 'Beaver' and should perform better than the Negro. We'll start testing in a few days."

My uncle circled the room with a noticeable limp, shifting from corner to corner opposite me. When the major retired for the night, Uncle Martin walked across the room to me. I was surprised all over again at how much he towered over me.

"I thought you may have been smart and run off to save yourself, or even been killed, but it turns out you're a German war hero now. You've got a medal there to prove it."

"It's nothing, Martin," I said, unsure of what my real identity should be.

"Quite a big hoopla for nothing." He reached out and put his hand on my shoulder. "You little shit, I had no idea where you were until I saw this." He pulled out the newspaper with the picture of my oval face staring off the page.

"Come with me," he said and hooked his hand under my elbow and led me toward the door.

In the dark lawn between the tents and barracks, Uncle Martin walked to the back portion of the camp, near a dilapidated utility shed.

When we got to the side of the shed, I stopped not wanting to walk into the shadows after my uncle.

"Are you going to kill me?" I asked.

"I wouldn't kill my family," he said. "Now come here." In the shadows, Uncle Martin stepped forward and hugged me. "You scared the Christ out of me, slipping off like that."

My head was in his chest, and I felt his chin lean onto the crown of my head. I hugged him and clutched at his back.

"I couldn't handle what we did to those men in the Ems."

"That's okay. I shouldn't have forced you like that."

"I couldn't keep doing it and I couldn't stop you. You'll die killing them like that."

"You didn't do any of that, so don't regret a thing." The shadow of the forest swayed behind him. When he let me go, I still held onto him until he stepped away from me and bent over into the bushes and pulled out a large backpack. "Here," he said, laying the large bag at my feet. "You have to get as far away from this as possible."

"What? Why?"

"I promised your mother I'd save your skinny little ass, and in this bag is how you're going to do it."

"Where would I go? Look what I'm doing here. The Germans will win, Martin, and the sooner they do, the sooner all this will end."

"That's not going to happen, Jacob. You'll be killed. I may not be meant to survive this war, and I'm okay with that, but I sure as hell don't want it destroying you too. I need you safe and alive. This family's lost enough. And that Major Oldif is using you like a piece of meat to lure other stupid Dutch kids who want to be heroes and have no idea what they're getting into. Your little fame here, Jacob, is a propaganda ploy and nothing more. You have no idea what these people really want, do you? What their Fatherland would look like?"

Uncle Martin kicked the bag at my feet. "I have papers, maps, a compass, a gun, ammunition, food, and enough money and gold, everything you need to start a new life. Now you have to make it out of Europe. Your German papers will get you far, but once you cross the Rhine, you'll need to start using all the ones in the bag. The pictures of you are from your parents' house and were pasted onto these IDs.

"I want you to get to England. I left a note with the names of several ship captains that can help you. If you find one of them, tell them who you are and catch a ship to Ottawa. There are good Dutch people there."

"You aren't coming too?"

"Jacob, my whole life has been preparing me for this. Stay and fight is what I'm supposed to do. I know this much if I know anything."

"But there's no way out, you said so yourself."

"There is for you and you have to find it. You can't see the whole picture here, but what you're mixed in with is vicious. Take this pack and leave, get out of Europe. Follow the instructions and find the men I listed. Find one of these men. They can help you once you get out of here. Your life is all that matters, not this war, not these countries, just your life. You're the last of our family, and we'll be erased if you're lost."

Martin looked down on me with his wet eyes. A large vein in his neck slipped under a blade of ink on his skin that rose above his collar.

"Don't regret what you've done. You can't. I don't. What else can you do, Jacob? You have to survive."

"Ensign," someone called to me. "You're pissing in the woods and missing your own party." Uncle Martin stepped back into the shadows and pulled the backpack with him. He propped it up behind a tree and turned back to me. I was looking at a condemned man when Uncle Martin said, "Come back later for the pack. You have to leave, Jacob, please, promise me you'll get out of here." I turned back from his shadow to the officer in the field behind me. The man staggered. He cupped a cigarette in his right palm.

"I'll be back in a second," I called to the man.

"Hurry, hurry," the man said. He swayed back and forth in the lawn and waited for me to finish peeing.

Martin stood behind the tree in front of me. I stepped forward and pretended to be finishing up. The man behind me mumbled a song to himself. My uncle nodded to me, kissed the palm of his hand and reached his arm out and cuffed the side of my head. "Get to Ottawa," he said. "You have to get to Ottawa."

"Will I see you again?" I asked.

"Meet me at that flagpole at one A.M." He pointed to the large field at the center of camp. "Be there at one."

"Ensign," the officer behind me yelled. "You're missing your party."

I turned and left my uncle in the dark woods. The officer, a man I'd never seen before, had an oily face with a scattering of dark, spiky whiskers. He threw an arm around my shoulder and started singing in a raspy falsetto as he led me back to the tent, where a gramophone now played.

Once the tent cleared out and the soldiers and officers who had gotten the most drunk stumbled off to their bunks, I snuck back to the woods and retrieved the bag. It was heavier than it looked, packed so tightly that it felt like a solid bag of bricks. I lugged it to my cot and stowed it in my locker. A couple hours later, when my few bunkmates were snoring, I opened the locker and started looking through what Uncle Martin had left me.

The first thing in the pack was a letter scrawled out in my uncle's handwriting that said,

> *You have to be the one to survive. Stay off the main roads as much as possible and use these cards to pass checkpoints if you can't find a way around. I used to work with some men who can help you once you get to Southampton in Britain, Lisbon in Portugal, or Casablanca in Morocco. In whichever port, ask around for Felix Courtier, Javier Méndez, Petrous Valspar, or Michael McCollum. Try to find these men. Wait in a safe port if you have to. If you find these men, tell them who you are.*

Inside the pack was a stack of German ID papers with my picture but different names. The pictures were from a series Martin had me take at a department store in Utrecht the year before. There were orders corresponding to each ID badge that had the person by that name for change of post and transportation. Each soldier listed was in transition from one base to another. There were more transporting papers, and huge stacks of money in different currencies. There were wads of bills: German, Dutch, Belgian, French, English, Canadian, Australian, and American. There were canned meals, matches, a Luger, and a series of maps on which Martin had written in where large German forces were and how to go around them. The suggested route ran along the northern woods of Germany, Holland, Belgium, and France, trekking west to show the nearest Allied shipping lanes, and a passage across the water.

With everything he'd given me there was enough paperwork and planning for ten evaders to slip out of the country. Whatever misplaced paperwork he had done, he had done so to procure all this. There were identity papers, passports, exit visas, and entry permits. He even had a French Legionnaire's papers that said, "Legionnaires, you ask for death and I will give it to you."

The pack had combs, a toothbrush, soap, wire cutters, and three compasses that were hidden as buttons. There were maritime maps with planned-out escape routes printed on thin silk that could be folded up and stuffed into a pocket without taking up any space. There was even a pair of special shoelaces that could be used as miniature saws to cut wires. The bag had been packed to use every last millimeter of space. There were twenty-four malted milk tablets, boiled sweets, a bar of chocolate, Benzedrine tablets, a ball of darning wool, water-purifying pills, a razor, needle, thread, fishing hook and line, a rubber water container, fifty cigarettes to smoke or barter with, and a brown tarp. The whole pack was an escape plan in jigsaw puzzle form. All I had to do was sneak off and put the pieces to work.

Uncle Martin's bag had shown what kind of man he was. His plans were so detailed that he must have been funneling supplies to escape lines and Resistance fighters like Ludo had suggested. I could see the hanged man and full mast sailing ship etched onto my uncle's skin when I shut my eyes, the marking of life and death he wore over his veins.

I lay in bed living a dozen different lives, projecting myself into a vast array of futures and then dropping one life and taking up another, each time jumping further and further from the confusion of the war.

Uncle Martin told me to get to Ottawa, no matter what. The

Dutch royal family had gone there, so if Edwin or my father were alive, they would have gone there too. The thought of them waiting out the war in Canada filled my head while I was carefully repacking the bag and putting it back in my bunk locker. But I'd also heard of German deserters who had been shot and left in the street for three days as an example. I didn't know if I had the courage for something so bold as escape.

At ten to one, I walked outside and headed to the flagpole. I didn't bring the pack because I didn't want anyone to see it. I scanned the edges of the field for the figure of my uncle to emerge or call me to him. Call me to get out of this place. The field at night felt as empty and vacuous as floating in the ocean in the Negro, waiting for the cruiser to come find me. When I was by the flagpole I heard a series of gunshots: *tat-tat-tat-tat-tat-tat-tat*. After each noise, a ship or U-boat in the harbor exploded. I dropped to the ground and looked into the trees for the muzzle flash. The shooter changed aim and fired at the camp buildings, seeking out planted explosives, which began to burst into flame. Soldiers ran into the field near me. They looked up for planes as four more buildings split open with orange flame and noise. I knew it was Uncle Martin in the camp. That was his parting shot.

In the wreckage of the camp, most of the crew and soldiers who were not injured or killed were still drunk as they tried to put out the fires. A captain found me cowering in the field and put me to work cleaning up. Had he not, I would have gotten my bag and run off then. He thought I'd passed out after the party and didn't question why I was there. I worked through the dark hours. Some soldiers talked about the air raid that had just hit us and thought one of their own had fired the gun into the sky after the planes. At a quarter past four in the morning, too tired to be of any use, I returned to my bunk to sleep.

Just before dawn, a heavy pounding sound came from the revelry field. It was a steady beating of a marching song I'd heard as a boy at camp. Now it sounded much deeper and industrial, like some large machines hammering out the rhythm. Outside the first tendrils of sunlight reached over the treetops. By the flagpole the dark shadow of a man swayed next to four, giant fifty-gallon oil drums that he swung wildly at with two long, metal rods. The rods jumped up off the tops of the oil barrels and he slammed them back down again. There were men running at the mad drummer. I recognized the outline of the bare-chested man, sweating in the cold from his wild swinging.

Two guards ran across the field. Pauwel turned to them while still pounding on the drums he'd set up in a half circle around him. The guards stopped. Pauwel was naked except for a shoulder holster that held a Luger. The guards called for him to stop, but he kept hammering. When one of the guards pulled out his own pistol, I ran over, waving my arms and telling them not to shoot.

"Pauwel."

"Jacob. I came back for this shit? Look at this place. This is shit." He pointed to the still smoldering areas of camp, then pounded on the drums again.

"Pauwel, what are you doing?" I yelled.

Pauwel looked at me with his deep black bags under his bloodshot eyes. His shoulders still worked the metal rods up and down but now more steadily, like he was echoing the ground's heartbeat.

"I'm playing in the sun," Pauwel yelled and opened his eyes crazy-wide toward the first sun rays topping the trees. "I'm going to be cleansed by the natural light."

"Easy now," one of the guards said as he walked up behind Pauwel.

Pauwel spun around. "Stay back," he yelled, and he helicoptered the rods over his head.

"Pauwel. Pauwel. Look at me," I yelled.

"Drop your weapon," the guard yelled from behind Pauwel. Something changed in Pauwel's face. He shut his eyes when the first of the sunlight cleared the trees. The warm light touched the back of my neck. The light caught the moving edges of Pauwel's metal drum rods, and then the beads of wet rust on the upturned oil drum lids. Everything for a moment was touched by light.

"Are you sleepwalking again?" I yelled to Pauwel.

Then the guard moved up closer behind him. Everyone was jittery from the explosions. Saboteurs were feared. They trained their guns on Pauwel, likely wondering if it could have been him who blew up the buildings. Pauwel must have sensed the man closing in on him, as he swung around with a rod high in the air and brought it down on the guard's head. The guard crumpled to his knees in front of Pauwel, who was about to bring his second drumstick down onto the man when the other guard fired his gun. The shot hit Pauwel's abdomen below the left side of his rib cage, ripped out his back, and popped through one of the oil cans. The raised metal drumstick fell from his hand and clanked off a drum before hitting the ground. A melted rose opened on Pauwel's back and seeped down over his buttocks as he crumbled to his side, next to the man he'd struck down.

"Stop. Don't shoot him. He's one of us." I ran to his side with my arms up and shielded him. "He's one of us."

Both men were put on stretchers and carried away. They were taken to the compound's medic, who had a long line of wounded to deal with from the explosions before he could stitch up the guard's head and spend the rest of the morning suturing Pauwel's wounds. The bullet missed all his vital organs but tore through his upper intestine.

While waiting for him to get out of surgery, I found out that his U-boat returned early because it had technical difficulties. It had submerged several hours outside of Kiel and gone west for two days when all the lights on board started to explode and pop out. "I mean all the fucking lights," a sailor told me. "It was the craziest thing. We were in the dark damn near the whole time. We had to turn back, but that took twice as long because we had to be extra-careful going about the smallest things. It was spooky. I felt a little crazy too. And the other U-boat that set out with us, we haven't heard word from them yet. There's no telling what happened to them."

Old visions of lights exploding all over Europe and shards of glass raining down on Nazi soldiers' heads flashed into my mind, and then there was my father, tall and kind and patient, opening his giant mouth to let out some new story, some soul-enriching story that would tell me who I really was and was supposed to be. But I couldn't hear the words. I tried to listen to that specter of my father floating through my head, but nothing came.

I was starting to grasp that I didn't understand this war or where I should be within it all. All the clear lines had blurred.

After Pauwel's surgery was over, they gave him a large dose of morphine. He was limp in the infirmary bed but his head kept thrashing back and forth.

"Pauwel, what happened?"

"The bubbles are in my blood. I have dark bubbles seeped into my blood," he said. His head was tilted back and rocking, smoothing out the pillow. Beads of sweat rolled off his brow and his eyes were open too wide. All pupil. It made me nervous. Later that night I held his dirt-smudged hand as he struggled to breathe. His rib cage sank when he exhaled, then he gasped, and a sucking noise rose from inside his chest. When the medic wasn't watching, I lifted his eyelid back with my thumb. The white of his eye was threaded with bloodshot veins that looked like raw red worms.

I stared at the spackled walls of the infirmary room by Pauwel's side that night, trying to understand what happened to him all those hours in the dark, and how a human being could capture the mechanical heartbeat of war with only a set of drums.

18

The Beaver was a wider version of the Negro and they said it could move faster underwater. The dock crew strapped me into the cockpit and closed the glass dome over me. Major Oldif stood on the dock with several engineers, checking off items on their clipboards, and never looked at me. The first training exercise had been fast-tracked because of the Martin's sabotage. I'd been keeping Pauwel company as he fought his way through morphine dreams and recuperated when I was yanked away to take the Beaver out for a submerged lap of the harbor, and then out to open water and back, to be sure it worked and they could push on with their production schedule.

"Hurry now. Hurry it up," Major Oldif kept saying.

It took me several hours to get to the open water, because there had been a British bomber raid hours before. German fighter planes had been sent to cut them off, which forced the bombers to lighten their load by dropping their bombs into the sea north of Kiel, and left kilometer-long strips of dead fish drifting on the surface. Fish bellies awash with gold and oil-slicked purple-silver drifted past me as the

Beaver slipped out on the ebb tide. The bow parted the fish so they fanned out in my small wake.

It looked like the sea had been poisoned along the northern shores into deeper water. All those dead fish. Almost everyone in Europe was starving and here were so many dead fish. I'd heard talk of what the Germans were doing to Jews, how the eastern front was erupting and the western front was waiting for a giant invasion. There was talk of Japs, Turks, Brits, and Yanks, but they were all out of sight. They were allegedly fighting or ramping up to fight all over the world, spreading out, shooting one another down. Still, it was all out of sight, too big for me to see how I, in my little tube out in the ocean, fit into any of it.

Uncle Martin had been right. I saw no larger picture, and though I did not know it at the time, that is what made me so dangerous. Now, I can imagine boys from camp, like rash-necked Timothy, Garth, Lutz, and all the rest becoming small parts of a machine that would grind us to bits.

When I returned from my run in the Beaver, I reported to the medic building. After performing a test, the doctor told me I had a very bad case of stomach ulcers. I then went and sat next to Pauwel and told him about the ulcers and dead fish, even though he was still unconscious, and I didn't know if he could hear me.

I dipped bread into coffee until I was full. Eating anything had started to feel like a chore, an acidic boiling in my stomach. Perhaps it was the ulcers that gnawed me, or maybe it was the fear that Pauwel would die in front of me, or of being in a midget sub again.

The coffee in my stomach made me feel nauseated. I propped my hand up against the wall and vomited it all up into a puddle at my feet. The smell rose up in vapors.

After my running of the Beaver, the crew was ordered into one of the only remaining buildings where Major Oldif gave us a folder with our new orders inside.

"We will be transferring our operations. Those explosions in camp have made it unsafe to stay here. Tonight the Beavers will be loaded onto trucks, and you will be transported with them to the west in the morning. Your mission will be to set out, protect our shores, and engage any Allied vessels you encounter. You will have thirty-six-hour rotations in your vessel, which includes going out and coming back. We will leave at 0700 for your new base."

We were silent as the major spoke. I kept my eyes on him and nodded as he talked, but heard only scraps, as my real thoughts circled like carrion birds. When he straightened his head and looked at me, I was afraid my disgust shone through like my skull was made of old rags, thin cloth.

In my bunk that night, I took out my uncle's gear and went to the desk and spread out the escape paraphernalia, starting with the passport papers and even vouchers from my navy command unit. The navigation and tide charts layered on top of one another covered most of the desk. I marked an x on the maps where Major Oldif had planned our routes once we cleared the German naval blockade. I ran my finger over the map and found a spot where there wasn't supposed to be much German military presence along the shoreline, not far from where we were supposed to set out in the subs. I drew a new route on the map that would have me leaving from the push-out port of Hamburg, where the trucks would take us. I lay the Knight's Cross on the desk. It would be so much easier to continue following orders.

The lamplight made the Knight's Cross glow in front of me. It was something *I could be proud of for the rest of my life,* the major had told me when he handed it to me.

On one of the false passport papers there was a blank line to write who my next of kin was. My mother was dead. My father had slithered off and may very well have bled out somewhere, and the current had swallowed my brother. I could put my uncle, but there was no telling how much longer he would be alive or which side of the war effort his name would place me on. So I left the line blank.

I stuffed Herbert Yarborough's passport papers and my own Knight's Cross into the pocket of the Englishman's rolled-up flight jumpsuit and packed it into the bottom of Uncle Martin's backpack. On top of that, resting against the side zipper for easy access, was the dead German officer's Luger and the one Uncle Martin had given me with a spare clip of ammunition. I loaded my own gear and charts in a plastic watertight bag, maps of the North Sea and North Atlantic, ten days' worth of dried food and canned meat, four canteens full of water, and a bottle of energy pills before closing the pack.

When I had finished, I took Herbert Yarbrough's barter kit and walked across the compound to the medic's office. Pauwel was still unconscious. The wounds in his intestines had become infected, and his temperature had risen the day before. There was no waking him up. No getting him to come with me. I took his hand in mine and slipped the three gold rings from the barter kit around his left ring finger and tucked that hand under the covers.

"I hope to see you again," I whispered, then left the room, walked back across the compound, and waited on my cot for our departure.

In the morning, I was still exhausted from the series of events since the party that I only wanted to sleep. The line of trucks with the Beavers had been covered with mesh camouflage so the loads looked like a giant cropping of alder bushes. There were twenty-eight Beavers being transported to Hamburg where they would deploy. My sailor's duffle bag with Martin's backpack inside was stored behind the seat in the cockpit of the truck that had my sub. I rode in the truck's cab with the boy driver. He was younger than me and had a lopsided face like he'd had a bad birthing. His right eye sat lower than his left, which made his eyebrows slope toward his right ear.

We split the convoy into three so as not to attract as much attention from marauding Allied fighters intent on shooting anything that looked military.

On the outskirts of the city we passed bombed-out buildings. A bus had driven into a crater. Its back end angled out of the dirt, and I imagined it full of people driving deeper and deeper into the earth.

"A shame looking at all that, isn't it?" my driver said. "I hate looking at rubble. Can't wait to trade this hunk of wheels in for a plane to get some payback. Maybe even take up one of these odd little boats you've got back here." He lifted his hand and tapped his knuckles against the truck wall behind him. He smiled at me with those big round eyes and crooked teeth. Of all the faces I've seen since, his somehow has managed to stay in my mind, that young boy driving a truck for his country. Happy to be a small part in the machine he never asked about. He smelled of sweat, cabbage, and diesel fumes, and never stopped talking.

We passed a shot-up lorry pushed off the side of the road and a burnt-out munitions train car striped with bullet holes on its side next to the tracks.

"You hear those bastards buzzing around sometimes, but they haven't bothered me yet," the driver said. "Those guys get flak-happy after a while. It takes them the longest, but they all snap. They go mad up there and buzz around shooting whatever looks funny to them. I don't blame them. They're in a world of hurt if they get shot down. Soldiers race out to find the RAF men and tie them to the back of their motorcycles and drag them behind. The road peels them like bananas." He bounced around in his seat like he was trying to unstick each butt cheek from the leather. He hunched over the steering wheel so his back arched into his neck and his torso looked like a thick, angled stump. "Our boys who go down over England, they don't catch them like that. Some of them carry razors in the cuff of their pant legs to cut their own wrists so they won't be tortured into giving up any information. One pilot chewed through his own veins to avoid having to tell the Brits anything."

As we drove, the boy's voice washed over me until I was deaf to him, and only let little bits of what he said sink in. I was so tired. Along the road, boulders encrusted with gray-green lichen blurred past.

"You know, the snipers take you out on your third drag of a cigarette. You light it and they find you. Your second drag they scope you and let you enjoy your last breath, and on your third they blow your head off."

We passed a long row of German panzers heading east. A coal barge cut the thin fog and passed under the bridge trestles. The boy kept talking.

"I'm going to get some time off and go hunt down some of those French girls in Paris. I've heard some of the guys talking about them. How you can take them out to be with you for the night. All the guys talk about it. I swear I'll get there and go crazy. Saving my money for it now. I'll be happy as a dog with two tails."

Two hours west of Kiel, the road was bombed out and splintered trees lay across the path. The second and third waves of trucks caught up to us, and several of the drivers pulled out chain saws to eat away the wood to allow the procession of trucks to pass through. The trucks eased forward over the destroyed road.

When we reached the outpost north of Hamburg, there was a small set of tent barracks set up in the woods about a hundred meters from shore. A crane with camouflage meshing sat next to a pier. One by one the Beavers were unloaded from the trucks and tied off.

My driver patted me on the shoulder after my Beaver was put into the water. "Heil Hitler," he said, smiling at me one last time before turning his truck around and driving off.

The crew rested until nightfall in the tents, at which point we would depart. I slept and dreamed of my father telling stories of Thump-Drag.

When it was time for us to go, Major Oldif was on the pier. He patted me on the shoulder.

"You keep doing good for us, ensign. I'm proud to have you on this crew." The major stood in front of me as the dome hatch clicked shut. The engine hummed as I slipped away from the pier into the greasy water of the harbor. There were commercial liners and freighters and lesser ships docked side by side and roped together. I cruised north on the path set for me, but at the opening to the North Sea, where I was supposed to turn north by northwest, I repositioned and went due west along the coast.

The waves were one- and two-foot swells as the Beaver cruised along the surface with no running lights. In the dark the midget sub motored through the night. To avoid being sighted by any airplanes at first light or spotters on land, I submerged the Beaver, diving so the nose plunged under, but kept it running five feet under the surface to pop back up any time if I needed to.

By sunset, after cruising through the day at five knots, having run 216 kilometers from the mouth of the Elbe in Hamburg, I calculated my position and steered southwest toward the little *x* on my map that should have been a long stretch of forested land without any large military camps west of Bremerhaven in Germany.

Several hundred meters offshore, when there was no sign of life, I aimed the bow of the Beaver downward and out to sea, where there were no lights anywhere and fired my torpedo. The torpedo released and pulled away. The force of it pushed the Beaver backward, and that familiar roil of water carved a gopher tunnel under the surface of the ocean. I prayed my shot would find no purchase but run out of momentum and quietly sink to the sea floor.

Once the torpedo was gone there was an extra three feet of clearance under the hull. Closer to land, I unlatched the dome lock and pushed it open. The moonlight curled upward into the sky as the ship air flushed against my face. With my backpack in my lap, I increased my speed as much as it would go, and steered until the hull slammed into sand and jerked me forward, my backpack padding the impact of the Beaver slamming to a stop. With my arms threaded through the front of the backpack so it adhered to my chest, I crawled out of the cockpit onto the forward planking of the sub and jumped from the bow, straddling the two worlds at once, not on land, not at sea. Not a part of Germany, not a part of Holland. Not a sailor, not a citizen. Just a fear-filled sack stuffed with bones and gristle. My feet plunged into the water and sank into the sand. The cold water cut into my feet and shins. Alone. Terrified. I worked my way through the surf, over the dark strand of the beach. Ahead of me the dark trees swayed, and I ran toward them and the darkness and cover they offered, carrying the true credo of any life: I enter unprepared.

19

I ran through the woods until my legs went numb from the cold and gave out. I hunkered down next to a felled tree, silent in the dark, listening for any signs of life coming to investigate my shadow sprinting for land. My shivering was uncontrollable. I stripped off my jumpsuit. The dilemma of clothing was now my focus. In a military uniform, there was risk of being consumed back into a unit, or some officer changing my orders. Dressed as a civilian, there was risk of being thought a spy and shot or shipped off to a camp. With the prospect of a German search party finding me at any moment, I decided to put on my German sailor's uniform and move forward with my own papers. My frozen feet sloshed around in my wet boots.

The land map and one of the button compasses from Uncle Martin led me southwest toward Oldenburg. I walked all night. By morning, icicles on trees hung down like blue fangs, and shone in the first light.

After eating a canned meal and wrestling with the acidic pains in my stomach, I leaned against a tree and crapped in a sick green splatter onto the leaves. I marched due west all day, only coming across one road, which was like a dark river that I lay in front of, making sure no one was near before sprinting across.

My feet were in horrible pain from the cold when a storm gathered like a giant bird.

I kept thinking of Ottawa. Of finding my father there. It kept me walking. This went on for three nights, skirting south and then north of anywhere on the map where a town might be, moving no more than sixty kilometers a day, paralleling several roads from deep in the woods, hiding in the snow. The snow and ice soaked through my boots and clothes and turned my skin pink, bright red, then white. Blisters on my feet bubbled up, burst, and formed again.

On my fourth day since scuttling the Beaver, the rotten blisters and sores on my feet got so bad they turned into trench foot and large sheets of skin peeled loose. By morning I needed shelter to fend off hypothermia and what I feared was frostbite on my toes. The wind swirled in my ears and I didn't hear the vehicle that turned onto the road behind me until the driver and passengers had me in full view. It was a German military jeep. I cursed myself for being careless. What a pathetic four-day escape. As the jeep came to a stop next to me, four soldiers got out and, at that moment, I cared little about what happened to me as long as I could get warm.

The slightest suspicion from them would mean their pistols would slip from their leather holsters, and they'd demand papers. I tried to decide which to show them. In my right pocket were the papers that said Private Lem Volmer, from Munich, in route to a guard station near the former demarcation line in France. Though there was my sailor's uniform. On either side of me the ditches and thick woods walled me in.

"What is this?" an officer among them asked. "A long way from the water, sailor."

"Yes, sir," I said.

"You're not German," the man said.

"No, sir. I'm a Dutchman."

"Ah, Dutch." He looked at me then, judging my reaction to what he said. "The Dutch have been giving us a lot of problems," the officer said. "Where the hell did you get that uniform?"

"I'm in the Kriegsmarine, sir. I have papers."

"You're not one of these border jumpers?"

"No, sir."

"Let's see those papers."

I kneeled on the ground next to my backpack, reached in and felt the muzzle of the Luger. I knew what Uncle Martin would do in that instant. How he'd be driving alone in these men's jeep within minutes. But that was not me. Next to the gun my fingers pinched the bag with the newspaper clippings and commendations I'd received from Major Oldif. My papers for the Beaver mission were in there. I handed my orders and accommodation to the officer.

On top of my paperwork was the certificate of ownership that came with the medal. DER FÜHRER was written in large, bold lettering below a picture of the Knight's Cross with a swastika in the middle. There was a seal pressed over my own name, *Jacob Koopman, Oberfahnrich zur See, Midshipman*. The officer read it, looked up at me, then back to the picture. Then he raised his arm and saluted me and told his soldiers, "This sailor wears the Knight's Cross."

As the other soldiers saluted, I saluted them back, raising my arm above my head, trying to uncurl my frozen fingers to face these men like they were my brothers.

"Very kind of you," I said. "But I'm freezing to death."

The soldiers made room for me between them in the back of the vehicle. We drove past more fields and into another forested area.

"How was the medal won?" the man driving asked.

"I sank a ship," I told him, letting the words flow out of my mouth for the first and last time in my life, as if they held no weight at all. The officer shifted in his seat to look back at me. "I was sent out again but had to scuttle my boat north of here and started walking but got caught in a storm. You're the first people I've seen since."

We drove through a small German garrison town. The first house we drove past had a huge Nazi flag hanging from it with the swastika against the bloodred cloth. It snapped in the wind as we passed. The streets were full of soldiers in sweat suits jogging up and down the road for exercise. One house had a group of officers out back taking target practice at a scarecrow they lined up against hay bales.

We drove through the center of town, passing a row of quaint old village homes. I imagined that inside the walls of some of those buildings were starving and terrified men, downed RAF lying fetal in piles of their own excrement, waiting in the darkness for the world or the war to end.

The soldiers took me to a small, forested mining compound well outside the town. About half a dozen large troop transport vehicles left as our jeep pulled in. The military green, canvas-topped trucks roared by us with their tops snapping in the wind. Each one that passed was empty.

"You can follow me, and we'll get you dry and fed," the officer said. His long stride was hard for me to keep up with.

He led me to a small bunkhouse next to a mining silo. "You can have that bunk for the night."

"Shall I radio your unit now?"

"Maybe we can wait until after I get some sleep."

"Not a problem. We'll radio them tomorrow. We'll have trucks going east in the afternoon if that will help."

"Thank you, sir," I said, already stripping off my wet clothes.

"That looks awful," he said and pointed at my bleeding feet. "Let me get the place warm for you." He walked to the end of the barrack, which was a small wood frame bunkhouse with eight beds that all looked unused. The rafters were untreated pine with nails poking through from where they'd shoddily laid the boards. A wood-burning stove sat at the far end next to a shower and toilet stalls.

"Take a shower, and I'll have this going when you're done."

"Thank you."

Once warm, my feet throbbed in pain. When I'd eaten, slept for a few hours, and dried my clothes off over the stove, I dressed and put my backpack on. I was terrified that the officer would take me into custody, so I started walking around the compound. There were soldiers at the gate. Those soldiers must have lived in the only other bunk room. At the food tent, when no one was looking, I squeezed the air out of bread loaves, stuffed my pack with them, and shoved in cans of noodles with meat sauce and sausage with gravy until my pack and pockets were full. Then I headed to the far woods on the hillside that rose above the compound and the gravel quarry to the right of it. I decided to slip out of the compound before my location was reported. As I walked to the woods another row of transport trucks rumbled in. The few soldiers who were outside started walking to the trucks.

"*Guten Morgen*," one of them said to me as he walked over.

"*Guten Morgen*," I said, walking to the face of the woods to make a show of standing behind a tree to urinate. When no one was in sight, I stepped farther into the forest and up the hillside.

Fifty meters through the trees and below me was a clearing where giant mounds of upturned dirt, clean gray gravel, and another substance that looked like a mountain of thick terra-cotta soil ran parallel to where I walked. In front of the first heap a bulldozer left idling burped out puffs of smoke that shimmied the main chassis. A row of troop transport trucks came in and snaked along the backside of the mountainous piles. Farther through the woods, soldiers led about twenty people of all ages off the back of one of the trucks. It looked like a family of seven was in the lead headed by a skinny dark-haired man and his graying wife of about fifty. They had two girls who looked to be in their twenties and a dark-haired young man around thirty with them. An old woman held a toddler to her chest. She whispered to and tickled the child as she walked out of sight behind the first knoll. Behind the family were men in dark blue jackets with those awful yellow stars on the chest. Several of the men wore wet and stained tweed jackets. Soldiers pushed the people around the backside of the gravel mountain. The largest cloud in the cold blue sky had an orange hole burned through its center by the sun.

The family was ordered to strip and add their clothes to the already arranged mounds of shoes, pants, undergarments, and jackets. Children's clothes piled up in their own mounds, frozen together in a giant lump the size of an automobile. When everyone was naked, they were led behind the last hill of dirt. I moved parallel to them from up on the wooded hillside and saw a giant pit on the other side of the hill. Clay stairs cut down into the dirt where it looked like a thousand-person puddle of naked bodies with interlaced limbs bubbled up from the earth. The bodies were powdered in white quicklime.

The giant tangle of bodies was so very human, yet the least human thing I'd ever seen. When the family rounded the mound and came into view, they hugged one another, but not one made a sound. They clutched one another as they were led to the pit. A soldier sat on the lip of the pit with his feet dangling off the side. In his lap he held a trench sweeper, a Maschingengewehr 42 machine gun. He was smoking a cigarette.

Once they saw what was ahead of them they all stopped. Soldiers pushed at their backs but they leaned away from the pit. Then a man with skinny legs and wire-rim glasses walked down the steps. He must have known he would be trapped in there forever. I waited for him to crouch down or try to scramble up the walls like a crab in a bucket, but instead he looked upward, away from what he stood on, and stayed perfectly still. The girls were pushed forward, and the rest of the group followed down the clay stairs into the pit. They were the first stark naked women I'd ever seen. The men walking down behind them seemed to be holding back tears. Even from as far back as I was in the woods, I saw how their flesh raised in goose pimples, and the old woman's body shivered around the toddler's chubby backside. The child's little foot hung loose and kicked at the woman's puff of gray pubic hair. When they were all in the pit, had walked, tripped over, and then stood on the pile of dead bodies, one of the daughters from the family pointed to herself and looked at the man with the gun and said, "Twenty-three years old," in German.

The man holding the gun pointed the tip of the gun at himself. "Me too," he said. Then he aimed the barrel at her and sang her a verse from "Lili Marlene," the same song I'd sung along to with all the soldiers at the training camp in Kiel.

Time would come for roll call, time for us to part,
Darling I'd caress you and press you to my heart,
And there 'neath that far off lantern light,
I'd hold you tight, we'd kiss good-night,
My Lili of the lamplight, my own Lili Marlene

When he finished his verse, he aimed, leaned back to brace himself against the gun, and opened fire. Flames shot from the muzzle, and the muscles in his arm shook against the recoil. The lyrics echoing up the mountainside were chased off by the *rat-a-tat-tat* of gunfire. The people in the pit fell in a bloody mist. Most were still. Some twitched. The girl who yelled her age was not quite dead. She'd been shot in the stomach and legs. Her back draped across her family members, her chest heaved upward as if trying to expel the bullets, and her head rocked obscenely back and forth, rolling over the collarbone of a dead man who bled from the throat.

Another truckload of naked men and women turned the corner and walked to the mound.

I felt the sudden sense of the world shifting, of morals and laws and civilized human behavior kicked loose. I lay down at the base of the tree. At that moment more than any other since I lost him, I wished Edwin was with me. I wanted him to see this, to look close enough that he could capture the moment in paint or charcoal so others could see. If others could see this, I felt, there would be no more allowing it to continue. I crawled on my hands and knees up the hillside, deeper into the woods so the soldiers wouldn't see me. There was another chorus of gunfire behind me. From the sound of the gun, the executioner had moved the muzzle from right to left and then back. It sickened me that I knew that. The cracking sounds echoed off the dirt mound and pushed on my back as I crawled.

When I could stand up without seeing the mounds of dirt through the trees I started to run. As I sprinted through the woods, taking long, panicked strides, more shots rang out, like a stone skipping across a river.

As I ran I couldn't stop imagining what lay beneath the snow at that mine camp. What other atrocities had been buried. What other lives had been packed tight beneath the earth. The tangle of folded bodies swelled in my mind. Limbs and digits running like roots through the dirt, stretching out and linking hand to hand, until some bucking jointed monster would dig itself out of this landscape of the damned and proclaim what a foul method it had been laid down by.

I couldn't let go of the image of the soldier's feet dangling off the edge of the pit. Hundreds of people in that pit beneath him, and it was only about two-thirds full. That the executioner seemed so casual sent an anxious nausea through my body and I wanted to vomit again. How would I navigate my way to safety? How, without any papers, could my father have been able to sneak through such a web of evil happenings?

Bare branches of alders and elms curved over my head. The straps of my pack dug into my shoulders. There was a salty, dry taste in my mouth. I didn't want to hear birds or airplanes or any other sound beyond my own heart and lungs drumming in my ears, drowning out the thoughts of the blood-covered people I'd seen in the pit, of how I, with the push of a single button, had easily killed more people than that.

20

From what Uncle Martin said, I had to move well west of Belgium to search out a boat to England, and if not there, southwest through Spain, and on to Africa, though North Africa was probably no safer. I kept thinking of Ottawa as a haven and the word became a three-step mantra as I walked.

Ot-ta-wa.

Ot-ta-wa.

I had sewn the identification papers and money Martin gave me into the lining of my backpack. In the right pocket of my jacket were my German navy ID card and the papers attributing the Knight's Cross to me. Those papers had my real name, height, hair, and eye color, and were signed by the commander of my naval brigade, Major Oldif. In my left pocket were the identification papers of a German SS officer named Dieter Adenauer, and Dieter's orders to report to Brussels. In my left pants pocket were Herbert Yarborough's papers and his small, black barter kit with the three gold coins, and three empty slots where the rings I'd given to Pauwel once sat. I prayed that if the time came, I'd pull the correct version of my life out of the right pocket.

I spent a day limping through the woods. At best, I blundered through this odyssey in a controlled panic. And all that time, regardless of how paranoid of getting caught I was, I still had the feeling of chasing someone, like blood was calling to blood. I kept imagining some tall, dark figure ahead of me, but every time I got close, he slipped farther away. All night I ran and all night I got no closer. At times it was easy to imagine being on a rescue mission, hunting my father or still seeking out my brother, calling his name out over and over.

When it was dark, my feet froze through again. The stale bread burned my ulcers. Inside my body was burning, and outside, I was freezing. I remembered reading in one of my father's history books about fifteen-thousand captured Bulgarian prisoners taken by the emperor Basil of Byzantine. As a warning to never attack him again, he blinded ninety-nine out of every one hundred of the men by taking out both their eyes. The remaining men had one of their eyes taken out so they could lead the rest home. That awful march was in my head, walking into that white nothingness, like I'd wandered off from my one-eyed guide and was lost in a country full of barbarisms.

The snow kept falling.

I was tired but lying down meant freezing through.

My feet burned.

Ot-ta-wa.

Ot-ta-wa.

Ot-ta-wa.

Halfway through a field I felt large-bore gravel underneath my feet before seeing the railroad ties. I could smell the creosote and tar oil. Nuzzling the compass up to my nose, I saw the tracks at my feet ran east–west and started following them heading west.

My boots landed heavily on the wooden ties, kicking up gravel. I could walk across all of Europe like this without being seen if the heavy snow kept up. My mind went blank on the railroad tracks. Snow and wind kept erasing my path. I imagined I was on some ladder stretching ahead of me through the whiteout. The ladder led upward, left the ground, ascended into the clouds. I recalled my father telling Edwin and me about the pillars of sunlight that burst through the cloud cover and drew giant glowing columns of light on the water's surface in the Ems estuary.

"Those are Jacob's ladders," my father said. He told us about the Bible story of Jacob, which is where my name came from. "Those are the ladders of light Jacob used to climb up to heaven on."

When a train came, I jumped off the tracks ahead of its iron breath, ran to the woods, and dove into the snow. In the white and silvered edge of the forest I lay motionless. All ache and stink. Beyond desire or prayer. I decided this was what the receding stars felt like at daybreak, or the last embers drawn over with sand. The front of the train had a plow that sprayed sparks off to the side. Rattling cattle cars trembled past, but it was too dark to see through the slats into them as they whooshed by. When the train rounded out of sight, I hurried back to the freshly plowed track, shook the snow off of my body, and started walking the cleared path, churning ice, dirt, and gravel up as I continued.

Several kilometers beyond where the train passed there was a steel bridge. The wind blew into my face, and I crossed to where the embankment created a lee. Halfway across I couldn't see anything. Going on seemed so useless as the soundless snow beat against me. The emptiness swallowed me, and for the first time I knew what it meant to become nothing. My brother had done that. Not dying. Not dead. But gone altogether. Disappeared.

Everything was white. Frozen. Empty. I took slow, methodical steps forward, letting my numb toes tap out each firm plank. The bridge tucked itself into the far hillside. Below the tracks, I hid from the wind by cramming my body into a fold of the bridge and hillside like a sparrow and only wanted to forget myself in sleep. To let the raw silk wings of rest lift me up into the milky mouth of night. Cold hours passed.

The first graying of the skyline in the east filled the ravine the bridge crossed over. It deepened with more morning light, and by the time I was ready to climb out of the crevice and dig food from my pack, the light was high enough to see the dark shadow of a cave's mouth farther down the ravine and the stream below that. I packed up my tarp and started making my way toward the cave. When I reached it, the mouth was a large vertical crack big enough to drive a car through.

Inside the cave I felt like I'd been swallowed by night again. My hands ran against the ribs of the dark, searching out the far end of the cavern. I couldn't see my hands in front of my face as I moved forward.

I wanted to retreat to the back, where I hoped there was a bottomless pit to jump into, or some underground river to sweep me away, or a cup of earth to sit still on while I recovered.

I pulled a small flashlight from my pack and stepped farther into the cave. The little light cut a yellow beam straight ahead of me. The granite crevasse walls rose up on each side. Not far from the mouth was an old blanket caked in mud and ice tamped into the ground. Large exposed slabs of granite protruded from every angle. In the dark mossy cave the air felt cool and fresh despite the clumps of rotting organic decay. The pitch of the earth angled up so the back part of the cave was dry but the darkness became absolute.

My options were to trudge back out into the snow and keep slogging along, or hunker down until the weather let up. I decided to gather firewood and dragged large dead logs back until the pile of wood was large enough to last a few days.

With kindling and a corner torn from one of my paper maps, I used matches to start a fire. I sat by it until I was warm, though when the feeling came back into my limbs, my toes were still numb. I pulled my boots and socks off. Two on the right side and one on the left looked like they'd been swatted with a hammer. Under the skin, a black color rose to the surface, old blood seeping out of the bones.

I placed the frozen firewood around the flame in a circle so it would dry. I pulled a tin of noodles with meat chunk sauce out of the pack and placed it on the lip of the fire pit to heat. In the tin, little bubbles started forming and popping in the sauce, splattering the sides of the can. It shocked me to smell something other than the cold air. When the noodles were hot to the touch, I wrapped a spare shirt around my hand and picked up the can and began taking large, ravenous bites and slurping down the blistering hot food. It burned the inside of my mouth. While I ate, and the fire was warm against my face, the thought of spending the rest of the war hidden in the cave settled on me like a blessing. I rubbed my toes, hoping some spark of pain, of lingering life, would jump up the knuckles and ache, but they remained black nubs no longer associated with my body.

Looking at my toes, I thought, these days cannot be days but lifetimes. This not mine, but a criminal's life. A victim's. Not mine, I raved.

The hammering winds and their primal whistling blew down the hillside through the deepest parts of that night.

Each moment in the cave, I felt my instincts gradually relax, yet some inner fear still spread through me. For as much as I wanted to recoil from the world, I knew there was no escaping the human kingdom. Life beyond the cave walls I now saw as manic, sickening, and starved enough that it was consuming itself.

The sun had crossed the ravine, and the direct light rushed up the far hillside where it pulled over my side of the hill like a retractable curtain. The day passed with excruciating slowness, and I lay in my tarp for the rest of it. I tested my memory of my family's house by mentally walking through it, seeking out the calming hymn of their voices in the dark. Time hung in front of me, dripping away.

The next day passed as the first had, and the days after that still. Long stretches of cold and dark, followed by a few hours of sunlight that touched the open lip of the cave wall where I'd sit with my eyes closed, letting the first warmth of a late spring lean into my eyelids.

"Breathe in the light," I told myself. "Breathe in the light."

My feet burned up through my legs as the heat from my body tipped into fever.

One moment I would dream of a butcher's stall at the fresh market. Lamb meat, marbled white and deep purple with fat; slabs of tongue; skinned hares looking ready to leap off the table; and the fat, pink quarters of capons. I'd imagine all that meat on a spigot over my fire and feel hunger clawing at the lining of my stomach. But the next moment I'd imagine a young girl with an oozing hole in her throat, red liquid gullies running over her bare chest where her fingers wrote across her abdomen in blood, smearing out her last words.

———————

When lucid, I studied my maps, considering all the ways to escape or get caught. My finger ran over every route until my eyes blurred and the colors bled together. I imagined the oceans flooding the land and emptying themselves, so that everything switched places, making people move to the newly dried space without any infrastructure they'd created on land. The map would have the water and land inversed, leaving a large, hulking landmass, some Pangaea before the shift and break of continents. That new mass would do fine for starting humanity all over again.

I'd heard of cave paintings in France, and wanted to etch some new creature into the wall. In the subterranean dank, I could try to mimic the silhouette of Thump-Drag my brother drew, could chisel and scratch my primal markings upon the stone as my friend Ludo had done, but add my own name. *Jacob Koopman. Charioteer.*

In the dark these grand and crazy thoughts kept me busy, away from the one thought I couldn't shake, which was that I was close to giving up, that my spirit was flagging. There was no getting to where I really wanted, a return to my life before the war. In the dark cave, with the falling snow shadowed by the night, I felt like a ghost, hovering in some purgatory.

In the cave I followed the instructions for my Benzedrine and Horlicks malted milk tablets which could be used as a meal. I used my water-purifying kit to get drinking water from the stream. I kept changing my socks, which I knew was important, yet I still couldn't feel my toes. Each night they blackened a shade darker. I held them close to the fire to try to cull forth any feeling but once got too close and burned the soles of my feet.

It was still unusually cold, but along the stream, where some of the snow melted off, were arrowhead plants, which the Irish called the antifamine herb. The large leaves had been frozen solid. I cut through the leaves on top with my dagger and followed the root down to the tuberous, potatolike bulb.

I fished in the stream and caught several eels to fry in my mess kit, I stomped on the mice caught in the gaze of my flashlight at the back part of the cave and boiled mice meat and dandelions, along with other roots I'd dug around for to make a stew. I found a dead raven whose chest had been hollowed out by what looked like a small vermin before it froze. There were specks of crystalized meat inside of it. I pulled the last of the feathers loose and brought the terrible-looking thing to the cave and boiled it in a pot. A toxic layer of sputum floated to the top, which I dumped out at the lip of the cave, and then I drank the awful soup, desperately needing some energy, beyond fear of some parasitic death. But I threw it all up. Once, I boiled raw snails for several minutes and sucked out their slimy insides, in order to save my canned foods. Though when I boiled rhubarb leaves dug out from under the snow, they got me sick, and I threw up for hours, which made my ulcer burn like hot coals and gave me delirious dreams.

In my half-sleep I dozed on and off, waking covered in sweat or shaking from the cold. The fire died down and instinct took over as I ferreted around the cave in a fever-induced stupor, tossing more wood on and piling some close to me so I could stay under my tarp. Hours went by like this. That desperate, spine-tingling feeling of being utterly alone made me curl up, and at the worst part of the night I began to hallucinate. I saw all the power line poles stretching across Europe like I was above them in a plane, but when I swooped in low, each one had a crucified child nailed into the wood. They yelled from pole to pole to one another and their awful cries spread everywhere.

Then I daydreamed of a shadowy world at the feet of two giants fighting above me. Each giant held a poisonous snake in his left hand, and they tried to stick the snake out toward the other giant to make the snake bite. I rolled to avoid their footfalls. I couldn't make out their faces, only the shadow of their movements, and they fought all night until a giant's sole descended on me, darkening the world in one quick snap, and I woke, sweating and fearful of a new dark beyond the cave.

21

The sun came up, and it was light, and when it descended it was dark and colder. Those two facts became my clock, my calendar. I became submammalian in that way. Then, on my eleventh day in the cave, there was the sound of sticks crunching outside. I tossed the blanket off, reached for the Luger in my pack, stepped away from the fire, kicked a heap of dirt at the flame, and leaned into the darkness against the wall. There was a stone jutting out that I rested my arms on to aim the muzzle at the cave's opening. My finger wrapped the trigger. My eyes focused in the dim light from the opening.

Someone's head peeked into the cave and then pulled back. Then they took another look and pulled back again before the dark figure stepped away from the shadows and was backlit by the sunlight. I aimed the gun at the person's chest and eyed my pack, sitting on the dirt next to my blankets and tarp. Without my pack of supplies and documents, there would be no changing names, no crossing borders through camps, no paying for food and ship's passage. Without those possibilities, I didn't know what the dimensions of my own life were—how wide, how long it could be, what say I was to have in any of it.

The stranger at the mouth of the cave took a step forward and waved a hand. "Come here," a woman's voice said in Dutch.

It was the first human voice I'd heard in what felt like an unimaginable amount of time. My forearms dug into the rock to keep me from dropping to my knees and wailing. Then a small, darkened figure stepped into the light. A child scuttled toward the woman and hid behind her legs. Their combined shadow looked like the lumbering shadow of Thump-Drag.

"Hello," the woman called into the darkened cave. Her voice was tentative and trembled in my ears. "Hello," she called again. She walked closer to the weakened fire and the slight firelight caught the gaunt angles of both their faces. She was young, and it was a little girl with her. Both wore the same dark blue jackets with little yellow stars on them that the massacred people at the mine wore.

"Look at this," the woman said and bent over my bag. When the girl went to open it, I stepped out of the shadow.

"That's mine," I said.

The woman screamed and the girl jumped back, mortified by my presence. The woman stared at the insignia on my jacket. The girl looked to be about six or seven. The woman, a few years on either side of thirty. Her eyes were the color of smoke, their centers as dark as polished coal.

"Please," she said, and then was silent. She had wild, curly black hair. The little girl had straight brown hair and her little hands gripped the woman's pants. Her eyelashes looked sealed together by crystalized snow and tears. "We saw the smoke from your fire," she said. "We only wanted to get warm."

The fire, my god. What a flagrant trail for someone to discover me.

"Who are you?" the woman asked.

"I'm a caveman." Each looked at the other. "Where'd you come from?" I continued.

"Please don't shoot us. We were on the bridge when we smelled smoke. It's so cold outside, we had to look for where it came from to get warm."

My gun remained leveled at them, so I dropped it down to my side.

"Sit by the fire," I said. The woman pushed the child ahead of her, closer to the fire. She bent over the girl and lifted her bare hands to the flame. I walked to the mouth of the cave and stood in front of it. Blue ribbons of smoke drifted through sunlight. How stupid could I have been? What bigger flag could I have sent up?

"Where'd you come from?" I asked. The woman stared at me, glanced at my German uniform again, and shuddered at the sight.

"We'll leave," she said.

"I'm not going to hurt you."

"You're a soldier," she said, and pointed at the gun.

The little girl's bare hands hung red and raw in front of her. Both their shoes and pant legs were soaked and covered in ice and mud. I holstered the gun in the inner lining of my jacket. I'd have to leave soon now too if the fire sent up my location. But I didn't want to leave the cave. I didn't want this woman or the child to be here. I hated them for their presence. I wanted more than anything for the world to be empty, but here they were, their presence screaming that that could never be. Outside, the low storm clouds frosted everything. It was no place to wander without direction in mind.

"Are you alone?"

"Yes," the woman said.

"Tell me where you came from," I said. "I won't hurt you. I'm a Dutchman. I won't hurt you. Just tell me where you came from."

"I'm from Amsterdam," the woman said.

"How'd you get here?"

"Train." The little girl hadn't taken her eyes off me. They were as deep as the cave we stood in and the reflected firelight sounded out their depths.

"Where's the train stop?"

"I don't know."

"What do you mean you don't know? How far is the station from here?" If the train stopped nearby, then this ravine was not as isolated as I'd hoped.

"We didn't get off at a station." She looked at me again. "We'll leave," she said.

Loneliness washed over me.

"When you're warm," I said.

My eyes moved down the woman's jawline to her delicate neck.

The two of them sat next to the fire, and within ten minutes the child curled up and slept in the woman's lap. Despite her obvious fear, her body succumbed to the warmth and what must have been utter exhaustion.

We sat next to the fire and were quiet for a long time, spending those strange, haunting hours in each other's company. I hadn't eaten yet that day and pangs of hunger flared in my gut. In my pack was eight days' worth of meals if I ate only once a day. There was a part of me that didn't want to pull out my food in front of these two, as I knew I'd have to share. But I was starving and ashamed for hoarding. I took out two servings of noodles and sauce with meat chunks and heated them by placing them close to the fire. The woman eyed the food the whole time. When the sauce bubbled, I handed one of them to her.

"Can you two share?" I said.

"Yes, of course. Thank you." She dug her hand into the container and scooped out a finger full of hot noodles and shoved them in her mouth. She tried to cool it against her tongue, puffing out her cheeks and taking weird, sharp little breaths. Almost immediately her face flushed red. She scooped more of the food into her mouth, and then shook the girl awake. "Eat," she said, and the girl, still half-sleeping, took the food from the woman's fingertips. She chewed with her eyes closed and ate the rest of the food the woman fed her without fully waking. When she was done chewing, the woman moved the girl so she rested on the dirt next to the fire. The woman then ran her finger along the inside edge of the container, rubbing off the last bits of food and licking her finger clean of the red sauce.

She stood up and limped to the far corner of the wall. I hadn't noticed her limp until then. She walked to the mud-covered blanket that had been frozen in the dirt and pulled it off the ground. There were camel crickets, potato bugs, and centipedes in the damp earth beneath it. When she shook it out, she laid it over the sleeping girl and wiped her own tears away.

That small, sad action made me feel so inhuman. I had only wanted to be far away from her, as looking at her and the girl showed me how stupid, awful, and miserable life in that cave really was.

The little one didn't wake up and I continued to stoke the fire and sat by it in silence with the woman. The back of the cave smelled like damp rotting leaves, pewter, and cold air coming in from some opening that created a draft.

Somewhere out of the quiet, I asked her name.

She kept looking into the fire with some profound sadness. "Janna. This is Mevi." She didn't mention last names. I understood. Last names made associations with people who were not there, people she may not have known the whereabouts of.

Janna had an oval-shaped face with a wide hairline and cheekbones sloping down to a narrow jaw. The little girl, Mevi, had a pear-shaped face with a pouchy jaw and cartoonish, round cheeks. They looked nothing alike.

I thought of resting my hand on the crown of the little girl's head.

"I'm Jacob," I said, the name feeling strange to hear out loud.

Mevi still slept. Her eyelids and fingers twitched.

Janna sat against the cave wall and took off her socks and shoes. She folded her right leg over her left, and flexed her ankle, which bounced up and down. The top of her foot had veins rising across the thin fan of bones beneath the skin. Splotches of bruises ringed her lower calves.

She saw me looking at her bruises.

"Is Mevi your daughter?" I asked.

"No."

"Who is she?"

"Are you a German soldier?"

"No," I said. I didn't know who I was anymore. "I took the uniform to stay warm. When the weather clears, I'll move on and won't tell anyone about you two if you want to stay here and hide. I won't turn you in." Would these two turn me in if I sent them away? Would we all get caught if we stayed?

Janna kept moving her ankle in small circles as if to loosen it up. There was a mole on the top of her foot. Her thin, crescent-moon eyebrows rose up to her bangs as she talked. She kept pulling on her earlobe as if triggering the words to come. She was soft-spoken, and at moments her voice stuttered. She looked down at her feet in the dirt and the fire cast a wild shadow of her feral hair on the rock behind her.

"We were put in the same train car from Amsterdam. A cattle car." She nodded her head at Mevi. "The other people in the car kept talking about what might happen to us when we got to wherever the soldiers were taking us. They were convinced we were going to be killed, instead of sent to labor camps." She started rubbing her bruised calf and ankle with both her hands. "The train car was packed full, but everyone shifted to take turns, trying to pull a loose overhead board apart. It took most of the night, but they got a hole in the roof, and I was one of the only ones small enough to get through. They boosted me up and I pulled myself onto the roof. Then they pushed Mevi up at me and told me we had to jump. That I had to take care of her."

"Did you see any very, very tall men on the train?" I asked.

"Tall men? No," Janna said.

The bruises on her legs must have been from when she landed. I imagined her on the top of the speeding train, how the wind and cold would have blotted out the senses, and that giant leap of faith she took.

Janna had the scent of chlorine on her clothes. She smelled it. "From the train cars," she said, almost apologizing.

She seemed on edge, perhaps not wanting me to ask what happened to her family. I sensed she had no answer or wouldn't want to give one. I pulled back and let the cave noises fill the void.

The people in the cars must have convinced her they were all going to die for her to jump off a speeding train with a child she didn't know tucked in her arms. I could imagine from what I'd seen at the mine camp that the people in her train car had been right. Some instinct must have been screaming inside of them. I watched her foot moving and understood how scared she still was, yet was somehow still managing to keep watch over the sleeping girl who had been thrust upon her.

I could see every part of her story and how it fit into the larger narrative. The German military had been telling a story for years and the whole country now believed it. I'd believed in it too as they told it with such flair, such verve and promise, that the words got into my bloodstream and ran wild. Their story was of one peaceful world where they could knock all the trouble out with that one violent push, and that story of a harmonious world had sounded so good to me when I was a kid at summer camp, and even later, when Major Oldif spoke of it. But I'd now seen the truth. That one story was meant to blanket over every other that existed. At that moment I knew where someone like Samuel, the air-writer from Delfzijl, would have ended up—where someone so full of stories, like my father, would have ended up. They didn't leave room for anyone else's story, all those beautifully odd tales that had filled my childhood.

When Janna and I went out to gather wood, Mevi was too scared to be left alone and silently followed us. She took hesitant steps down the hill and kept her eyes locked on Janna, a hand on her coat. We laid two long sticks between us to use as a stretcher for the wood that we stacked perpendicularly on top of. The two of us made enough trips to build a few days' worth of round-the-clock fire.

While sitting around the fire admiring Janna's silhouette in the darkness ahead of me, I felt a deep want and sadness.

Any time either of us woke in the middle of the night, we stoked the fire. The flittering shadows twitched on the cave walls. The darkness formed staggering shapes overhead. If I had to piss, I walked out to the side of the cave's mouth and peed down the hillside. I hadn't shit in days. My limited food intake was burned up to keep my body going.

When she slept, Mevi twitched and chirped like Fergus used to. Her dreams built and crescendoed to a full-blown night terror. She had a coughing fit, curled into herself, tucked up her knees, and spasmed with each breath. Her cheeks glowed red and glossy as if painful. I sat next to her and wished I knew some purification ritual I could employ. When I reached out to touch her shoulders, the muscles trembled under my fingers. She talked in her sleep. Said the names of people she loved. Her grief was a night-blooming flower. She called out their names and then stood up and started walking around the dark looking for them, exploring the frozen world she had jumped headlong into. The firelight illuminated her face. Each fleck in her eye led to another. Her eyes were endless that way, a map to more maps. Of all the ways the human heart chooses to leave trails for others to follow, the eyes were my favorite and maybe the most crushing. Her eyes revealed the raw truth that life would spare her young form no grace and no fury.

I led the sleeping girl back to her blanket next to Janna. Janna's smooth and delicate forearm and hand were uncovered. I wanted to lift her hand and have it touch me—to hold it between my own hands. Each fine fingertip looked incredibly soft despite the dirt under her nails.

The arched curve of her hip made me start rocking back and forth, trying to shake some of the loneliness out. My shadow shook against the wall, a monstrously humped body rocking over the stone. The light from the fire flickered against the cave wall. Mevi was still whimpering and Janna's eyes were open, glowing orange in the firelight until she snapped them shut. I swear I heard them close. I lay there looking at her face, and sending secret messages—please touch me here, here, here, and here. Then I watched my own shadow again, dancing on the wall, my darker, truer form. I shut my eyes and imagined more advanced people than me, etching figures into the stone, tracing their own mysteries.

Much later that night, Janna's eyebrows flicked up and down in her sleep. I was rotting away with ache, red lines of infection roping up my legs, and in the dark I was convinced touching the bone of her hip would cure me. I could fold my lips over her earlobe, gum at the small hole there that had once probably held glass earrings. I wanted to consume her without really being able to want her—my body wasn't strong enough to want her the carnal way my mind pictured—so I wanted her in a more intimate way, some sort of cannibal love that could give me my strength back, or at least comfort me with human closeness.

Pushing my blanket off, I moved closer to her, belly crawling over the space between us. Her eyes played games against her closed eyelids. My hand reached out for her face. My splayed fingers rose over her chin as close as they could without touching her and lingered in the space over her mouth. Her warm breath passed through my fingers. I held my hand like that for minutes, communicating the underlanguage of want. The miracle of her breathing calmed me—the desperate part of me. Then I rolled back to my blanket, and felt sleepy and depressed, pulled it over my head, and held that same hand in front of my mouth and breathed into it, pretending it was still her life touching mine.

How could I have felt lust at that moment? What a sad sack the body is. What a sad sack it was always going to be. I imagined what my inner desires would look like if they took some form outside my body, and the image of such a creature streaked across my mind and began haunting around there. There he was, the foul knot of want and loathing and hate and need, his body hunched over, in an impossible curl with his lips sealed shut around his own phallus. His hairy shoulders and arms waved around out to its side, trying to gather flesh with its want-ing hands. It emitted a horrible, whimpering cry between breaths. This subhuman, bare-assed, hairy-balled monstrosity streaked past, full of raw want and shame and hunger and inertia. The image was so horrify-ing I wanted to find it in the scope of a rifle and riddle it with bullets, fell it, and then unload round after round into its curved spine, zip up the legs with bullet holes, and blow out the back of its skull. I wanted to dismember that part of me. Take off the wanting fingers at the knuckle. Anything to no longer associate this thing with myself. I was afraid if there ever was a judgment upon our lives in this world, I would be judged by this creature, this parasitic want dragging me down.

When the snow stopped in the morning, it gave way to heavy rain. The stream at the base of the ravine reddened and swelled over the top of its banks, and where I'd been melting snow for water, I now had only to walk to the stream and dip my cup where it eddied over unfamiliar ground.

Mevi and Janna drank from my full canteens. That day was almost the last of my food supplies. What was left after that was only energy pills. So we each took the Benzedrines and shared two cans of sausage and gravy heated on the lip of the fire. When the sun was up, I went back down to the water. Mevi tried to follow me and fell. She hurt her elbow, and I scooped her up and dusted her off. Tears welled in her eyes but she didn't make a sound. I wanted to do something to comfort her, so I tapped the tip of her nose and aimed her back to the mouth of the cave with a pat on the head.

I'd become infested with lice since Janna and Mevi arrived in the cave. The little white specks clumped up on my arm hair and all over my body. They jumped in quick, perfect arcs across my forearm. I tried to ignore them until they got so bad I had to try something. On the banks I stripped off all my clothes and ran my hands over my oily skin. My blackened toes, now dried dates, penis slack and shriveled. I lowered my feet into the water and dipped my body under the flowing surface. There was some unworldly and astonishing feeling buzzing around me as I submerged in the frozen water.

The cold made my body shrink in on itself, but I held on to two rocks under the surface and let my body and legs shimmy back and forth behind me. The dull clanking of stones pushed over one another by the current filled my ears. If I let go, I'd at least momentarily enter the world Edwin had gone to. When I jumped up, the air bit my skin. I put on my underwear and carried the rest of my clothes up the hill to sit and get warm by the fire.

Halfway up the hill I saw Janna upstream. She squatted near the water. Her back to me. Her open jacket hung down her sides and brushed the ground. Spandrels of light wound through her black curls. I could not see what she was doing and kept walking up the path. When I passed a thick-trunked willow tree, I saw her wipe a sheath of dry leaves between her legs, then place the bloodied leaves into the water, a crimson raft that spun circles in an eddy before pushing downstream. Mesmerized for a moment, I turned and walked back to the cave as quietly as I could so she wouldn't see me.

"I'll have to go find food tonight," I told Janna and Mevi when we were all in the cave. "You'll stay here. We need to get those yellow stars off of your jackets. You'll have to lie about who you are from now on. You were too trusting with me, but now be sure to lie to everyone else."

Janna looked at me and nodded. Mevi said nothing. She never said a word while awake. With my Nazi dagger's tip, I cut the stitching of their yellow stars free and pulled the loose yellow threads out of the cloth. We watched the stars darken and burn in the fire.

I dressed and waited until the downing sun cast a layer of pink behind the ridgeline. Then I packed my backpack and checked each pocket with my various ID cards. The weight of the pack dug low into my back.

"Is this good-bye?" Janna asked.

"Almost," I said.

I climbed up to the train tracks and started moving west, taking each fearful step trying to will myself back into the nightmare, doing everything to convince myself this was a better alternative to starving to death. My blackened toes threw off my balance and each foot protested in pain.

Several kilometers from the cave, the woods opened up to a large farmer's field. I climbed a horse-gnawed fence post, crossed the boundary stones, and walked through a field with clods of tedded hay to the stable. I peeked through the slats in the wood and knotholes. When I was sure no one was inside, I snuck around to the front door and eased it back, making sure no one in the nearby farmhouse could hear. The inside of the barn smelled like animal breath, wet fur, alfalfa, and urine. I swept my flashlight past two workhorses and a starving old cow. A three-way tipcart full of cut hay and a plow were in one corner, and in the other was a pig pen with four piglets. I scaled the mildew-darkened wall of the pen and grabbed one of the piglets. It kicked and made a deep squealing sound that originated from the tip of its corkscrewed tail and increased in volume as it squeezed out. I tucked the thrashing animal against my chest, closed my fingers under its chin to keep it from biting me, and ran to the barn door. I shut the door behind me so whomever I stole from wouldn't lose anything else to the cold, and then ran back to the tracks. The animal struggled under my jacket, and its split feet pushed into my side.

In the woods the pig still thrashed against my chest. I didn't dare loosen my grip as I wouldn't be able to catch it if it got free. With the piglet pinned to my body, I pulled my dagger out of my pocket and slipped it under its throat. The animal gurgled out a last breath, loud enough that I knew I was right to not have killed it in the barn or taken more than one. Warm blood leaked out over my hand onto the ground, and it fought for a moment until it went limp in my arms. The smeared blood was thick and warm as I laid it out to see what to do with it next. I'd never killed an animal before. With the piglet laid out on its back, I used my dagger to carve an incision down from the slashed throat to and then a circle around its anus. From that cut I scooped the viscera out of the body cavity. The purple liver, the maroon heart, and crimson coil of intestines and organs flopped onto the wet ground. The blade tore loose the attached tissue, and when the animal was emptied, I picked it up by its hind leg and let it dangle at my side on my way back to the cave.

The piglet would feed us sparsely for a few days. With grilled meat in their stomachs, Janna and Mevi would get the color back in their faces. Mevi would talk. I would find us a safe place to go together. But I knew the meat wouldn't last. Closer to the cave, the night got even darker.

A few feet inside the mouth of the cave, two open and watchful sets of eyes looked at me from beyond the fire. Those eyes glowed like fiery animals in that darkness. I looked at them for a moment, strangers really, the woman who took such a miraculous jump and the child who hadn't spoken since. I stopped moving. I laid the piglet on the ground and saw how insufficient it was. How insufficient I was to the task of these two lives. I knew I could go back to get another piglet for myself before continuing west along the tracks. It would be so easy to place a stack of thirty, no, a hundred marks under the piglet's foot. An offering to Janna and Mevi and turn to leave. Turn from them.

My mouth had gone dry. I tongued the inside of my cheeks. My skin tasted like acrid pig blood. I rubbed my tongue there for a moment and wondered what sweetness was left in life to buoy me against such bitter, bitter disappointment.

I let the fantasy of leaving them play out. The pig would be eaten. Only the marrow-sucked bones would remain. Janna and Mevi would have enough strength to push on into the forest, to find some better safety. But hidden in my fantasy lay a terrible truth about myself, a deficiency of courage, or an inability to care for others. Leaving them when I could take them with me seemed like the gravest crime, one I would never be able to rectify. Leaving them, I realized, would have brought a deep ice floe of hurt like what I felt seeing my father drop to his knees and slither away.

No.

That would not do.

"I have something for you," I called to them.

In the cave I busied myself trying to cook the piglet. Being busy felt important to hold off that fear of tending to these two. I built a spit out of sticks and twine to roast the pig on and then cut pieces of it for both Janna and Mevi. I held out the meat for them and to my surprise felt life pushing upward in me. I wanted to feed them all this meat, then reach into those starving fantasies of food I'd been having and feed them for the rest of their lives. I wanted to save them, and that was like a switch for me. I could hide in a cave the rest of my life, but these two could not. These two needed better than that.

So, after we tasted the pig, and then kept eating it, devouring it whole to push back a hunger that felt like it was trying to rip out of us, we gathered our things and walked out into the darkness.

"I'll find somewhere safe for you," I said to the little girl as we left the cave. "I will."

I imagined the wind curling around like a banner floating in space. As I exited the cave's mouth and turned up the ravine, they followed, and I allowed myself a small, transcendent moment of feeling alive again. As I watched them, I had a deep and swelling love of trees, their sway and dance, and thought how goddamn beautiful this world would be if we'd never been allowed to touch it.

I led Janna and Mevi back to the farm I'd stolen the piglet from. It was the only place I was certain there'd be food, and it was away from the cave. It was all I knew to do. From deep in the trees we waited a whole day, trying to blend into the shadows Edwin was so adept at creating, watching for any life on the farm. Only once, in the evening, an old woman with a shotgun and a metal bucket walked into the barn. When she left without the bucket, and latched the door shut, we snuck into the barn and hid in an empty stall.

"You sleep first," Janna said.

Curled on the ground with the scent of hay and horse sweat working up the memory of Hilda, I fell asleep, but not for long. The pig meat in my stomach was churning. I shot up.

"What is it?" Janna asked. Mevi slept cradled in her lap.

"Nothing," I said, but I crawled from our stall and only made it to the next before I had to pull my pants down and let the awful puddle of my shit splatter all over the barn floor.

It took everything in me not to moan in pain, and the sound of my body was as animal and foul as the swine.

I crawled back into our stall as embarrassed by my own body as if I'd crapped like the dog at my mother's dinner table.

"Sorry," I whispered.

"It was the meat," Janna said. "Fat after nothing will make us all shit like that."

She'd done me a kindness by being coarse. Easy.

"Thank you," I said.

She nodded and smiled at me. Not smiled. I do not think in our time together I ever saw her smile, but her face performed a small softening. A gift to me.

"Your turn to sleep," I said.

She nodded, then shifted her body to ease Mevi onto the hay and curled around her.

In the morning, at the first sign of light, I sent Janna and Mevi running into the woods as I snatched another piglet and ran after them like all the purpose and drive had been renewed in me.

22

As we walked, Mevi reached her hand up to hold mine. Her skin was cold and clammy and I tried to cup all of it in my fist. I ran my thumb over her tiny knuckles and it felt like the simplest version of love. Language was still stunted deep in her throat by fear. But here was the truest form of communication to ever exist. This was all I needed.

A large pine unzipped by a lightning strike oozed sap over its charred trunk. We sucked on the sap. It made my mouth water, and I swallowed the sweet spittle while watching Mevi lap at the bark like a malnourished bear.

The dark hours smelled like wood smoke and lasted the longest. It was during the dark hours that I understood each day was its own living thing in that country. Though the sky was purple at dawn, the color bled away all morning until the sun crested the treetops and left a golden sheen on the tracks.

We followed the tracks, veering always west in the direction of the Dutch border. Me always chanting Ot-ta-wa. The shape of the cattle in the fog blurred as they moved across the field. They were amorphous, as if my brother had rubbed off their sharp lines with his dampened fingertip. The Germans patrolled the main roads, but they were not hard to avoid.

As we huddled together at night we went over our story. I showed them the soldier's ID I carried.

"We need to have a fast answer ready if asked. You are my wife or girlfriend," I suggested.

"I am your older sister," Janna said. "This is my daughter. She doesn't talk."

"Okay. My older sister," I mumbled. Hurt.

The train tracks ran through a small town that had a whole series of bombed and abandoned row houses. We walked through, thumbing the last remaining kitchen cupboards, peering into rooms, trying the doorknobs, and pushing our way into the hidden corners.

"Look for fruit flies," Janna told me. "They'll lead to scraps."

On the ground floor of the second house, there was the frame of a giant harp with all its strings broken. I picked it off the floor and stood it up in front of me so the thick strings hung down slack. I bent down and walked through the body of the harp like it were a door, but everything on the other side was still bleak and empty.

A dusty drop cloth held the shape of the ottoman beneath. Cobwebs hung from the ceiling.

In the basement I found Mevi standing in front of a collection of decorative spoons that hung from the wall, each by two small nails at the base of the neck. She let her fingers touch one, then the next.

Every time I pushed a door back, it felt like someone would crash out past me, or dive to cower in some corner. In my mind, I'd been playing a sort of game with my father, hide-and-seek. My father was always ahead of me, like a ghost laying down secrets in the morning mist. Any moment I might turn a corner and find him crouched behind a tree, peering out from behind the edge of a building, watching over me, or waiting for me to come save him. When it was dark and cold, the thought was comforting. It gave me that inner push to move forward, sleep less, be more aware, as there was no knowing how it might happen that he, we, might be saved.

"Can you tell me about your family?" I asked Janna. I wanted to hear her talk. To hear a voice. I wanted to hear a story.

"What do you want to know?" she asked. She was looking at me then like she first had. Like I was the soldier. Something imposing and scary.

"Just to hear," I said, and it was true.

"There is not much to tell that doesn't hurt to think about right now."

We left the row houses and weaved among the trees in the darkness like dogs, like Fergus, letting that extra sliver of skin shut over our eyeballs to protect us from briars. Deeper in the night we crept through fields, alongside roads, and a ruddy gray canal. When we found another train track, we followed it to the southwest.

My feet pounded in pain. The curled black toes felt like soggy pieces of rubber. Each time I looked at them it was with a sense of horror, as if they didn't belong to me, but were something else entirely, like dead squids that hung limply at the end of my legs. They gave off a rotting stink I could almost taste.

If God did have his finger on my shoulder, I thought, he was trying to flick me off the ledge.

From deep in the woods, cowbells jingled in the distance. A sheepdog barked. My eyes were always trained for the shifting of sentries. When it was a few hours before dawn, the soft orange glow of a fire shone in the woods. I had the girls hide while I snuck toward it, staying crouched low to the ground. When I was close enough to be sure it was only an old man by himself, I stepped out of the woods to get warm by the fire.

The man slept sitting up. He didn't have a jacket on. The sharp sticks of his collarbone stuck out against his thin shirt. The backs of his hands seemed creased and concave, the bones curved inward and sunk toward his palms. A knot of shaggy, graying beard rose off his loose, bone-colored face. There was a rattle deep in his lungs when he breathed. I sat across the fire from him for a moment to get warm and propped my feet up to the flame. When I looked back up at the man I saw his polished, dying eyes.

"Hello," I said in German.

Firelight glinted off the white stubble skirting his neckline. The circle of skin around his mouth sunk in like a pocket over his toothless gums. The man's right eye rolled back into his skull. The left eye was black and held the flame's vivid reflection on its glass surface.

He stared at me without moving.

"Hello," I said in Dutch.

Then he nodded. He lifted his hand up to his mouth and started to gnaw on something. When he brought his cupped hand down to his side I saw that he was eating a tulip bulb. The man picked up the rest of the bulb and stuffed it into his mouth where he started to gum at it. He had a jagged ridge of yellow teeth and eyed my uniform as if I were about to steal his last scrap of food.

All those dead fish floating outside of the harbor in Kiel flashed into my mind, and I imagined gathering them all into giant wicker baskets and leaving the silver and glistening piles of fish at the feet of this old man, or at the mouth of the cave for Janna and Mevi to stay hidden away and fed, or multiplying them like a bedraggled Christ and swallowing them whole myself.

I waved to the girls to come get warm and walked the perimeter of the fire, collecting a pile of logs and branches to stock the fire, and hunched my body over it. The old man still didn't talk, but his eyes kept opening and closing. Janna and Mevi stared at him. Took him in. I was amazed yet again by their resilience. I piled more wood, put some next to him, and when I looked up, Janna had reached out and touched his thin shoulder for a second, trying to communicate some sympathy and warmth. It was one of those small, crushing gestures that stay with you.

We walked back to the tracks, leaving him there to pass the remainder of the night alone.

The tracks wound west, and I limped along them. We were hungry. I was starving. I craved bacon and bacon fat, warm bread, clean meat, and purified water with honey in it. I wanted sweets so badly I licked sap from a tree again, but it only left a pine flavor coating my teeth. The baskets of fish from Kiel harbor came to my mind again, but this time the fish had gone mealy and the foul stench clung to my skin.

In a field covered in hoarfrost we found discarded clothes, books, and a brown leather briefcase, which Janna opened. The inside was custom made to hold small glass vials of oils and powders. The top half had a chart on what to mix to make different perfumes. The three of us kneeled in front of the open case. Each vial had a piece of tape with a name written on the top. Mint. Citronella. Peppermint. Spruce. Eucalyptus. Rosemary. Lemon oil. Juniper oil. Rosewood and myrtle oil. Cinnamon water. Clove. Larch resin. Vanilla water. Lavender. Nutmeg. I took a chance and drank sips of the oils, one after the other like shots of schnapps.

"Here." I handed the bottles to Janna and she handed them to Mevi, each of us drinking a third.

Janna took the bottle labeled *Spruce* and sprinkled it into a puddle at the cup of her hand and rubbed it under her armpits and across her chest. The smell was so intense she looked at me with a new fear in her eyes.

"I had the thought of us getting caught when someone asks what's that god-awful stench," she said.

I stood up and felt the mix of lemon oil and cinnamon water coating my empty stomach.

"Don't worry," I said, "by nightfall we'll all be pissing some of the smelliest perfume in Europe."

We left the case on the ground and walked through the rest of the field, reading it like a narrative. Scatter your silver spoons and candle collections. Your jewelry and bound books. Knit pillows and pressed drawings. They mean nothing now.

At the border of Germany and Holland, there were cement pill-boxes with 16mm-machine-gun mounts spread out every fifty meters along the open fields. Most of them seemed empty, but I led us south and well behind them until there was a place to pass unnoticed into our own country. Several days later, with a sister and niece I'd gathered along the way, I hobbled into Utrecht.

The few soldiers in town didn't ask us about our business, and I used several ration cards and marks Uncle Martin had given me to buy bread, carrots, radishes, and cheese. I rearranged the papers in my pockets to have the ID and orders of the soldier to report west to Brussels ready.

In Utrecht, we spent a night in the basement of a bombed-out house. Utrecht was southwest of Delfzijl, and I wanted to go back to see if there was any sign of my father, by the old fort or in the house. I believed that if he was alive he would have had to go back. He'd need to know what happened. He would have had to.

Uncle Martin would have taken care of Fergus for as long as he could, but I suddenly wanted nothing more than to be at home with that dog traipsing through the house. Janna and Mevi could come. I tried to imagine my home. The way it had been. What I thought of instead was my uncle's tattoos. I could see the bare-chested trapeze woman, her glorious blue-tipped breasts, and then the black, shaded, full moon looking down at a tall man, hanging from a tree by the neck. One side was for life and the other for death, his body containing both.

In the morning, we went around the city looking to buy some salve for my toes and more supplies for at least another week of scurrying west. In an alley a man with jaundiced skin bent down to a puddle and brought the dirty water to his mouth. I felt sorry for him but wanted to be away from the reek and gauntness of other starving men.

Mevi just took in all that hunger and hurt like there was so much it pushed all the words out of her head to make room. I wanted to push her eyelids down and kiss each one to keep them closed. My brother had been wrong to think he wanted to see everything, or had not lived long enough to know all the starving men that cross one's path.

At the cheese and produce shop, the woman behind the counter had a long, angular face with arched eyebrows and watery eyes. In front of her on the table were heads of red cabbage, leeks, turnips, carrots, and onions that I wanted to bite into like a starved beast; taste the freshness and dirt. The woman had a toddler who cried inconsolably. Something about the small boy reminded me of a monstrous radish: filthy, damp, and bitter with a round red face. The child eyed me in my uniform with an uneasy mix of fear, confusion, and some deep-seated anger, with hungry, hungry eyes. I listened to his wail, and felt a strong desire to slam his head onto the marble floor to shut him up, to see a bright color seep from his skull. I was shocked to look down and see my hand cupped, as if palming the boy's head, only then realizing how twisted my thoughts were becoming.

We followed the wrought-iron garden fence into the park. A gravel path led to a grotto with a stone statue of a river nymph. On a bench in front of a hedge of budding ornamental shrubs, we ate bread and tried to figure out what to do next. I needed a doctor for my feet.

Mevi tapped Janna's leg and pointed down the path. Almost a dozen German soldiers turned the corner, coming our way. We were out in the open and they looked like a patrol. A terrific swelling of energy rose up in me and more than any other time in my life, I felt a screaming need to survive, if not for me, than to protect these two with me. Seeing those soldiers, the fear of Mevi ending up at the bottom of a pit crashed down on me. It was too late to make a run for it, and I thought all was about to be lost.

I patted the bench next to me, motioning for Mevi to sit down. I eased back and stretched an arm comfortably over the back of the bench around Janna, and watched the soldiers come. As they got closer, they abruptly stopped. They weren't carrying rifles but musical instruments in dark cases. Breaking to the right, they started walking to the gazebo to practice for a concert. I shut my eyes. How ridiculous. How ridiculous the world was at that moment.

"What should we do?" Janna asked.

I sat on that bench, trying to think of an exit point from the city, but my feet were too sore to go through another long stretch of time outside in the wet and cold. I needed help, and I didn't know which identity to try. What person to become.

"Do you want to continue on your own?" I asked them then.

"No," she said. "No."

As a threesome, we walked into a church to seek shelter. Janna and Mevi sat in a back pew as I walked up to a small altar and a stained-glass window of Jesus with his arms spread out to the congregation. I wasn't sure if Jesus was calling his flock to him or sending them out into the world. Light lingered on the altar, the communion table, the pressed vestment cloths, and the giant, opened Bible with a red ribbon tucked between the pages. Part of me wanted to limp forward, fall to my knees, crawl across the chancel, slither to the tabernacle, eat the bread, and drink the wine, then steal and sell the gold.

Footsteps came down the aisle. A fat man with a scarred face in a brown friar's robe walked toward me. A slight wheeze followed each exhale.

"Are you here for confession, son?" the man asked me.

"I think so," I said.

"Then right this way." He lumbered into the confessional off to the side of the altar. I followed him, and we each sat on our own side of the booth.

"Father, I need help," I said.

"We all need help from time to time," he rasped.

"No, it's my feet, they're freezing and I need somewhere to hide."

The friar was quiet for a moment, and I didn't say a word. The red chair smelled of incense.

"Your fellow soldiers will be able to help you," he said.

"I am not one of them, Father."

"Then what are you?"

What am I? That's what I didn't know anymore, what I hadn't understood since the war began and everyone was forced to take sides. I was a cave-dweller. An animal in the twilight. A vagrant of the snow. A Dutchman. A Nazi. An orphan. I couldn't answer. I scratched at the wood on the pew with my fingertips.

"My son, what can I do for you?"

"My feet," I said. "I need someone to doctor them. Please."

"Son, I think the other soldiers can help you."

"Father, please. I'm not one of them." I wanted to tell him about Janna and Mevi, but at the moment I thought they'd be ignored or worse for being Jewish and falling in his line of sight. "Just look at my feet."

The friar stood up, opened his door, and then swung mine open. He stood there, imposing and as wide as the door frame. I'd made a mistake. I reached into my bag and rooted around for the Luger. The friar lifted his cassock and pulled out two Colt revolvers, one in each hand, that he slung from his belt line. By the time he had the guns leveled at my head, I hadn't even grabbed the handle of the Luger.

"Jesus," I said.

"Please, watch your mouth in here, young man."

"You're carrying guns in the church?"

"What are you reaching for?"

I slumped back. The bag fell to my feet. I didn't see a way to get by him.

"Well, son. I guess you'd better let me have a look at your feet to judge for myself," he said.

I kicked off my left boot and reached down to peel off the sock, and the friar let one gun drop to his side and lifted his other hand to block his nose from the stench. My second and third toes on that foot were solid black. There were red lines under the skin, leading across the top of my foot where the entire thing had become infected.

"Why haven't you gone to the soldiers to have those taken care of?"

"I told you, I'm not one of them."

"Is the other foot like that?"

"Only one of my toes on that foot is frozen."

"Okay then," the man said, holstering his guns under his cassock. "Who are you?"

"Someone who needs help, that's all."

"You have to understand, no one can be trusted in these times. The Gestapo dress up like downed airmen in order to infiltrate the escape lines. Even telling that story does damage. It makes people nervous. I can never be too careful." He stroked his ginger-colored beard and looked at my rotting foot again. "Let's see what we can do for you."

"You're not going to turn me in?" I asked.

"You're not going to give me a reason to, are you?"

Specks of dust drifted through the rafters. The friar's breathing was still labored.

"No. I'm out of options. I need your help."

"Like I said, we all need help sometimes."

"Then, I have friends too," I said, and pointed to the back of the church where Janna was holding Mevi tight as if ready to dash from the church.

The friar led the three of us to a room behind the altar. "You stay here for a bit. When it's dark, we'll find you some help."

We waited there for hours. I struggled to remember the ritual of a Mass. The standing, sitting, and kneeling. Lining up for communion. I couldn't grasp finding solace in such a habit. I wanted no Christian bread or Jesus wafers now. After being alone with my thoughts for so long, I only wanted the hot breath of words. More words than I could take in. Anoint me with voices and the stories of those I love, an outpouring of everything they know. That alone would be worth falling to my knees in worship.

When the friar came back, he motioned for us to follow. We walked out the back of the church and through the park where we'd been sitting earlier. We cleared the park, and kept walking to the outskirts of town. When we passed people on the street, even soldiers, they nodded to the friar and didn't stop us.

I asked him where he had gotten his guns.

"Maybe it's best we know very little about each other," he said.

"It's only that I've never met such a heavily armed man of God before. Not even a poorly armed one."

"Well, one of the guns is for any German who gets in my way, and the other is for me if I fail to hold them off."

We continued in silence past the city limits. Painful kilometers, leading us through farmlands.

When we reached a farmhouse set off by itself, the friar knocked on the door and we waited until an old man opened. The man wore scuffed rubber boots, wool pants, and a brown sweater with a coarse collar popped to cover the back of his neck. His cheeks were pitted, and a purple filigree of veins webbed across his swollen nose. He looked at the four of us, and I saw he didn't recognize the friar.

"May we warm up at your table for a minute, sir, before we carry on our way?"

The man hesitantly stepped aside. Inside, an old woman stood in the doorway. The old man had a laborer's powerful hands. His wife was stern, upright, with big eyes that took us in. She gave a slight, sad smile to Mevi.

"Very cold out there tonight. We're sorry to be a bother, but like I said, just a moment to warm up."

The old man pulled out three roughly hewn chairs at his table for us to sit down. The friar looked around the house and then set his eyes on the old man. "A lovely house you have here, sir." He pulled a torn playing card from his cassock and laid it on the table in front of him.

"Thank you," the man said. He looked at the card, and then for a long moment at each of us. He stood up and walked to a cupboard behind him, and when the man turned his back the friar fingered the handle of one of the revolvers under his cassock, his white cord with three knots swung off the side of the chair. When the old man turned around, he brought the matching half of the friar's torn card to the table.

"Very good," the friar said, letting his hands slip away from his sides. "This young man here could use some help that is beyond me."

"And who is this young man?" the old woman asked.

"I'm Dutch."

"And?"

I looked at Janna, then back to the old woman. "I'm trying to escape conscription. They're with me," I said, nodding at the girls. Janna looked surprised by my confession, but I kept my eyes on the old couple, who, to my surprise, decided to let us stay. The first night they fed us beans, potatoes, and cognac, which warmed me and I could feel the blood start to circulate, but also made my feet throb. The old couple let me change in their bathroom, and when they saw my feet with my three curled-up and blackened toes, they both covered their mouths.

Mevi stared without flinching.

"Maybe take her to the back," the old woman said to Janna, motioning to Mevi.

"You have to do something about those toes, boy," the old man said.

He had been a soldier in the Great War. He said he'd seen frostbite before and knew how bad it could get if not dealt with.

"He can't go back to town. There are too many soldiers, and there will be questions," the friar said.

"We'll help you. But this won't be pleasant."

They got me drunk that night. The liquor was sharp and sour and felt like acid in my gut, swishing over my ulcers. I sat in a chair until I could barely hold my head up, and mumbled about Janna and Mevi, the old man dying in the woods, and a giant stepping on me. The friar grabbed my chin and poured more liquor down my throat. Then they put ropes around my upper legs to cinch off the arteries, and then more around my upper calves until my legs felt like sausages in casings. Then the friar laid his giant body across my chest so I couldn't move. The old man had his wife pour alcohol all over my feet. A giant metal pot of water boiled nearby. She had bandages, a jigsaw, a mallet, and a flat-mouthed screwdriver with a sharpened tip that would slice through bone when her husband hit the handle with the mallet.

The old woman put a wet rag in my mouth, and the water seeped down my throat and choked me as I bit into it. It was under these crude conditions that the old man amputated three toes on my left foot and one on my right. Thick, phlegm-green pus oozed out of each, followed by black blood. When he cut, my toes made a soft thud against the porcelain plate. More black blood drained from the dismembered toes, and then turned pink and normal-looking again, as if I was making my feet sick. My blood soaked into the wadded cloth until he cauterized the wound with a knife his wife had kept on the stovetop burner until it throbbed bright orange. Strange smells filled the room. The friar's face was bright red from straining to keep me from bucking loose.

The friar pulled the rag from my mouth, held his scored face close to mine and whispered, "Were you sent to find out the escape routes?"

I bit down on the inside of my cheeks.

"Tell me," he said, slipping a free hand from my shoulder and pushing it on my throat.

"Please, don't do that," the old woman said, putting a hand on the friar's arm.

"We have to know for sure," the friar said. "Who sent you?" he yelled into my face.

Pain pulsed through my body. My teeth sought each other through the skin of my cheeks. The room moved at an angle. The asthmatic red face interrogated me, Colt revolvers that were looped into the friar's cassock dug into my gut.

"No. Let him go," I heard Janna scream as she rushed into the room. Her sleepy little half of a shadow followed behind her, taking it all in.

The friar easily held Janna back as I shook my head no, pinched my eyes shut, and whatever ghastly expression the friar saw on my face said enough. He let go of my throat and resumed pinning me down.

Soon after, they placed the burning metal against my third toe stump, and I passed out.

I don't remember anything that happened after that. I didn't dream.

I awoke startled, disoriented, my heart booming. The deep thrumming of my own pulse and short breaths let me know the urgent force of life hadn't left me. I was still drunk and had a horrible fever. Hot blood pooled inside my stomach.

In the distance a calf bawled. Folds of cloth and quilted blankets were wrapped around my body. My hands began groping at the blankets to feel my legs, to run my palms down my shins, over the ankles, and along the fanned-out bones of my feet to the thick padding around my toes. The two white wads of my bandaged feet bobbed up from beneath the blankets. I stared at the gauze but could not yet imagine the obscene gaps between my toes.

Fear came to me in shuddering, breathless gulps. My clearest thoughts fluttered off like gypsy moths. My body sank back into the sweat-soaked bedding and darkness.

When I woke again, everything seemed far away. Or I was far away, like being pulled out of a photograph. Yanked away from a woman talking. Janna. Janna in the center of the room, far away. She was saying something. It seemed urgent. I wanted to be near her. To walk up to her but everything between us wavered.

Nothing felt real.

Then I felt her hand pushing on me. On my chest. Her fingers splayed, each resting with a gentle force. Her hands touched my chest the way I'd pushed on the tombstone Ludo carved for Edwin. Then there was nothing again.

I woke a third time and there was the girl. Mevi. Her face close to mine. I willed my mind to rise up from the fog pinning me down, but then she was gone.

My eyes opened and closed in a blur. The old woman who helped cut my feet came in with a steaming cup of hot coffee and a bowl of beef broth, and laid them on the small nightstand next to the bed. She walked heavily and wore a thick, tweed skirt and gray sweater. She wiped her hands on her brown smock and then placed a palm on my forehead, then against my cheek, cupping it, which eased some of the desolate feelings that had come to me in the night. She tapped her crooked finger against my collarbone, and smiled with blackening teeth.

"You had me worried for a while, boy."

When I came out of my stupor the next afternoon, a crochet counterpane was tucked over me. My stomach burned, and both of my feet throbbed all the way up to my hips. The old woman was there. Behind her was a radio tuned to an illicit English station. I heard snippets of news while tossing in bed.

"Who are you?" I asked.

"It's better we don't share names, dear," she said.

Half asleep, and half awake, I lay and stared out the window and thought of going to summer camp with my brother and Ludo years before. There, we had tossed one another up and chanted our names. It shocked me now how casual we were about marching in our uniforms, aiming guns, and lobbing grenades. How all that we had been training for unfurled before us, how easy all that had come.

The memory faded, and I became lucid for a moment. I faced the old woman.

"Where are they?"

She shook her head no.

"Where are they?"

"They left."

"What. To where?"

"They told you when you woke. The woman told you. She thanked you. You were awake."

"When will they be back?"

The woman shook her head no again.

"Why? How long have I been sleeping?" I pushed myself up in the bed, but lay back down when the weight of Janna's hands on my chest felt real again, felt like something very serious and not a dream at all, but stones pushing me down.

The old woman rubbed a rag over my forehead, and the feel of it on my skin, of someone tenderly reaching out to me when I felt so alone, brought wracking sobs up my spine. I choked. "No. Where? No. Where'd they go?"

"It's best not to know."

"What. Why. Why now?" I rolled onto my side to cover how raw I felt. "Why'd they leave?"

Though I knew. Even then, newly freed from the fever dream, I knew. I was not a worthy shepherd. Not for them. To them I was a stranger. But to me they had become much more. To me they were a renewed purpose. A tangible direction. Jesus, was I to lose everyone?

"The friar?" I pressed on.

The woman pressed the rag to the back of my neck. "Yes."

"He took them someplace safe?"

"He brought you here. You're safe. He'll take them somewhere as well."

When I stopped crying, I rolled back to the old woman.

"Will *he* tell me where they are? If I go back to him, will he tell me?"

She let the rag fall open, then lay the cool cloth over my face so I could not see her.

I kept my eyes closed then and pretended to sleep. When she bent down to feel my forehead I could smell the starch on the cuff of her shirt, the dark odor of boiled vegetables, and the warmth of her breath. When she left the scent lingered, a presence I held on to for comfort.

Once my fever broke, the horrible pain in my feet lessened. It took another week before the swelling went down, and I could stand and start to take a few baby steps. My balance was off. I had to relearn where to put pressure against the floor. The large gaps between my toes felt all wrong. I would put too much pressure on one side of my foot to overcompensate, and at times, the phantom weight of my missing toes ached inside my bandages.

I wandered their home. Now with the girls gone the desire to keep going faded. My appetite for food or love or sex or even safety slipped beyond me. I wanted everything to go black again.

There were a few pictures of the old farmer who took me in as a soldier when he was younger. Looking at them made me feel guilty for running away from my war. I wished for his bravery. I told the old lady as much.

"I'll get you all killed," I told her. "You're risking too much."

"The old have less to lose, dear," she said, patting my shoulder as she set a bowl of broth in front of me.

There was another picture on the wall of a young man with a wide, stern face similar to the old man's. "Is this your son?"

"Yes."

"Where is he?"

"We don't know."

On the wall was another old photograph of a large family standing in front of a small log home. The family bunched together around an old man laid out on a wooden cart that was propped up to face the camera. The old man wore a suit and his long beard had been brushed out, and his hair looked wet and pushed back. At first I thought he had large eyes but when I looked closer, I saw that they had been painted over his closed eyelids. I'd seen pictures like that before. Easterners took pictures of their dead to keep some trace. As pictures were very expensive then, these funeral pictures were an event to dress up for. If you couldn't travel to see a relative, you could see the picture of them being put to rest. There were old women, rough-looking bearded men, and stern wives with broad children of all ages, some cradled in their mothers' arms and others as tall as their fathers. It would be a fine way to die, propped up like a meat puppet and surrounded by loved ones. It should be the way we all die.

We had been eating their potato rations, and once, after a bombing close to town, the old man brought back the head of a cow that had been killed. He said he had to use a fellow farmer's double-handed tree saw to get it loose. He carved the meat off the bone and they both rattled around the kitchen frying it up, and boiling it into a stew.

That night, when I sat down at the table with them and had a meal with them for the first time, the food she laid out almost made me weep. She'd made beef casseroled in beer and served with raisins fried in a pan over the hearth. That night we feasted, but I had a terrible case of the runs. I was strangely happy about this as it meant at least my bowels still worked.

Later that night, the old woman had me lie down on the kitchen floor with a towel under my heels. From a mothballed closet in the shadowed corner of the room she brought out a sewing kit with a polished cherry handle. She undid the bandages at my feet, pinched the rounded eye of a needle, and lanced my cloudy blisters. Each rotting abscess let out a nauseating stench. After that, I limped around the old couple's house feeling like Thump-Drag himself.

Then I repacked my backpack and readied myself to move on. I left two hundred guilders and the gold coins from the barter kit on the pillow of the mattress they'd given me.

"Thank you for everything," I said.

"Your fast, running days are over," the old woman said. "Hide when you can. Please hide."

Over the next several days of moving west, I stopped in old barns, office buildings, and basements of deserted houses. One home looked ancient, like the small cottages I'd seen with Edwin and Uncle Martin in Borkum, one of the Frisian Islands, which had once been inhabited by whalers. Some of the oldest homes on that island had whale-bone fences surrounding the property.

A Messerschmitt buzzed overhead. The black crosses on the under-side of its wings were visible. I stumbled over tree trunks and brambles as it passed. I was always falling, then worming my way forward.

My feet always hurt. Each breath pressurized the feeling I was obli-gated to carry everyone I ever loved free of this mess. When walking I felt like the beating of all their hearts replaced that of my own.

Outside the town of Guttenfield, there was a parking area and a large sign staked into the ground that read Guttenfield Zoo. There were no cars, and the broad, iron gates were closed and chained shut with a thick iron padlock. A smaller sign hung from the gate on which it had been printed Please Don't Eat the Animals' Food. The apostro-phe and the word *food* had been crossed out with a white brushstroke, so the sign now read Please Don't Eat the Animals.

I kept working my way past farmhouses with thatch-roofed barns and a shadowy castle draped in fog along a river. It felt like I'd marched through centuries, back to some barbaric age. I imagined kings, with fur caps and dark beards, who hunted in the woods along the river, wandering the castle's firelit hallways. I ate what little food I could scavenge and rooted around for snails on the forest floor, dig-ging the meaty parts out with the tip of my dagger. They tasted like diluted salt and slipped down my throat like hunks of phlegm. After eating, I doctored my feet, changing the bandaging, which soaked through from all my walking. My bare feet showed the charred nubbins where my toes had been, each pinched off like the end of a sausage link.

I crossed into Belgium and made my way to Bruges. There were people in the streets of the city: a French mountain man in a full-length bear-fur coat; an old man with a Lord Kitchener mustache; and a small girl in a shabby smock of a dress, holding one handle of a bag tethered to a tired-looking woman with greasy, brown hair. The bulbous end of a baguette stuck out of their bag, and the little girl's dark eyes watched the bread as she was dragged along by the woman's grip. Around them was the rubble of buildings left in the wake of the Allied bombings. The old couple had given me a change of clothes, farmer's clothes, but the city people eyed my hobbled gait with suspicion anyway.

There were posters on the walls: Nazi propaganda intended for Belgians and Frenchmen, as the British at the time were sinking French naval ships in the Mediterranean to keep them from falling into German hands. The posters said thirteen hundred French sailors had been killed by the RAF. So the Nazis wanted the French and Belgians to take up arms against the RAF. The posters helped me decide on an escape route through northern Europe. I figured the less time in France the better, as the country would likely have every kind of displaced person, and the allegiances would be too varied to navigate safely.

My first night in Bruges, as I slept in the main square of town, prisoners were roped together and shuffled through the streets to the train station. Floodlights filled the air overhead, sweeping back and forth. If I watched the lights long enough, they turned into stars that had become mobile, swirling around in space.

23

The Knight's Cross was now sewn into the canvas lining on the inside of my backpack. The orders of a soldier, Hedrick Sherman, were in my right cargo pocket. Hedrick was due to report to guard detail on the islands out in the English Channel, which the Germans had taken over. The orders were dated for two months ago, but I took ink and carved a potato with a relief of the new date and pressed it onto the forms. At the train station in Brussels, the guards glanced at the papers, my uniform, and then let me board a train to France. It was filled with immigrant workers, other soldiers, and civilians who looked like this was part of their quotidian lives. It was easier to blend into the crowd than I'd anticipated.

In Rouen, where the tracks would have crossed the Seine River, the bridge had been destroyed. Everyone unloaded from the train, and were ferried across on a small barge to the other side, where we boarded another train and kept on going west and then north to Cherbourg.

When the train got to Cherbourg, I'd intended to steal a boat and work my way across the Channel, but all the small passenger boats in the harbor had been sunk, and soldiers even took axes to the hulls of the little dinghies. My only other option was to wait in a military compound for a boat out to the island of Jersey to take me to my fake post and try to steal a boat from there.

I spent the night debating whether I'd made a huge mistake staying to the north to try to cross the Channel as opposed to going south, through the Pyrenees Mountains, and trying to work my way to Gibraltar. Though there was no way of knowing if I could have made it such a distance. I decided to start practicing a story about being late arriving to my post.

In the morning, with the identity of Hedrick, whom I decided had been delayed after having his feet wounded in a bombing raid in Utrecht, I boarded the boat to Jersey. It was a fisherman's boat, not that different from Uncle Martin's. The boat's owner was a Frenchman who had also been conscripted into service. His name was Fabien. Fabien's face was narrow and rigid, and he wore a thick bird's nest of a beard. In the wheelhouse with Fabien, we spoke English because Fabien's German and my French were both poor.

"This is a good boat," I said to him after we pushed off.

"She's been good to me." Fabien eyed the water ahead of him.

The only other person onboard was another soldier, who had gone belowdecks to sleep. I asked Fabien about how he'd come to be a ferryman, and told him my family had done the same thing. I shared that I was a Dutchman and couldn't wait for the war to be over. "I would like nothing more than to jump the Channel and travel to Britain," I said, watching Fabien's reaction. He looked at me out of the corner of his eye.

"Dangerous talk," he said.

"Profitable though, I imagine."

The two of us sailed in silence for a while. Belowdecks, the other man slept. From Cherbourg to Southampton across the Channel it was a mere hundred miles, and I contemplated pulling my gun and making the two men blow by Jersey and sail closer to England. But in the end, I took a gamble, and was frank with Fabien.

"In here, I have papers," I said, kicking at my bag.

"What kind of papers?" he asked.

"Papers for the other side."

"I see. Both lucky and dangerous for you," he said.

"It is, but it could be a big advantage for you."

"How so?"

"I can pay you to take me closer to the shore, I'll row the rest of the way."

"We'll get blown to hell before we get close, and what would you row on?"

"I can pay you for trying. Get me close enough for an honest shot at fighting the currents with your inflatable life raft."

"That's crazy."

"I have money. A lot of money. You could take care of your family through the rest of the war."

"You're a crazy kid, now be quiet."

"Fabien. Listen to me. All you need to do is get me close enough to row the rest of the way."

"Even if we didn't take fire, the rocks on shore would cut you to ribbons, and if that didn't happen, the British would eat you whole."

"Get me close. I'll deal with those things."

I leaned into Fabien and begged him. "Drop the other soldier off, wait until dark, and we'll run without lights. I'll help you navigate. When we're within sight of land, any land in Britain, I'll pay you, and you can turn back." I pulled a stack of francs from my backpack. "This offer expires as soon as I see land on Jersey."

"What about the other soldier? He'll know something's not right."

"You wake him up and tell him I've already gone ashore. I'll hide in your steering hold until night when you push off again. I'm going to be paying somebody to help me get there, might as well be you. It's a lot of money. Consider it."

When Fabien pulled his boat up to Jersey, I ducked down below the wheelhouse console and hid with my backpack in the slimy bilge tank. My Luger was stuffed in my jacket pocket, ready to draw if Fabien changed his mind.

At the dock, he tied the boat off with the help of several soldiers, and then woke the man in the holds.

Every sound on the fishing boat was familiar. I listened as time passed. I practiced the story I would use if I was found in Yarborough's RAF uniform once in England. I was shot down over Delfzijl, in Holland. I'd been in hiding and had worked my way back. My parents came to Britain after the Great War. I was born in Holland but grew up in London. That was my first mission, and I bartered with a fisherman to smuggle me offshore.

In the bilge I pushed away the feeling I had become Herbert Yarborough, sentenced to the dark, by convincing myself I was close to fulfilling a promise to my mother and uncle. I was close to escaping. I had to be. I had to believe that.

After the sunset, Fabien came back to the boat. When he cast off, he called for me to come up. He went into the holds and pulled out two oars and leaned them on the stairs heading up to the deck.

"I hope you don't get me killed, but if I die, I'd just as soon have my pocket full of cash."

I pulled out the Luger and placed it on my right thigh so Fabien knew I had it. Uncle Martin would have done the same, I thought. Then I gave him the money.

"We will be fine," I said, knowing all the dangerous submarines flittering along and under the surface of the water.

The boat worked its way east of the island, out of sight of the sentries and their giant searchlights set up to detect RAF raids, then turned north and headed for England. The chop was several feet but the boat handled it well. The inflatable rescue raft was blown up on the back deck with two oars inside. My papers, maps, cash, gun, clothing, and the English airman's jumpsuit were in my pack. I pressed the jumpsuit out with my hands, then changed into it. It fit, but the sleeves and legs ran below the knobby bones of my ankles and wrists. I put the English airman's papers in my pocket. I stepped into Herbert Yarborough's skin.

Back in the wheelhouse, Fabien looked at me and whistled. "You are one impressive young man." He pointed the bow to a small cropping of lights off in the distance. "That's where we're headed. There's a small town east where I'll drop you, but I have no idea what it's like now. I haven't been there since the war started."

"Okay," I said, and turned away from Fabien. I ate the last of my dark bread to have energy for fighting the currents and got into the raft. There was nothing else for me to do. I put on a life jacket and looped a small length of mooring line between my backpack and belt. A small canvas dry bag from Fabien's holds was filled with all my German soldier's identifications. I planned to cut it loose from my pack at sea so no one in Britain would find them.

When I was ready, Fabien undid the line, cast it into the boat, and waved.

"Good luck," he said.

Set loose in the ocean, the rubber floor of the raft was the back of a giant serpent—a huge, pulsating muscle. It was hard to steady myself while feeling separated from the swells by such a thin strip of material. Drifting from Fabien's boat, I remembered a line from a poem in my father's study years before. It didn't matter that I couldn't remember who had written it. They might have been anonymous, taking on new shapes and forms like me.

And now I am on the wide, wide sea, alone.

The shadow of land was a few kilometers away, and as soon as my oars touched the water, I fought my way toward shore, riding up the side and down the slope of each swell. My back ached fighting the current from sweeping me away, and in my battle I became aware that nothing, not one future moment, was promised to me. A skin of sweat coated my body by the time I heard the surf breaking on the rocks. The white wash and spray of water blasted up and off the shore. The oar blades slapped the water, and the handles rubbed the calluses on my palms raw.

As I splashed through the night, a giant spotlight snapped to life from a bluff and swept over the water so the light engulfed me. It bounced off my body, and I raised an oar over my head and started waving it back and forth, back and forth, then put my hands over my head and started waving them.

The tide pulled me out a bit farther, so I took the oar and started fighting my way back. The light still swallowed me. I slipped the dagger from my boot and cut loose the packet of German papers and dropped them over the side of the raft, away from the spotlight. Then I used my prized *Blut und Ehre* dagger to cut open a sewn-in pocket inside the backpack to loosen my Knight's Cross. With the medal in one hand and the dagger in the other, I plunged both hands into the sea and opened my palms. Both fluttered down like golden flashes of fish.

Closer to shore, where the raft was going to smash into the rocks, I jumped. An icy blackness swallowed me. I reached for anything solid, finding only mouthfuls of water, until I wasn't sure if I was under or above the bitter surface. I felt myself being lifted higher into the blackness on the shoulder of a wave. Rollers slammed me down as I struggled to the surface. Mouthfuls of salt water went down my throat, and my soaked clothes weighed me down into the swirling, black cold. Waxy arms of seaweed wrapped around my feet until the incoming tide freed me and pushed me toward land. I was flotsam—free—sure I was about to die.

Then the waves lifted me up and over the rocks and pushed me in with the breakers. I rolled through the muck by clutching the beach and dragging my body forward. My arms and two stripes of muscles running down each side of my spine were raw and burning from rowing and straining to keep myself from slipping below the surface of the swells. When I crawled out of the surf onto the sand, the spotlight was still sweeping over the water looking for me. With the last of my energy I stood up, grabbed my bag, and ran to a cluster of boulders along the bluff and hid.

Several minutes later there were small flashlight beams walking down the far hillside and combing the beach and the large spotlight went out. I heard British soldiers calling to one another to look for the raft among the rocks. They stayed a long time looking into the water but eventually went back up the hill toward the source of the spotlight. I sat between the rocks in the dark and felt to see if the knobs of cash in the pack were still safe. After waiting a shivering hour, I changed out of the RAF uniform and into civilian clothes between the rocks. I left the RAF uniform and paperwork on the ground like I'd shed another layer of skin, the last remnant of Herbert Yarborough, and crawled in the opposite direction of the soldiers, toward the distant town rising over the bluff.

24

In town, several soldiers drank coffee and smoked cigarettes outside a café. They were straight-backed, lock-kneed, clean-shaven men in khaki uniforms with long-sleeved leather jackets and tin helmets. They had unbuttoned their jackets to be able to fold their arms tighter around their chests to stay warm.

The town had been bombed, and several of the old buildings now stood in concave rubble mounds sliding into the streets. There was an open merchant's store in the town center that I went inside and told the man behind the counter I needed new clothes. Inside there was an empty wine barrel full of walking sticks and carved canes. Ivory and bone handles with rosewood or ebony shafts. Some had faces for handles. Bearded Romans. Bespectacled royalty. Hooded Bedouins. I could imagine my face as Edwin drew it, carved into such a stick, then a hand palming it and covering the world in darkness.

With the pounds Uncle Martin had given me, I paid for a pair of gray flannel trousers, a tweed overcoat, leather boots, and a shirt. Then I went to the train station where cars and military jeeps lined the road. I hired one of the drivers to drive me west to Southampton, where

Uncle Martin had written there was a good port to find a ship out of Europe. I had made it, but I still didn't feel safe. The whole time walking through town, buying clothes, and even in the car driving away, I expected a hand to grab my shoulder and pull me back.

The car ride took two hours, during which I laid out my paperwork in the backseat. All I had left was my own Dutch ID. Jacob Koopman, of Delfzijl, Holland. The picture and the writing seemed like they belonged to a stranger.

As we drove, RAF bombers crossed the Channel.

In Southampton, the driver dropped me at the port. Europe was across the Channel, which was full of military vessels and submarines. Whatever boat left this port would do so at great risk, but I didn't know of any other options. I wandered the docks, eyeing the sides of the docked freighters and cargo boats. If there were crewmen at the gangway, they told me the same thing. Their boats weren't going anywhere, or that they didn't have enough crew to make their next trip.

"Do you know Felix Courtier?" I asked one of the gangway watchmen.

"No."

"Javier Méndez?" I had the letter from my uncle in my pocket, and by midafternoon I'd asked after each name. "Petrous Valspar? Michael McCollum?" No one in the harbor knew these men.

After I had inquired at almost every ship, a man with a black mustache and a slumped, heel-scraping gait walked up to me on the dock. He wore a grease-stained coverall with the sleeves rolled up, exposing the dark hair that covered his gorilla arms. The knuckles of both his hands were capped in gnarled scabs.

"You the one asking for folks?" he asked in a Irish accent.

"I am."

"Mind if I ask what it is you're interested in doing?"

"Find a friend of a friend."

"Looking for work, are ya?" he shifted back on his heels, and his massive chest ballooned out.

"Looking for a ship overseas. I'd work for it if I could."

"Is that so? Tell me, who are these people you're looking for again?"

I listed the names Uncle Martin had given me.

"No. No. Don't know any of those fellas, but I may be able to help you out. I know a boat bound for New York as soon as it can crew up. It's outside of town at the old dock if you're interested. Go ask around there this evening."

Later that afternoon, I started walking out to the pier. More planes flew overhead crossing the Channel. I pictured the distant town those planes would sight and bomb, and then imagined the continent on fire. The raising orange glow I'd seen over Rotterdam and Delfzijl.

I walked to the old port where the man had told me I might find a ship. At the dock was a small lean-to covering a large corkboard that had messages in many different languages stuck to it. There were pictures with directions of where the person who left the note went, who they were looking for, what had happened to them. A whole board of hundreds of layered notes, letters, and pictures; it was a monument to the lost. A last hope for the living. The board made me feel sick, as I knew it would be miraculous if anyone found a note left by someone they knew.

To Neil Von Poppell,

We are going to my cousin's in Halifax. Please send word of your safety. We waited for you as long as we could. May God Keep You. May we meet again for the Cherries.

Lucas.

To Margaret Margareta,

I have the kids, my love. Our hearts are full of your dreams and they keep us well. Rest if you have left this world, and rest well. If you have not, look for us. I will drop our name loudly everywhere on this earth that we go so people will remember, and you can follow the trail of my voice, follow the love it sings out to you.

Vincent Margareta.

To Bobolus Yakaveti,

Your Brother will put us up in his apartment in New York. His address is 1567 Franklin St, Apartment 12 B, Queens, NEW YORK. We will look for work to send money.

Your father, Sol.

There were pages upon pages of Dutch names too, and addresses for where they could be reached, stories from people who didn't know where they would be as they had no money and nowhere to go. Many picked an arbitrary date to meet back at that very spot. That seemed to be a trend in the notes. These notes contained a fierce hope, as much for the writer as the written-to, that they would meet, and with any providence, they could have some control over the date, the place, the if, and the when.

Many of the dates on the letters had passed, some of the more deeply buried by over two years.

I had to stop reading, it was all too much, such glaring loss. When I turned away, I saw a dirty, old freighter ship docked at the end of the wooden pier. The *Royal Crest,* a small cargo ship flagged out of Liverpool. It was docked to this borderline-defunct pier with no lights on it and a dilapidated dock house. The ship looked empty except for someone standing watch on the gangway. When I got closer, I saw it was the fat Irish sailor.

"Still looking for a ship, are you then?" the man said.

"Is this your ship?"

"It's the captain's," he said.

"Do you really need crew?" I asked.

"That's right. You'll need to talk to the captain, though."

"Is he here?"

The man walked up the gangway to a radio by the open hatch and called for the captain. The old boat's blue trim was in need of paint and covered in rust bubbles.

Several minutes later, the captain, an older Portuguese man, came down the gangway. He had tanned skin and a horseshoe of wispy gray hair over his ears. His lidded green eyes were pinched close together. A cigarette-stained, yellow mustache curved around his mouth and pointed at his loose, jowly cheeks.

"The kid says he's looking to crew up," the watchman said.

"He does, huh? And who is the kid?" the captain asked.

"My name is Jacob Koopman."

"And where is Jacob Koopman from?"

"I'm from Delfzijl, in Holland."

"In the northeast on the left bank of the Ems, across from Germany? Yes? What'd you do there?"

"Germans have been there for a few years now. They made me work in a local factory, and I worked on a fishing boat with my uncle."

"So you worked for the Germans?"

"Sir, they gave my family food rations, which I needed for my mother. When she died a few months ago, I ran away. I'm trying to get as far from them as possible."

"Well, we should put a gun in your hand and send you back to get them out of your town."

"One small gun won't get that job done," I said.

The captain pinned his eyes on mine. "You're right. Now tell me about the fishing boat."

"A large trawler. I navigated it, helped fix the engines, and did all the docking. I knew every nail and board of that boat."

"It was your uncle's boat?"

"Yes."

"What was his name?"

"Martin Van Deerjack."

"Martin Van Deerjack, huh. And what did this Martin Van Deerjack teach you about cargo ships?"

"I've never been on one."

"So why would you be any use to me?"

I'd thought of that answer. "I'm guessing everyone else knows how dangerous leaving this port would be, which is why you can't get a crew and why you're still here. I can crew for you, navigate once we're out of port and underway, and do whatever you need."

"Your uncle taught you all that?"

I thought of Lieutenant-Major Erich Oldif and the dents in his head. His clipboard. All that training I'd had at the naval camp. "Yes," I said.

The captain stepped close enough to smell me. "Do you know the story of the frog and the scorpion?" The mustachioed man standing on the gangway bit back a grin when the captain said this.

"Yes," I said.

"You do? Well, Mr. Jacob Koopman from Delfzijl. You know what I feel like at moments like these?" the captain asked. "I feel like the frog."

"I just want to work my way out of here, that's all," I said.

"Good, because the scorpion goes down too for causing trouble. Isn't that right, Peter?"

The guard's mustache rose up like a hair curtain, revealing a crooked grin. "That's right, sir."

"Let's see your papers?" the captain said, and I handed over my own identification for the first time in months.

"Well, Mr. Koopman, I could use you," the captain said. "But seeing how you already tipped your hand as to wanting to get out of here, and will probably jump ship in the first port you like, I won't pay you for your work. I'll see you across the Atlantic, and I won't have you tossed overboard if you do what's asked. Can you live with that?"

"I can."

"Then I'm Captain Fernandes, and this is Peter, my first mate. We have eight other crewmen, and you make our ninth. Peter will show you the ship. We'll leave first thing tomorrow morning. I suspect you'll be staying aboard until then?"

"Yes, sir," I said.

"Good. Welcome to the crew."

We agreed upon the work I'd do—standing watches, doing engine rounds, and galley duty—and like that, I was to go back to sea. The watery depths were becoming for me the most familiar and terrifying expanse of the earth.

Later that night, Captain Fernandes walked down the dock with a crowd of people. I was on the back deck watching and counted over sixty figures marching behind him. The captain pointed to the cork-board and the people all stuck something to it. Each carried packs on their backs and in their arms as they moved up the gangway. Captain Fernandes led them to the holds where they spread out on the deck.

"You will all stay belowdecks until we're underway. I'll let you know when you can wander about the ship." When Captain Fernandes turned to leave the holds, he saw me standing there. "I didn't say how much galley work there'd be, now did I?" He smiled at me. "There will be more pots to scrub than maybe you thought."

Before we launched from the pier, I met the rest of the crew on the bridge.

"We're taking the northerly route, south of Iceland, rounding southern Greenland, and down to St. John's, working our way to Hali-fax, Boston, and New York," Captain Fernandes said. Then he had me and another one of the crew hoist a white flag with a red cross on it and fly it high so any periscopes could see it. "Give that one a little kiss for me first," he said as he tossed it to me.

The bow of the tramp ship cut through the early morning fog and the white mist brushed over the decks. Behind us stood the last of Europe, dimly lit by the halation of the shore. The smoke and light above the land looked like a giant, six-fingered hand, waving good-bye.

I remembered a story my father told me years ago, when we were on the *Lighthouse Lady* on the way to camp. My uncle was at the helm. My father told me how Poseidon sent Thump-Drag inland with the oar over his shoulder to build a church in his honor. I had grown up believing all those stories as gospel truths. That one especially, emphasizing Thump-Drag's clear knowledge of his purpose. Now, I knew better. Now I could see Thump-Drag tired of his walk, throwing away the oar, and going about his own directionless life. That made sense to me. That was a story I could believe.

By noon that first day at sea, the ship was west of where I had washed ashore several nights before. We went slow to avoid the heeled-over warships that littered the coastline. Some of the downed vessels were held on submerged rocks. The waves traced a white foam outline along their sides. When the sun went down, I twisted all the lightbulbs aboard off or covered them for us to run in the dark. When it was pitch-black, the captain allowed the people in the holds to come up on deck. Peter stayed at the helm and the captain walked among the passengers.

"I need to show you how to use our life rafts," the captain said. He had me and another crew member demonstrate how they inflated and how to load into them. "If we're torpedoed, you'll need to do this, so pay attention." He spoke in slow, direct terms. Then the other crew member translated what the captain had said into Polish. The people were of every age group. A few children were huddled up against the adults. They all focused on the captain and the large inflatable raft in front of them.

"Who are these people?" I asked the captain later that night in the crew mess room.

"Refugees. Much like yourself, I would guess." He chewed on a spoonful of stew.

"From where?"

"Poland and Czechoslovakia," Captain Fernandes said.

I looked around us, and felt something inside me shift. I pictured the notes they pinned to the board in Southampton. I knew the ultimate Nazi goal of having one race and one grand narrative. Their effort to bind the continent together had failed by the mere presence of these people on board. Boats departed from every corner of Europe, and on each, there burrowed little tics of survival stories embedded in each of the passengers. These living refugees gave me hope. The continent itself was still populated with great storytellers, perhaps even some crawling through every contested border and shifting in currents beneath the very ground that was invaded. There was no mono-story, only the great, broken narrative of raw, throbbing life.

After we ate, the captain asked me to follow him to the wheelhouse. "Okay, Mr. Koopman. I'm going to show you how to steer this ship. Your job will be continental avoidance. In other words, don't hit anything. If you can navigate a trawler, this won't be much different. Only, it takes a lot longer to stop. You can start as the second set of eyes on the night watch."

The first several days went like this. I slept in a crew bunk, woke, and helped wash the dishes in the galley and put them away. Then I ate, and sat watch with Peter, or Captain Fernandes, whoever had the watch at the time. I also had to wipe the engines, immaculately kept twin diesels, and do what Peter assigned on the outer decks of the ship, dabbing grout on the exterior so the ship looked rusted and old, which, I was realizing, it was not.

While under way, the passengers who weren't sick ate salt bean soup out of tin mess kits from the ship's galley. The conditions weren't very good for those aboard, but it was a passage of escape. Every flat surface had a sleeping body on it. Many of them hung on to their bunks or the pipes along the base of the bulkheads as the ship pitched back and forth. They retched into vomit buckets that slid across the deck. The fetid air was so very human and pungent that I covered my nose with the cuff of my sleeve every time the buckets needed to be cleaned.

When Captain Fernandes came into the holds, he walked around the bunks looking at his passengers. He coughed something up from deep in his lungs. He bent over and hacked phlegm into a hankie he pulled from his coverall pocket and held the dark discharge in front of him, and then folded the hankie in half and slipped it away. He stopped. At the foot of the bed where a man was lying with his arm over his forehead, the captain leaned down and placed a hand on his chest, patting it, reassuring. A sweet gesture. He walked from person to person, smiling at them, touching them, performing a kind of ministry.

Everything important to me had been taken away or destroyed. These people had probably gone through the same series of losses and were left holding the wreckage of their own lives. Any of them could have been my family, and for a time, that is what they became. I realized that looking into these strangers' faces. Each was my brother and father. The women were my mother, Hilda, Janna, and Mevi. The boys were Ludo and Pauwel.

The captain moved about them and I realized he wasn't giving them last rites, but quite the opposite; he was willing them through. I watched him and thought maybe there were lesser gods who did walk among us. Lifting up others when they needed it most, offering an invisible push on the shoulder that can lead them back to the rest of their lives. Though, maybe that responsibility was for us all, to reach out when we could, to set the floor so people couldn't free-fall forever.

I was touched by his interactions in the holds, and I knew if there was such a thing as redemption, it was quicksilver that must be recaptured each day.

When we came to a patch in the ocean that was glass-calm, the captain idled the engines of the ship. The crew opened a side hatch and

352 — DEVIN MURPHY

let down a rope ladder. The smuggled passengers climbed onto the
rub rail and jumped into the freezing sea. Cramped and lice-ridden,
they leapt out into the ocean and splashed around like children, con-
secrated, briefly cleaned and renewed. I watched from the bridge's
wing station as the people whose old lives had been snagged away
from them through the upheaval of war, shocking and surely violent,
now floated on their backs in the sun.

A porpoise drifted up to the swimming crowd and the tip of its fin
cut the water, which from the surface looked like a shark.

"Oh boy," Captain Fernandes said. "Here we go."

At once, the swimmers screamed and swam wildly back to the ladder. I was startled by their sudden pronounced and fervent desire to
live, and felt I'd never heard a more joyous and powerful noise.

Once we were again under way, the bow of *The Royal Crest* cut through
the waters southeast of Iceland. It was four in the morning, and I
shared the bridge watch with Captain Fernandes. He had me organize
the ship's flag drawers. China. South Africa. Russia. Argentina. A flag
for every nation on earth to hoist up the flagpole. He plotted the ship's
course and prepped the navigational charts. On watch with him, he let
me ask questions about the ship and took the time to explain everything.

"Tell me about that uncle's fishing trawler you were on," he said,
and I did, telling him about the good times I had spent with Uncle
Martin on the water.

"How far out did he go?" the captain asked.

"All over the North Sea."

"For how long would he go out?"

"A week or more at a time by himself. Only a few days if he took me or my brother along." I didn't mean to mention my brother.

"Was it your uncle who had you looking around for Captain . . . What was the name?"

"Courtier. Méndez. And a few others."

"Huh."

We were quiet for a while and the night was calm around us.

"Who are the people in the holds, really?" I asked. I expected him to tell me to mind my own business, but he didn't.

"Financial backers from the major Canadian and American cities pay good money to have people smuggled out of Europe, and very few ships will attempt the trip because of all the carnage caused by U-boats."

"How long have you been doing this?"

"A long time."

"Since the war started?"

"Depends on which war you are referring to." His lidded eyes flared open so I could see them glisten.

"What will you do after you deliver these people?"

"I'll go back. An Allied invasion fleet will be trying to get into Europe eventually, and if they do, nowhere will be safe. Every bit of the continent will be contested and this shoddy little ship will be needed more than ever. There will always be the business of refugees."

The captain's candor made me nervous. He was clearly working a secretive business, and yet he spoke openly. Still, I wanted to know more. "How have you managed to avoid getting caught?"

"There are ways. You figure them out and perfect them."

"Do you have to lie about who you are to cross borders?"

He looked at me for a long time, then broke his gaze and faced the water. "You know, I once saw a burning oil slick sucked up by the eye of a cyclone while at sea. It pulled fire up into a blazing column that moved over the water like God's fiery finger, tracing a new fault line. A fault line that, if it had crossed our path, my passengers and I would have all died. How could a man-made border mean anything once you've seen something like that?"

I wished for other boats like the *Royal Crest* to leave every port in Europe. I wanted my father, Uncle Martin, Ludo and his family, Hilda, Mrs. Von Schuler, Mevi and Janna, Herbert Yarborough, the armed friar, the old couple who took my toes, and all the starving, scared, and wounded to be saved before the military tide that had swept into Germany could be pushed back, kicked under, by some giant revolt.

"What would you do if you had the opportunity to save somebody?" the captain asked me.

I cupped my hands around my face to shield him from seeing the gloss of my eyes. I had been relying on my calculations and rough instinct for so long, I had trained my mind to oscillate away from the deep, feeling part of me. The place where I held the knowledge that I hadn't been able to save anyone. But this man must have sensed my distress, my guilt, and I was fearful that if my thoughts were exposed, the whole continent of the past would heave up and crash over me, swallowing me in an unforgiving and savage swoop. In the silence he asked, "Are your parents gone?"

"Yes." I began crying into my hands.

"Siblings?"

"Yes."

"Your uncle?"

"I'm not sure."

"That doesn't surprise me. He was always a cunning one." The captain's eyes were on me again in the darkened wheelhouse.

"What?"

"Your uncle. Really tall. Tattoos. Whistles through that funny gap in his teeth when he talks too fast."

I stood up so fast I felt a cool push of air against my wet face. "You know him?"

His smile was detached, and his probing eyes contained many strands of consideration. Of me, of what he should say. Of the way this night might unfold. "Not as Martin, but I know him."

"I don't understand. Are you one of the men I was asking for?"

The captain nodded. He looked out the windows and scanned the water then turned back to me.

"Are you Courtier or Méndez?"

He nodded again.

"Which one?" I asked.

He arched his eyebrows and gave me a subtle grin.

"Both?"

He nodded again.

"And Valspar and McCollum?"

He nodded again.

I had a hard time comprehending what I was hearing. "Why are you telling me this?"

"That's a good question." He started to say something but began a fit of deep, stomach-folding coughing into the crook of his arm. I waited until he finished.

"Peter heard me asking for you in the port?"

He nodded.

"That's why he sent me to you. To see who I was?"

"You got it," he said. "You know, it's been my experience that it's the incidents we can't control that make us who we are." We sat without speaking for what felt like a long time as the bow cut through the rolling swells. I pictured a tower of fire swirling over the water, and knew political boundaries meant nothing when weighed against a single human heart. I did not know the captain's motivations, nor he mine, but that night I understood I had crewed up with a shadow ship.

After that, I walked the decks with Captain Fernandes on his night rounds. He scanned the holds, laden with ripening fruit, sprouting potatoes, and burlap sacks of grain giving off the concentrated odors of earth. There were heaps of dried fish; pallets of concrete and rebar; reams of paper, barrels of liquor, molasses, and tar; and all manner of assembled products from years of crossing and recrossing the equator, stretching from pole to pole. And hidden in the holds were people who were forging ahead to a fresh start.

On one of the night rounds, we went to the engine room and watched the blurred-out wheels of the twin diesels and the steady force of the plunging pistons, and I let the hum of orbiting machine parts and electric light seep into me. Standing there with the engine songs and the scent of spent oil and bilge water was sort of like receiving Holy Communion for me. In the holds beneath the waterline, looking over the machinery that pushed steel bones of the ship through wave after wave, I felt at peace being on the ocean, and with the idea of being a stranger to no port but always moving on. As if noticing my interest, the captain had me follow him around his vessel, as if showing me what his life was really like, why and how he did what he did.

"If our schedule holds, we'll dock in Halifax to refuel. Half the passengers will be dropped off there and will make their way to communities in Maritime Canada that have paid for their transport. The rest will be delivered to Boston and New York, where I've arranged paper-work for them.

"We'll then return to Halifax before heading back to England. If you want, I'll pay you for the next trip if you want to stay on. I can show you how to do this. There aren't many who do this work and it's good work. Your uncle was good at this. He probably thought the same of you when he gave you that list of names."

"What if you get caught?"

"All boats fall on a bitter tide."

"You might be killed."

"Nothing's for certain." He hacked up something wet from deep in his lungs.

"Not if you do this kind of work."

"Some foolhardy things are well worth doing." The dim light re-flected off his bald patch. The captain told me to think about it, and when I did, I felt as solitary as I had in the darkest moments in the cave. I thought of the thousands of people who could trace the ocean's waves back to their homeland, to a life now lost. It was horribly selfish to have been concerned only with saving myself when there were all these oth-ers who needed saving as well.

I imagined what my life could now be. I imagined Québec, Ot-tawa, or somewhere in the States, or South America. Somewhere on land. But the land was full of lank flags, and the earthly history of boundaries claimed and fought over and reclaimed. At sea, the flags were taut and snapped violently in the wind, as if alive, and the waves kept creating and erasing the shape of the world. Powerful yet tran-quil, the roll of the sea was significant to me in ways my heart could only murmur, and could not be put in words. For me, the choice felt natural. The ship offered life at the edge, beyond the borderlands, beyond common language, beyond the past and all it carried on its shoulders. The sea offered constant motion, a running toward the future, unburdened from the past. Yes, I knew the sea was for me.

We worked our way northwest toward Greenland to avoid heavy military traffic. Late one night, everyone seemed awake and restless. The top deck was covered in bodies huddled together in their threadbare clothing. Several old women had climbed the back ladder in knee-length nightgowns that hugged to their torsos and fluttered behind them like wind socks. They reached one hand at a time forward along the rail until they found a place to lie down. The low groan of the props churning three decks below spoke to the rocking slap of the bow skimming the water, but no one spoke. One of the few refugee passengers that I'd met, Earl Sardenski, a retired steel smelter and widower from Warsaw, was so close to the starboard side railing his free hand leaned at the wrist against the safety railing. He had a son in Atlanta who had paid for his passage. His fingers curved upward and cut the wind off the side of the ship. The ship was a fine-hair-length south of the Arctic Circle between Stromfjord, Greenland, and Baffin Island, in the Davis Strait, which was too far north for our destination but we hoped took us clear of U-boat traffic. The water was calm as black ice. The running lights were all off except for forward navigation markers; the ship slipped stealthily through the night.

Slow waves of green lights washed over the sky. Chemical-reaction green absorbed into the sable night and flowed as if the source of everything green lay somewhere up in the north. Jarred loose from the ice sheets that choke the passage through Baffin Bay, the great light diffused softly through old animal bones lodged in the ice caps, in its deep fissures and cracks, and it scrubbed the atmosphere above the top deck—some new kind of clean. Green crept over the northern curvature of the earth, pulsating ephemeral matter that rose and settled in the passengers' eyes as they lay. We watched the slate surface of the sky waxed clean by the living motion of aurora borealis, spreading laterally, each wave drifting, dissipating, and pushed off by the next strange sheet of light. It was as if the sky were performing green miracles over our small, northern corner of the world.

"What a gift," Earl said.

I studied his face. We had temporarily avoided whatever wild, red-eyed force that brings us all, one day, to oblivion. We probably had more in common than I dared to ask. I had endured disgrace, humiliation, loss—loss of hope, loss of self, loss of ever reemerging whole. I was left spiritually broken, alone in every sense, intimately familiar with calamity, and yet, still alive; I could still recalibrate myself to what had happened and go on.

"This looks like the dawn of Creation," Earl said then in Dutch. Hearing him freely speak Dutch, I was cleaved open to where my family was kept, each member a burning light, both illuminating and blackening my heart. I saw Hilda floating above me in the sunny woods. Ludo chiseling all our names into stone. Edwin staining colors into a canvas. The sun calling out images from my uncle's skin. My mother banging on the organ keys. My father palming light in glass. Thump-Drag traveling from this long story to some new, even larger epic.

Earl and I were the last to walk back into the holds that night. In the crew mess room, the majority of the passengers were awake, tired, and sickly from the motion of the ship. I sat with them and listened to them talking. A child cried in the holds. Her voice was a golden echo. I looked around and saw in their faces how their lives were in shambles. Watching them made me deeply ashamed, to have never thought of what parallel dramas of suffering were unfolding alongside my own.

I wanted to go back and shield everyone who felt sick with danger, to rescue everyone who needed saving. There were so many, I knew, who were trapped and lost and without hope, waiting for something to change. I had the training to be a boat runner, and if Holland could no longer be my home, the water would be.

It occurred to me I should have written something on the message board in Southampton, but I knew the odds were stacked against me that anyone I loved would have ever found it.

That night, in the galley, I did not yet know how I would spend my life—all the ships I would board, all the names I would assume, all the people I would take from one tumultuous place to somewhere new. Hundreds of trips. Thousands of people. A life spent working for Captain Fernandes, then Peter as captain, then for Uncle Martin, who showed up unannounced on a dock in Buenos Aires after tracking us through the Southern Hemisphere a year after the war ended.

Uncle Martin.

Uncle Martin standing at the end of a pier.

A miracle of sorts.

It was Uncle Martin who years later helped me pay for my first ship. It was on that first ship where I became a captain, a smuggler myself, ferrying lost souls from Xiamen, China, to Taiwan with Kuomintang members fleeing the mainland; from Pusan, Korea, to Fukuoka, Japan, before Seoul was occupied; from Berbera, Somalia, to Cape Town with those desperate to escape Ethiopia's Red Terror; from one great upheaval to another.

I did not yet know how right Captain Fernandes was: how steady business would be.

It would be much later that the dreams of my father walking into the heart of our own ruined town would begin. Standing at the lip of the rubbled factory. Seeking out the gravestones of his family. Only finding one, his wife, my mother's, whom Uncle Martin decided not to bury at sea after I left him. If my father was alive, he would have had to go back. Any man would go back. I did. I saw my mother's solitary stone in a field of names separated by grass and clover.

I try to imagine what my father does then. Why he doesn't go home and start again. Pick up the tools he'd once made a life with.

I've asked everyone I could if there was a trace of the man. "Such a tall man," I'd say. "Perhaps at the edge of town. Trying to stay out of sight." But no. No one knew.

I could not ask Hilda either. I found her name printed on a plaque flush to the ground in the same field as my mother. I knelt and traced each letter of her name with my fingertip.

HILDA.

I could not ask Ludo. Both his name and his mother's were etched into a masterfully carved wooden cross in that same field.

All of their markers held the same date.

I try to make peace with the names in that field.

I try to make peace with the names that are not in that field.

I try to make peace with my father. The industrialist, the businessman, the teller of stories, an oar over his shoulder, looking for a new place to begin again.

In the cargo hold of Captain Fernandes's ship that first trip, I only knew I had lived long enough to have my own story to tell, and that night in the galley, under the mess hall lights, manically, with great energy, I told those people, tired old men, displaced women, and sea-sick children, a purged story in my native tongue, something I'm not sure all of them could understand. But in the rocking dark, they sat wrapped around every word.

25

Thump-Drag's mother died giving birth to him, so he was raised in the town's orphanage. As he grew, he developed a giant hunchback and a dead clubfoot that he would swing ahead of himself, and it made a heavy thumping sound before he dragged it over the ground, churning up dirt and gravel as he walked. The other children in the orphanage gave him the nickname, and it stuck even after they had all been adopted, leaving him behind newly christened.

"The old lady who ran the orphanage took pity on Thump-Drag and let him sit with her as she sewed in the evenings. Eventually she taught him how to sew as well. But when he was old enough to work, he was sent out to the gas pits. The gas pits were inside the town walls but far from all the homes, and were where everyone went to get their fire for the night. The pits sat where the land leveled out and was too arid and dry to grow crops. They were far enough away from the village that Thump-Drag had to leave early, clopping his way each evening out to the old gas mine.

"The gas mine was covered by a large piece of stone with several long ropes and chains attached to it. As it got dark, everyone in the town came out with their long, unlit torches propped over their shoulders. They talked about their crops, their families, their lives, and what news they had of the great army to the east that had begun marching in every direction. Thump-Drag heard them whispering to one another all the while set on his nightly task. He took up the chains and ropes, tossed them over his shoulder, that large knot of muscle, and started to pull the giant rock, which slid away from the open mouth of the gas well. As the giant rock slid off the geyser, a steady *whoosh* of gas flowed up into the air. The people with their unlit torches saw the shimmering vapors, billowing between them and Thump-Drag, who grew wavy and distorted. Now they could only hear the steady thrum of the gas and then the *thump-drag* of the clubfoot approaching the open mouth of the geyser.

"Everyone watched as Thump-Drag took a piece of flint rock and threw it very hard at the base of the geyser. They were all still talking among themselves, taking for granted that moment Thump-Drag was so tuned into, when that first spark rose against the shale rock, followed by the swallowing sound of a giant flame igniting. Then the giant plume of fire shot out of the ground. The people in line came up and each handed a torch to Thump-Drag, who stuck it into the pillar of flame and handed the lit torch back, until everyone had a touch of fire.

"Then Thump-Drag lugged the stone by the chains over the plume of fire so the fire was put out. He turned and watched as the line of people walked away with their burning torches. Their line of flame cut through the dark and split the night in half. The individual flames spread out so he saw the layout of the small village in the distance, and how each person took their fire into their own homes, and how their walls lit up with orange shadows from their freshly lit hearths. He gathered his own burning torch and walked back to his small hut, strangely happy that all those people who had ignored him or shunned him for so long could make it through the night, seeing in the dark, finding some warmth by the light he helped bring them.

"By his own fire, Thump-Drag sewed quilts and tapestries and elegant shawls. He sewed family crests onto uniforms and blankets that people brought to him; sewed baby clothes for little children whose parents would never let him touch, wedding dresses for women who never looked at him, and military uniforms for men who could easily slay him. They would come one by one to his hut in the afternoons, wait at his doorway and tell him what they needed or wanted, and they'd watch for a while as he began to sew. They'd tell him what they wanted their sewing for and, as if under some trance in the doorway, they'd tell him their most secret hopes and deepest fears. In this way, Thump-Drag became intimate with the very marrow of his village. He heard too of the encroaching army's desire for the village's gas wells, for their nightly soft burning light.

"The next night, everyone in line was talking about what they should do to defend themselves. Many wanted to fight, but they would be outnumbered and likely slaughtered. Many wanted to surrender, but there was no guarantee they would not be enslaved. Everyone was afraid. Everyone had heard whispers of what the army had been doing as it crossed the map.

"That was when Thump-Drag told them he had a plan, but would need their help. No one wanted to listen to the town curiosity at first, but he was honest with them, and told them that there was no harm in trying what he suggested. So, they did what he asked and brought him all the material they could. With the gathered cloth, he started sewing a tremendous quilt to cover the whole town. It took everyone working through the days and nights to complete the giant, seamless cover.

When it was finished, Thump-Drag had them drag the beautiful cloth over the walls so that the entire village was draped by it.

"'We are doomed,' some of the villagers said once they saw what their plan had led to. The city now looked like a false hillside. 'We have let this idiot convince us that his harebrained plan of hiding our city will work. The invaders will see it is not a hill.'

"But Thump-Drag was not through yet. He persuaded each of the people in the town to sew themselves a pouch and bring it to the gas well. When they had done so, Thump-Drag removed the stone, but did not ignite the plume. He took each pouch and held it over the tower of leaking gas. The sacks filled with the gas, expanding taut, and once filled would have lifted into the air if he had not tied them off into a knot at the bottom and tied a little string to each. He then tied each string to the wrist of the person who sewed the pouch, so it floated above their heads as they walked to the center of the town. Thump-Drag had to hurry as the army was closing in on the covered gates of the city. The first ranks of their divisions lined up around the front gates, while the rest filed in behind.

"Once everyone had their pouch filled, Thump-Drag closed the well and met them in the middle of the town. Thump-Drag went around and whispered to the townspeople a fragment of a story he had heard them speak, one they had inadvertently told him over the years. Thump-Drag would move on as each townsperson found his own voice and strength, and spoke of her own life.

"Then he used a dagger to cut loose the gas pouch attached to that person's wrists, which then floated up against the giant quilt enveloping the town. As Thump-Drag continued moving from person to person, sound infiltrating the spaces between, their stories filled with fear and longing as they spoke. The vibrations from each voice pushed each person's pouch upward, only to come down again from the weight of the tarp. Up and down, up and down, the pouches jumped.

"The approaching army demanded that whoever was speaking come forward or that they would burn the entire city down. The first townsperson Thump-Drag had approached crawled out from under the cloth. He was a young man with a lame arm who continued to tell his story, until his fellow townspeople heard his death scream.

"Upon hearing the scream, yet another person presented herself to the army—speaking of what she had known: the taste of cherries, the feel of a horse's mane brushing the soft skin of her wrist. Others joined, a chorus of stories chronicling every human emotion and fault they knew. The army kept demanding that the speaker come forward, and as the townspeople heard the second, and then third death scream, they spoke even louder. Every voice that was silenced outside the tarp brought dozens of more voices from under the tarp forward. Each story pushed at the pouches levitating overhead.

"These stories sank into the soldiers' ears, and with each swing of their swords yet another story emerged: it was as if the voices were multiplying with each attempt the soldiers made to silence them. This made the soldiers wonder if what they were doing was wrong and they became more and more confused, and more and more anxious.

"The townspeople, understanding that they were soon to die, started speaking in unison, their voices clapped together, their pouches rising higher becoming a force against the giant cloth Thump-Drag had made. Small pockets of the cloth rose, as if they were rising bubbles, and the whole cloth started to move and shimmy.

"The soldiers surrounded by the dead bodies were awestruck as they looked on. They heard an overlap of language that sounded like so many things, a creature at once foreign and familiar. They grew scared. They had awakened something awful, they realized, something beyond their abilities to destroy. They regretted what they had done and backed up from their prey, backed away from their leader's orders, which had no purchase among this greater noise.

"The great army fled, having killed, having witnessed the sound of their killing, and having heard, still louder, the chorus of those stories when shared together. There was no denying the strength of such a thing, and no way to erase it from their being.

"From under the cloth this pulse echoed through every heartbeat, and whoever heard it understood that it is the little stories of our day that hold the only things of value in this world.

There once was a town where a nimble roof was raised by people telling their stories, powerful yet full of grace, set to the simple base rhythm of *thump-drag, thump-drag, thump-drag.*"

ACKNOWLEDGMENTS

This book is the product of having many wonderful people in my life who I will always be thankful to.

My deepest gratitude to my agent, Rayhané Sanders, who is a fierce, smart, lovely visionary. Her belief in me will always be one of the greatest gifts in my life.

My editor, Laura Brown, whose intelligence and grace is as clear as mountain water. Thank you for bringing this book into the world. It's so nice to be in such good hands.

Thank you to everyone at Harper Perennial who made this book happen and to Trent Duffy for helping get it all right.

Steven Schwartz who shaped my writing life and personal life for the best. Thank you for setting such a high bar for me to strive for and cheering for me along the way.

Jonis Agee whose radiant goodwill and support always lifts others closer to their distant goals. You were one of my favorite people the minute I met you.

Special thanks to my great teachers, Rick Simpson, Charles Gannon, Stephanie G'Schwind, Judy Doenges, John Calderazzo, Leslee

Becker, Todd Mitchell, Judy Slater, and the late Gerald Shapiro. To all my friends and colleagues at St. Bonaventure University, Colorado State University, University of Nebraska—Lincoln, and Bradley University and all points in between including: Thomas Coakley, Jennifer Bryan, Theodore Wheeler, Clarence Harlan Orsi, Karin Babine, Jill McCabe Johnson, SJ Sindu, Ben Lumpkin, Mike Nett, Nick Theodorakos, Tom Cullen, Kevin Gilligan, John Wright, Lee Newton, Rob Prescott, Kevin Stein, and Thomas Palakeel. Also Chris Harding Thornton who swooped in and saved this novel. Jonathan Starke, my most trusted set of eyes, thank you for everything. To all my students who make my work a joy.

Hans Jonker and everyone that came after.

Michael and Debbie for opening your home and hearts to a creative writing graduate student. A big risk, I love you. To David, Jori, Allison, all the Sheades, and Herb Miller for becoming family.

Sabrina and Chantal who sang to me when I was a child. To Jamie, Quinn, Tessa, Brynn, and Kendall, my heart is always with you.

My parents, Tony and Mariette Murphy, for your holy and wild spirts that showed me how to find beauty in all things and loved me unconditionally. Thank you for filling our home with books and covering the walls with joyful visions of the world.

Hyat, Nora, and Jude. I had no idea how special the world was until you entered it.

Becca, after all these years of swimming in words, I've found none as beautiful and pulsing with life as you are. I'll love you forever.

DEVIN MURPHY grew up near Buffalo, New York, in a family with Dutch roots. He holds an MFA from Colorado State University, a PhD from the University of Nebraska-Lincoln, and is an assistant professor of creative writing at Bradley University. He has worked various jobs in national parks around the country and once had a three-year stint at sea that led him to more than fifty countries on all seven continents. His fiction has appeared in more than forty literary journals and anthologies, including *The Missouri Review*, *Glimmer Train*, and *Confrontation*. He lives with his wife and children in Chicago.

Insights,
Interviews
& More . . .

Meet Devin Murphy

Agnes Rasek

DEVIN MURPHY is an assistant professor of creative writing at Bradley University. His fiction has appeared in more than sixty literary journals and anthologies, including *The Missouri Review, Glimmer Train,* and the *Chicago Tribune*. He lives with his wife and children in Chicago. ∽

The Making of
The Boat Runner

I believe you have to grasp onto a wide variety of experiences and embrace all aspects of your life to write the book you're meant to write. Novels are gifts from one person to an unknowable other. It is why I'm an awful critic. I have nothing bad to say about someone who attempted the form, who lived the life to tell the story. Since writing *The Boat Runner,* I understand exactly what Gustave Flaubert meant when describing his infamous character, Madame Bovary. "It's me," he said. "*C'est moi.*" You put everything of yourself into a book.

When I poured everything of myself into *The Boat Runner,* I was surprised the story centered on a character who morphed into a well-intentioned Dutch smuggler. But then I really began going over the details of my own life and this character emerged and seemed inevitable.

My mother, who is an artist, was born in occupied Holland in 1942. At twenty-one she came to the United States as a nanny to the Dutch Consulate in San Francisco, where she met and married my American father, who is a philosophy professor. They moved around the country for years until I was born near Buffalo, New York, where I grew up feeling distanced from a sense of family history. This meant everything about both sides of my family, especially the Dutch side, was a source of mystery. ▶

The most fascinating, shadowy figure from my maternal family was my Dutch grandfather, Hans Jonker, who passed when my mother was nineteen. Hans was a Renaissance man who played the violin, bred new strands of orchids, and painted in his spare time. For the majority of his career, however, he was a head electrical engineer at Phillips where he ran a radio tube lab. During WWII, he was forced into hiding to avoid conscription by the Germans who wanted all engineers and scientists for high-level military work. There were rumors that he'd sought refuge in a monastery, fled to England, or was killed. This meant my Oma, while caring for my mother and her three other daughters during wartime, would go out looking for her husband. This story sat latent in my mind for years.

While I was in my twenties and working at sea, feeling farther from my own family than ever before, I started calling home from pay phones around the world to ask my family direct questions. Why were we so transient? Who were my relatives? What was Hans Jonker really like? As it turned out, my mother had old letters, paintings, pictures, and haunting stories from her father and her own life that I'd never heard. My mother shared memories of GIs giving her chocolate in the streets of liberated Holland that fascinated me. Most importantly, I found out she has scar tissue on her ears from bombings near her home when she was an infant. The damage to her ears went undiagnosed her whole childhood, and she spent her school years having a hard time hearing in classrooms. Paying attention was a challenge, so she took to entertaining herself, drawing and creating art. My mother would go on to become a career artist who welded giant sculptures from discarded steel, and painted the most incredible images with pastels and acrylics that hung on the walls of our home. This inspired the need for art and creativity in the Koopman family.

These nuanced understandings of my heritage snuck into my writing, and then strangely empowered me to employ events from my own life—specifically, the more than three years I spent working various jobs on a half dozen small international expedition ships. I love ships, living on ships, the sea, and traveling, and the spirit of that experience has very much informed this book. In my twenties, I saw shipping ports in every corner of the world, and witnessed how ships hold the potential to change the direction of any life at any time.

I later married into a large Jewish family in Chicago, and in doing so, became very close to my wife's two grandfathers, who are now both in their nineties. One lived on and off vessels as a frogman in the Pacific campaign of WWII, and the other had been a medic who helped liberate the camps in Europe. I've had long conversations with them and used their stories to understand different perspectives and ▶

religious backgrounds when writing about the war. At a family party, the medic, Joe Sheade, took out pictures the size of a stick of gum that showed heaps of pajama-clad bodies taken from the liberated death camps. He's kept these photos in his wallet for over seventy years. "So I don't ever forget," he said. His willingness to look directly at something so ugly to keep perspective haunted me.

Then the last piece of the puzzle for me was research, which I did *a lot* of. Almost everything I discovered, story I heard, or event I learned of that took place during the war became something I held up and asked, "Would this show the impossibly complex and ethically messy reality of one Dutch family's life during the war?"

Yet, even after all this, my editor challenged me to go back and revise with an eye for moral and personal dilemmas for Jacob. It was with this in mind that I wrote the scene where the boys at camp lead Jacob to the burn pits to toss rocks at the rats. One of the boys makes an offensive comment, comparing the rats to a Jewish propaganda poster, and, both desperate to fit in and relieved not to have been the focus of these boys' menace, Jacob agrees. He is immediately reminded of his beloved Jewish teacher who called out, "Yeladim," to gather him and his classmates, and he is flooded with guilt. This is this scene that troubles me the most. This scene arrived from my own children's teacher calling to them,

"Yeladim," this word that breaks my heart with the love and care it sings out. It has become my favorite word, and after writing that scene, and knowing it was right for the book, it hurt, and still hurts. It makes me uneasy to include those anti-Semitic sentiments, something I feared readers would judge both Jacob for allowing and me for writing. But I felt that I needed to push all cowardice and self-censorship away when writing *The Boat Runner*. These events were ugly, to be sure, which is why we must look and look closely at them.

This is very much a work of fiction, but it is built upon a historical and personal scaffolding of real people and true events. Now, I hope others will read this book and see this family's impossible situation, and how the circumstances that create great upheavals have morphed through time, jumping borders, races, and oceans. I hope this book does its job and entertains, evokes empathy for others, and leaves you more alert to those around you and the unique depths of their lives. But more than anything, I hope this story connects some unknowable reader to the receding shadows of our past, especially those of the darkest times, which is where we learn how essential it is to find the power of our own voice. ᓚ

Devin Murphy's
Short Story
Off Dead Hawk
Highway

The older Girl Scouts kick out the
screens of their bunkhouse at night and
wander the open fields at the back part of
the ranch. They often walk down the
dirt road my cabin is on to get to the
horse pasture. I can see them in the dark.
They move like timid deer—taking
quick dashes ten yards at a time and
stopping to assess the night around
them. They betray themselves by
laughing when one bumps into the other.
I keep my porch light off so I can see the
stars. The girls never pay attention to my
cabin tucked along the tree line or me on
the deck as they line up along the fence,
stepping on the first plank to lean over
the top and coo to the horses. They wave
carrots and apples they've hoarded from
the mess hall. I like watching them—the
slow saunter of the horses approaching
and nuzzling the girls, their movements
breaking the stillness of the night,
fireflies touching the space around them
like thin blue flames.

By morning, the undertow of the
mountain will have pulled the girls back
to their bunks, and the horses will be
slick with dew and honey-colored in the
pasture. The bear grass will bloom like
fists of light pounding up the hillside,
and by afternoon, rainstorms will

darken the sky and strike the ground with lighting before blowing over and leaving a calm I have only ever felt in these mountains.

My boss, Joe, rents the horses from an outfit called Sombrero that lets them free-range in the mountains during the fall and winter. The horses are all starved and half wild by spring when they come to the Girl Scout Ranch. Joe had us wait by the horse trailers when they arrived to send back the ones we thought were too sick. If we could fit a dime between its protruding ribs we wouldn't let it off the trailer. The ones we kept had to spend two weeks being retrained by the wrangler girls.

So when a wrangler calls this morning from the stable and says an old horse has died, Joe says, "You fellas misjudged one," and we have to go out in the rain to get the dead horse before the campers see it.

Joe drives us to the pasture. The pasture runs along an incline with a large cup of earth surrounded by lodgepole pines with rainwater pooling over the roots. My coworker, Kurt, says that later in the summer the rain washes away the topsoil down to the clay, "and the clay gets slicker than snot."

Kurt and I take the tractor into the pasture. It's slow going—the wheels can hardly catch in the mud. In the trees lies a dark brown quarter horse. Its head is sloped downward enough to see a row of yellow headstone-shaped teeth embedded in the gums. Its unfurled ▶

tongue lies on the ground like a dull pink ladle.

"We'd be better off just letting the mud swallow the damn thing," Kurt yells over the engine noise.

The other horses are in the open part of the pasture. But the one they call "All-But" is watching us through the trees. All-But has everything but one eye. The eye he has is a piercing cloudy blue. That blue eye is on us as Kurt ties a sheep-shank knot to bind the dead horse's back legs together. He hooks a chain to the knotted rope and loops the chain on the back of the tractor where I stand as Kurt drives. He eases the tractor forward slowly so he won't tear off the legs. When the chain is taut, he leans on the gas, and the old horse pivots from the pot of earth it died in. Once we get it out of the trees it starts sliding easily over the wet mud. As it runs over jagged rocks I notice chunks of the hide and meaty patches of the horse's side left behind it. Joe holds the gate open for us so none of the other horses can get out.

"Drag it as far into the woods as you can, and toss some brush cover over it," Joe says. He has on a mesh baseball cap and the beads of rain are running down the back of his neck. The cold does not change his posture or his directness. He seems like he's done everything a hundred times. Kurt drives past the horse barn towards the woods, away from the little girls' cabins. On the gravel and root path going east on the mountain the horse's body gets caught on a broken root that gouges under its ribcage and snares it like a fishhook. We change the knot and tie another one to its front feet to drag it loose. Dragging it by the front leaves the head swinging backward at an awful angle. I watch the neck snap as we drive. A quick *pop* breaks through the steady tractor noise.

We untie it in the woods at the end of the camp's property. The hide has been scraped raw and the last ten yards of mud we moved it through are blood-smeared. This high up, there is too much bedrock to bury it, so we use jigsaws to cut away at the surrounding trees' lowest branches and pile them over the horse until we can no longer see how mangled it is. Part of me feels like we should light the pile on fire.

I ride on the back of the tractor as we return the way we came. The rain washes the copper-red blood marks and clumps of horse fur away from the trail. There are already turkey vultures flying in wide spirals above the slope we left the horse on, the black finger of their beaks tracing the mountainside. The birds cut through the sky like they are scrolling something on the mountain's thermal updrafts—a language of nature's neatness, its cycles of wind, that I am hoping will tell me how to start my life over.

* * *

When I was young, my father, who was from the mountains of Montana, left our family and went back west. Since then, ▶

the west has always loomed in the distance like a place you could disappear. That's why I came, and when I first arrived and started working last winter at the ranch, I spent my off-time staring out my cabin windows at the white loneliness of that mountain field. It was too cold to go anywhere even if I had a car, and that trapped feeling had me so cooped up I'd want to wander off on the snow-covered mountainside and disappear. The only thing in the cabin to occupy me was a bunch of old books about how to be an outdoorsman that categorized all the trees and animals.

There was a book called *Pertaining to Sparrows* written by a woman who must have loved those birds more than anything else in the world. She even wrote about the sparrow's predators as if she were afraid of such birds herself. She described a small falcon called a kestrel, with its rusty blue-gray cap, lightly-spotted breasts, and the way it beat its wings before swooping down on smaller birds or insects, making a shrill, *killy-killy-killy* noise. There were other books that spoke of the migration cycles and showed pictures of Steller's jays, purple martins, rock wrens, goldfinches, and grackles. I sat looking out that frozen window trying to imagine all those birds returning, calling to each other through the canopy of the subalpine forest. *Shee-e-e-e, C-Ough—C-Ough, killy-killy-killy.*

During the days, the only way I could settle down was to keep my hands busy, and keep my mind focused on plowing the road or cleaning the facilities center. Then we started rewiring the electricity in the camper cabins, installing a new furnace for the activities center, building new partitions for the horse barn, and by May, I had passed the winter immersing myself in any project Joe had for us. If I was lucky, I would have worked hard enough during the day to be content and sit on the deck at night. I could ease back into the rocking chair and let the night settle around me— listen to the new language of daily work, silence, and the wind speaking of life on the mountain.

Discover great authors, exclusive offers, and more at hc.com.